VERONICA WEBB SIGHT

Veronica
Webb
Sight

Adventures in the Big City

••••••••••••
Veronica
Webb
•••••••••••••

MIRAMAX
B O O K S

New York

ISBN: 0-7868-6338-2

Book design by Christine Weathersbee

FIRST EDITION

10 9 8 7 6 5 4 3 2 1

For Momma,
my rock and my anchor,
with love, respect, and gratitude.

ACKNOWLEDGMENTS

Thank You:

The Webb family, Russell Simmons, Herb Ritts, Steven Meisel,
Kevyn Aucoin, Sam Fine, Marpessa, Stephane Marais,
Julian D'Is, Andre Leon Talley, Bethann Hardison,
Lelanni Spencer, Oscar James, Andre Hurrell, Puff Daddy,
Lance Yates, David Schiff, Gleb Klioner, Sherry Berman,
Neal Hamil, Kathy Quinn, The Fords, David Hershkovits,
Reggie Hudlin, Kim Hastreiter, Isaac Mizrahi, Bernadine
Morris, Bernie and Owen Wincig, Ingrid Sischy, Azzedine
Alaia, Pamela Hansen, Glen O'Brien, Arthur Elgort, Karina
Castaneda, Jack Masserelli, Elise Konialian, Jason Weinberg,
Graciella Bravlasky, The Artist Formerly Known as Prince,
Karl Lagerfeld, Betty Bertrand, Kristin Powers, Susan
Dalsimer, Paul Schnee, Harvey Weinstein, Teri Agins,
Terry MacElroy, Martin Brading, John James, Paula Karaiskos,
Simon Dukas, David Brown, Didier Rubini, David Cashion,
Lynda Obst, Howard Rosenman, Elizabeth Saltzman,
Jane Rosenthal, Patrick McMullen, Patrick Demarchelier,
Darren Keith, Sante D'Orazio, Andrew MacPherson,
Bruce Weber, Todd Eberle, Frits Berends, L. A. Reed,
Tim Rosta, Elisabeth Novick, Victor Matthews,
Hercules Webb, Peggy Sirota, Lisa Lucas, Tunde Whitten,
Peter Lindbergh, Edith Spezialli, and Bill Davila.

CONTENTS

VERONICA WEBB SIGHT

INTRODUCTION

Please Allow Me to Introduce Myself

MOTOWN

N ormally, when I introduce myself to strangers it's at a party with a drink in my hand. I tell you something about my background, and you tell me something about yours. And we get to feel each other out. After a few more sips of giggle water and a vibe that we might like each other, and then we might begin—gingerly—to trade secrets. Secrets about our point of view, what we want, what we got and what we don't seem to be able to get. And then, in the phase known as friendship, which takes a long time, we'd arrive at the point where this book starts.

I'm willing to admit everything. I'm going to throw down the glove and let ya'll know what it took to get to the here and now. Most of it's a fairy tale and the rest is what reputations, enemies, gossip, and nightmares are made of . . . Some of you might know my name or my face because I had the quirky fortune of modeling for twelve years. I'm where I am right now because I was born with fantasy, moxie, and drive. And because of my mother, who I honor above everything in this world, with the exception of God, who she introduced me to, she's the gentle gardener who tended to me while I grew wild.

I'm from Detroit, the proletariat Hollywood, a place where blue-collar working people revolutionized the way the world dreams. I bounced out of my mother's womb during a blizzard in '65, into the twilight of Motown's golden age. As a kid the cars and the stars that came from my town dazzled me. Every car from a Pacer to a Cadillac was like a modern pharaoh's chariot. Almost everyone my family knew had a job on the line at an auto plant that made those cars. It wasn't uncommon to catch sight of Eddie Kendricks from the Temptations, Smokey Robinson, the model Wanakee, or Supreme Flo Ballard after school in the shops downtown on Woodward Avenue. Automobiles and entertainers made my imagination go berserk. I knew every dream needed a vehicle, and I was looking for my ticket to ride.

I started experimenting with who I could be: "Artist" seemed like a good career, full of romance and adventure, with a chance for posterity, so I concentrated hard in art class. Ballet class was another passion, being a ballerina meant I could see the world. Movies were super important to me. I'd watch any movie that came on TV, and when I was old enough to take the bus I split my afternoons between the art house films of Herzog and Fassbinder at the Detroit Institute of Arts and Bruce Lee movies at kung-fu theaters in the 'hood. I thought about modeling too, dedicating a lot of time to tinkering with my clothes, and ill-chosen drugstore cosmetics. I never achieved the look of a magazine layout, and there were no outlets to become a model in Detroit anyway.

English class was the only place, academically, where I excelled. I discounted becoming a writer at the time, probably because it came too easily to me. One day I reasoned, based on the "spaghetti principle"—throw everything against the wall—eventually *something* would stick. I ached with hope in those days that one of these versions of myself would be a passport to a magic kingdom.

With my sisters: Teresa (left), Jennifer, and me.

Childhood and adolescence felt like a holding cell, or an obligatory waiting period before I could get to real life. If I wasn't working on something creative or fantasizing, I was moping. It just seemed like nothing spectacular ever happened to me.

I kept journals from the time I was nine. In the spring of '80, just before opportunities started to unfold, this was how the world looked to me. 3/20/80 "All the sudden it's hot. I feel restless and stifled, but at ease. My world is not large enough. I hope that one day I can make it accommodate me. Everyday my need for romance becomes more prevalent. I'm never satisfied except through writing. I want the world to be quiet and pass its own reality test. I'm suspicious of my constant pangs for romance. I'm questioning whether or not I'm facing up to what

I need to provide from within, or some task that I have to fulfill. Or is it just that I want something else to consume that energy I'm keeping at bay. I really wonder what I'm doing. Day-to-day living seems pointless. I expect something monumental to happen everyday. For life to be more of a linear trajectory toward making my dreams come true. I expect to see this major metamorphosis of intellectual ideas fall into place at an amazingly accelerated pace. I have such a strong desire for greater intellectual, spiritual, emotional, all-around involvement I had to start keeping a journal." Most days in the summer seemed the same. "Ate chicken and popcicles. Went to play in an abandoned building. Got chased out. Went out of the way to go to the suburbs to watch MTV. Came home. Had vague interaction with my parents and got in bed with my journal."

With my daddy.

My mother had let my imagination grow wild—and that was the only playground for being wild. My parents kept my actions under tight surveillance. Having sex or doing drugs were punishable by death in my household. My father made it clear that if me or one of my two older sisters were ever to come home pregnant before we were out of college—and married—he would beat us half to death and then throw us out in the street to die. Drug use had the same penalty. My father's temper had a hair trigger, and he was guarding the doors to perception and passion.

My daddy didn't play. One summer, the week school let out, I must have been about seven, my sisters were just in high school, and they made the defiant move of staying out an hour after curfew. When the streetlights came on they were supposed to be in the house. I don't know what they were thinking but by the time they tried to get in the back door my father had locked it, the dead bolts were twisted shut and the screen door was latched. No matter how much me, my mother, or sisters begged him to let them in my father was unmoved. You know my sisters spent the night on the porch and all three of us were grounded for the entire summer, right? Those were the rules: If one of us did something wrong everybody got punished. In those days I was raw with hope that something would happen.

And then something did.

MAC ARTHUR PARK

I got my first ticket to ride in '80, my freshman summer of high school, in the form of a scholarship to Parsons School of Design in Los Angeles. I thought I'd go out and take the world by storm. I had six weeks—that seemed like plenty of time. It was the first time I was away from home. I was fascinated when I moved into the dorm across the street from MacArthur Park in Los Angeles and saw how other kids were getting down. One student was taking liquid acid, he said his mom was a psychologist and she let him do it. Everybody was shacked up with a new partner. And it was just "whatever." I was one of the youngest kids in the program, too scared to spread my wings and try anything out. I made a decent showing in my classes and had a whole bunch of crushes on older boys that never went further than making out once or twice, and then I got rejected. My social life was pretty uneventful since I wasn't having sex, didn't take drugs, didn't know where to get drugs, didn't know anybody famous—and worst of all, didn't even know how to drive. Every so often one of the older kids would have pity, or take a liking to me, and bring me along to the Whiskey A-Go-Go, or Perkin's Palace, to see a band like X, the Bad Brains, or the Cramps and hang out in the parking lot or on the sidewalk afterward and drink beer. It was a punk-rock scene in those days. And I learned two things very quickly that still help to this day: The right clothes and haircut can get you over. And how to hold my liquor. If you don't master an understanding of that, you can't be a model.

I went back to Detroit at the end of that summer with a new confidence. I had been somewhere and done something nobody else in my school had done. And I was really obnoxious about it too—I borrowed punk-rock style and attitude and flaunted it like I'd invented it. I was in the phase of adolescence where I wanted attention, but if anyone questioned me about my new getup (I looked like an early incarnation of Madonna) I'd die of embarrassment. My parents couldn't know that I was dressing like that so I'd get to school early, and duck into the bathroom like Clark Kent and transform myself with eyeliner and accessories into "Miss Super Cool." The only reason I was dressing this way was that I wanted people to look at me and wish they were me. I wanted indirect attention from people so I could hold sway over them and choose who qualified to be friends with me. Adolescence is such a whack phase of life.

I suffered through my sophomore year of high school fixating on Prince and David Bowie and movie characters like Holly Golightly in *Breakfast at Tiffany's* and Louise Bryant in *Reds*. I worked odd jobs, rebelled against my parents (under my breath) and prayed for a handsome prince to come rescue me. My ambition to be a ballerina gave way to learning to smoke cigarettes, drawing for five hours a day, and committing a catalog of music trivia to memory. The goal after school everyday when I wasn't baby-sitting or working as a cashier somewhere was to get to my friend's house, smoke cigarettes, listen to new Marvin Gaye and Talking Heads records, and make drawings to submit to art schools for scholarships. One day on the way to my friend's house, art supplies under my arm, wearing a music-oriented outfit complete with contraband accessories, a young man in a business suit said, "Excuse me, miss. Are you a model?"

I was so flattered! I'd been recognized! No way was I going to betray any positive emotions in my expression. I was a

In my mother's kitchen, thirteen years old.

teenager committed to attitude and angst. I used my arrogance and said, "I could be. Who are you?"

"I'm an agent," he answered, smooth and unruffled as his silk suit. Now I was thrown—I had no experience with anything like this, and I flipped through my mental Rolodex for a reference as to how to play this scene. I came up blank. He was an attractive, trustworthy-looking man. He introduced himself and said he "scouted for Hudson's," the big department store on a corner near where we were standing. Hudson's stretches high into the sky, occupying an entire city block. The store is a Detroit institution. My aunt had worked there as an elevator operator for twenty years before she retired. I bought all my school clothes there every year. It was a place I trusted. I told him that I was on my way to an "appointment" and tried to sound sophisticated and already in demand. He told me if I wanted to be considered for the catalog job, he assured me I'd get it, I'd just have "to show up now." I asked if it was okay to bring a friend with me. He said, "Sure, bring as many friends as you want." He gave me a complicated set of instructions to his office on some high floor of the department store. We shook hands and agreed to meet as soon as possible. I floated to my girlfriend Erin's house like I was filled with helium, and blurted out the story. Her father was listening and said I should ask my parents if it was OK with them. They could take me, but neither I or his daughter were going anywhere.

I rode the city bus home envisioning *Vogue* in bold type above my class picture. I told my sisters I'd met a modeling agent on the street and that they had to come with me tomorrow morning so we could see this man and start making money. Who knew where it could lead?

The next morning I approximated some cheesy version of what I thought a model would look like. Remember this was 1981, practically the pioneer days, most people only had three TV channels and there wasn't a lot of information out there about the fashion business. I had to make it all up, and I wasn't too far off—I wore my big sister's dress. The dress was a baby blue wraparound Qiana disco number from Merry-Go-Round. My older sister Jennifer went with me. She was about to enter medical school, and if she could handle cadavers in gross anatomy class, she could deal with a modeling agent. We hopped the elevator up to an administrative floor of Hudson's. When we got off there was no one at the desk. We were happy not to have to negotiate the receptionist. We breezed down the long, narrow, silent passageway following the directions exactly. We walked past locked office doors: There were no windows in the corridor and packing crates lined the walls. We passed a pay phone covered in dust. I didn't register this. I was practicing a runway strut in case the agent or someone who could possibly have an effect on my career came down the hall. No one was going to take me by surprise. Jennifer started getting spooked. I wasn't trying to hear what she was saying. I've always been hard-headed. I was determined to swan into this man's office and be on my way to a modeling career. I insisted we keep going. Just one more turn, and we were there: a dead end. Nothing but an abandoned janitor's closet. I was so furious that this wasn't the end of the rainbow that I just stood there dumbfounded. It took me a minute to wake up to the sound of my sister saying, "Veronica, we gotta get outta here. Now!" And then my eyes opened to the situation. We made it back out onto the street safely. When we walked back into our house my sister Teresa, a year younger than Jennifer, who had been against my going in the first place, was sitting in the living room by the phone shaking. She'd left work at the bank early, she looked so bad we thought the bank had been robbed. She looked at us like we were crazy.

"When you left to go down there for the modeling thing," she said, "I got a cold feeling like something wasn't right. I called the executive offices of Hudson's and they said they never contract or recruit or do shootings downtown. Whoever told you that was a con artist. Anything could have happened to you. Security was looking for you all over the place. I have to call them back now and let them know you got out of there alive."

Jennifer, me, and Teresa.

The three of us looked at each other and decided not to talk about it anymore. I went up to my room and cried my eyes out, leaving snot and mascara all over the place. I told myself that modeling was just an impossible dream, and that I wouldn't think about modeling ever, ever again.

NEW YORK NEW YORK,
BIG CITY OF DREAMS

The summer of '82 I got another scholarship to Parsons School of Design, but this time in New York. I wanted to go to New York since I was five because it looked so good in the movies. I just knew if I could get there something would happen.

I'd lived in a dorm before and had learned the ropes. I knew how to put on that "new college personality," behaving like "been there, done that." I don't know how exactly I pulled that off considering I just got "there" and hadn't "done" anything yet. Life was all about going to Food, a restaurant in SoHo someone told me Andy Warhol owned, and hoping he might drop by so I'd get to meet him, or hanging out in Washington Square Park in the day and club and party hopping at night. I was so busy setting up my social life for my imminent return as a college freshman at Parsons the following year, getting the lay of the land, and ingratiating myself with the cool cliques of kids, I barely made a B-minus average in my classes.

When it was time for college in '83, I didn't get accepted to Parsons on a full scholarship basis. I just wasn't that talented. I might have been but I concentrated my area of study on running around and hanging out on the streets. I was wrong to think I could get away with it. I messed up a good opportunity. The realization stung.

I'm scared of cats, but I'm thankful for one catlike quality I have—I usually land on my feet. I did get an academic scholarship to The New School for Social Research. Big Ten school it was not, but the location, Greenwich Village in Manhattan, and the price—all the classes paid for—were right. My family was happy that I wasn't going down the starving-artist path.

I packed three weeks in advance for my trip to college. I was ready to get out into the real world, and I thought my life would instantly become "aesthetically perfect," as I had written so often in my journals. When I got to New York the first entry in my journal was completely to the contrary:

> 9/30/83 Have been in New York for a week and am scared shitless. I feel totally insecure about everything.

I thought that was over when I found my clique. We called ourselves the ska-zulu crew. We were a bunch of kids knitted together by our love of fashion and music. All we cared about was hip-hop and ska music, dancing, drinking, and getting attention. Which would have been a potentially profitable pastime if we were in a band, but we weren't. I just didn't know what I was supposed to be serious about, having fun or studying my major. The pattern had to do with my thinking I could just spend my life having a lot of fun and there'd be no consequences. The days went like this: wake up with a hangover; get a hot dog from the street vendor to cure hangover; go to class; eat lunch; explore the Village; go back to the dorm; do homework. The cutoff time for homework whether finished or not, was ten P.M. Going out to clubs every night was imperative.

By eleven P.M. the ska-zulu crew was assembling on a stoop on St. Mark's Place, in our slavishly planned-out thrift shop ensembles. Everybody would have a forty-ounce of malt liquor in a paper bag and we'd talk about music, who we wanted to sleep with, and cap on fools strolling by. What we were really waiting for was an opportunity to knock us down. I spent most of my money on clothes and alcohol and felt brilliant. And I was good in school. I was taking classes like The Grotesque in Fiction, Hidden Injuries of Class and Race where I did well, and some math requirements where I failed miserably.

The early eighties were fabulous for club life in New York. The Mudd Club was popping. The Mudd Club was this shabby little warehouse space tucked away in a dark service alley in

TriBeCa. David Byrne of the Talking Heads, and the late painter Jean Michel Basquiat dee-jayed there a few times. Artists who symbolized the cutting edge from the Sex Pistols to Grace Jones came to party. Danceteria was a hot club, too. I remember seeing Madonna hanging out at there before her first single "Holiday" became a hit.

I thought I'd find the miraculous delta of the quicksilver rivers of fame, fortune, and love at a club one night. In two short months I started to find out otherwise.

10/26/83 Dancing, drinking, and going out all the time is so seductive because emotions are running high and deep. Unedited praise and insults flowed out of my mouth night after night. I slept with this one who should have belonged to that one and who belonged to this one who wanted me and so on and so on. The discos, parties, and club love have worn off, I feel like my insides are falling out. There's no sanctuary to protect myself against myself, or myself from the world. Even by killing off 98 percent of what is vulnerable to the world, my vulnerability to myself is dangerous and constant. I moved away from home and I'm genuinely lonely for the first time in my life. I'm transferring these feelings onto boys. I'm projecting an ideal lifestyle companion fantasy onto them and I get disappointed when things didn't pan out.

I see myself the most clearly when I'm depressed or when I'm elated. In between those times I tend to create problems I can control. Nowhere relationships, screwing around with my weight, smoking too much, drinking too much, in order to feel like I have some sort of dynamic power over my life. I've been so hung up on guys who were hung up on themselves. I was so hung up on making someone love me to satisfy my ego that I felt like it was eating me alive. I hated the fact that the people I projected my unrequited love onto were even alive because the things I felt for them created such a void in my own life. I wrote in my journal, 11/5/83 "I can't cry. I can't hide. I feel trapped in a tiny town—yes, New York—I feel fenced in by hostility, narrow-mindedness, insecurity, and loneliness. I don't know what I need or even what I'm looking for. I don't like being drunk and I despise, detest, abhor soberness. I don't like being near anyone in this fucking town. I want to be alone, but there's nowhere to go to take my mind off of myself. I have no options, no comfort and no sanctuary. I HATE THIS!! I don't want any pressure from the outside world. Release Valve! Later . . . I feel like I'm mimicking myself. Everyday the same blather about some boy who doesn't fulfill my desires, the same blather about homesickness, constant blather, never any resolution or release. Just awful. I don't know how to change my life. How to get away. How to help myself. I fucking need help! No one can give it to me now but a professional. I think I can cry now but my impulse to contain it is too strong. I did come to one ineffective resolution. I should either stop going out on Thursday night, or stop talking to boys."

I did stop going out for a little while and took a vacation from passion, thrills, and depression. Interestingly enough I was able to do it without numbing myself. That lasted a week. Then I was back canvassing the downtown circuit of clubs—Danceteria, A-7, Mudd Club, Area, C.B.G.B.'s.

I was having fun dancing and drinking and dying inside, looking for love. By 11/12/83, I was back in the same hole again: "Now I'm sad and losing sight of my goals in rapid fashion. I don't have much to keep me going, besides the expectations of my parents. I need something to balance my life. I don't know what's going on with me." I was confused, even though I thought I knew everything in the world I was unable to see the course of my actions. I was too proud to ask my family for guidance and comfort in the areas where I was failing. If I had, it would have saved me a lot of pain, but then I wouldn't have been a teenager.

Pretty soon, I dropped out of college. I didn't know what I was looking for, but it was something besides good grades and a diploma. Clubs were the nexus lexis of romance, fame, and fortune. I treated partying like a full-time job. Wanting all the trappings of an independent, glamorous, adult, bohemian life takes personal and professional skills—none of which I had. Then the story of my sex life started unfolding.

My mother taught me not to get married. She thought women should wait as long as possible so that who you are as an individual is solid by the time you make your marriage vows. Like a lot of women I was conditioned by convention and society to think that having a man is the ultimate validation. And of course, it was supposed to turn out just like in the movies. It's a ridiculous idea, because it's not based in reality. How are you going to meet someone and end up happily ever after in ninety-eight minutes? Sounds like a simple truth but I had to learn the hard, hard way. I bounced from one dead-end romantic liaison to another. I began to get a complex that I was inadequate. It's a more debilitating emotion than feeling unloved. I didn't get over it until I was thirty years old.

I met a young painter named Darius who was supporting his art as a restaurant cook, and we decided instantly and impulsively to stick together. He invited me to live with him in an apartment on the Hudson River. He rented it from Doris Horowitz, who was like a surrogate momma. Her son Ad Rock was living there and his band the Beastie Boys was beginning to take off, with the single "Cookie Puss." Most weekends the band would pedal their equipment to gigs on their bikes.

I was working part-time as a cashier in a swanky SoHo boutique to finance the details of nightclubbing. For five days a week, I stood behind the counter wearing an apron, ready to serve the wealthy young clientele who came in to buy state-of-the-art home furnishings, with hefty price tags that were way out of my reach. Occasionally, customers would ask me, "If you or one of your friends might be looking for a job as a maid, I have some work for you." Or they were throwing a party and needed some extra help. I thought that by dropping out of school, I'd lose the feeling that life was passing me by. My station in life was becoming clear. I never thought that this would happen to me—I was going nowhere fast.

One hysterically busy Saturday, a guy in his late twenties with wild eyes and long black hair, wearing head to toe black leather biker gear, cut the line. "Excuse me, meiss," he purred in a heavy French accent, "arrre you a mo-del?" Indicating my apron, I said, "No, I'm a cashier. Would you like to buy something?" "Non," he said. "You 'ave ze kind of features zat are pop-u-laire right now. You must call zis agency. Tell zem Val-in-tane send you. I am a coiffeur, how you say hairdressaire. Zey will take you right away." He sounded like Inspector Clouseau. It was hard not to burst out laughing. Valentine produced a business card from Click models. I shoved the card in my apron pocket and watched him leave. My co-workers crowded around wanting to know exactly what I was going to do about it. My first thought went to that day in high school when I had been lured up to the shipping room of the department store in Detroit. I suddenly remembered reading a headline a few days before, about a guy who was traveling across the states posing as a scout for Elite's Look-of-the-Year Contest. He would lure unsuspecting hopefuls into his car and super-glue their eyelids open, then rape and torture them in gas station bathrooms. The idea of following through on Valentine the Frenchman's lead gave me a cold chill.

I met my boyfriend at the flea market after work that day. We'd moved out of the town house on the Hudson into a dump in the no man's land between Chinatown and Little Italy. We lived like crumbs above an abandoned storefront and a sweat shop. While we were shopping for our apartment I told him about the French hairdresser's proposal. In the middle of the story, a well groomed *G.Q.*-attired man came up to me and asked me, "Are you a model?" Me and my boyfriend were stunned because we looked like a hip-hop, punk-rock *American Gothic*. I still had on my apron from work and was holding a broom in my hand that we'd just bought and my boyfriend was wearing dirty kitchen whites. In my mind I was thinking, "Okay, these guys have a ring and they're working SoHo." He said his name was Rick Gillette and he was a makeup artist, and producing a copy of *Mademoiselle* he starting showing me his tear sheets.

"What's a fucking tear sheet?" I asked, with the raw edge of a teenager. He explained that those were the pictures you worked on in the magazine and you would "tear the sheet out and put it in your portfolio." Oh. I wanted to know what was in it for him to send me to an agency. He said they were friends of his, it would help the agency make money, show the industry he had an eye, and he'd get a 5 percent finder's fee. He suggested that I go to Click, and not to forget to mention his name when I showed up.

We trudged back to our apartment with a new lava lamp, a broom, and an ashtray. My boyfriend Darius said that he was jealous, but he was happy for me too "'cause now you're on easy street." Darius acquired a fondness for amphetamines that I turned a blind eye to, because he was going to work everyday and making paintings. I didn't have enough experience with drugs to know how quickly this could turn into a bad problem. He said it was time we started celebrating our new-found fortune. He took a bag of some stuff he said was crystal meth out of his pocket, threw it on the cardboard box we'd covered with a blanket and called our dining room table, and cut it up in lines and showed me how to snort it. The plan for the evening was to do a little of this happy powder and go out dancing or something. It must have been about seven o'clock. Well past midnight I still couldn't get my face out of the saucer. I thought I was invincible, my nose was bleeding, my mind was racing; I was so fucked up that I thought this was really great.

Finally, we were ready to go out. I had been hearing noises, I thought someone was trying to break into our apartment through the fire escape. Things went from bad to worse once we got outside. I felt thousands of tiny parasites worming around under my scalp and the palms of my hands. I was clawing at my flesh trying to get them out. Then I saw them coming out of my boyfriend's arms. We stood on the corner loudly arguing about what to do. We agreed to take a taxi to the emergency room at Bellevue. When we checked in the nurse asked me kindly if we had taken any drugs. "Drugs! You bitch, how dare you! Can't you see I'm infested with parasites!" I proceeded to curse her out ghetto style, pounding on the Plexiglas window until she starting shaking and crying. But that wasn't enough. I ran around the emergency room trying to organize a mutiny among the other patients. I was Norma Rae on narcotics, until the nurse called security to put me in a straitjacket. I spent the night in the psycho ward at Bellevue being interviewed by a battery of psychologists. I wasn't trying to hear what they were saying to me, all I heard was my mother's voice in my head. "If you ate a piece of cake and it made you dizzy and crazy and you passed out that wouldn't be funny, would it? You wouldn't want to eat that piece of cake again, would you?" Walking out of Bellevue into the bright sunshine, rumpled, soiled, and humiliated, I decided that was it for me and drugs. I stayed drug free during my 20s, which probably saved me a lot of money and trouble considering how many other good ideas I would have for mistakes.

··········
GO-C
··········

I went back to work for another week, shaken and out of it. Payday came, and I was looking at my bullshit paycheck for

$125 in the employee room. My manager came up to me all uncomfortable, she said she didn't know how to tell me this because she had never had to fire anyone before who she liked. "Your work just isn't good, and I have to let you go."

That was the kick in the ass that got my courage up to go to the Click modeling agency. I remembered that Hudson's incident, and I made a bunch of phone calls to the Better Business Bureau and to *Mademoiselle* and checked everything out. I went to the office in Carnegie Hall, and as I was getting on the elevator Elle MacPherson was getting off, she was a few years into her career and in prime position to become a superstar. Elle breezed by me in all her squeaky-clean, cheesecake Amazon splendor. I was a grimy ungroomed club kid sweltering in black combat boots and a tight black wool dress with purposely frayed edges, eating a cheeseburger wrapped in tinfoil, wondering where I was going to fit into this scheme.

It was a whole new world when I walked into that office at Carnegie Hall. Everyone was speaking foreign languages, quoting big figures for model fees, making travel plans and blithely untouchable. I was concentrating hard on acting cool and nonchalant, when really I was petrified of rejection. Without any credentials other than the genes I inherited from my parents and the token I bought to make the trip uptown, I got an unusual reception for a newcomer.

The owners, Frances Grill and Alan Mendel, said, "We've been waiting for you." Frances was in her late forties, heavyset, and swathed in a complicated black dress. She smoked a cigarette out of a long holder. She had an accent like a Brooklyn truck driver, the contrast made her seem like quite a character. Her partner, Alan Mendel, had wild, long, hippie-style brown hair and a beard. His outfit sent mixed signals. He was wearing an upper-crust Ralph Lauren suit complete with golf shoes. My cheeseburger was lauded by everyone in the office as a "charming accessory." Frances said it made me "look like a modern girl on the go." They were making moves to get me started right away. They introduced me to my booker Gretchen. Gretchen would be the person responsible for tracking my daily appointments and pitching the agency's new discovery to photographers, magazines, and advertisers. All I had to do was lose ten pounds (I was 5'10½" and 130 pounds), get the right haircut—they had someone in mind—and get some "test pictures." I was sent to a photographer, and I was responsible for buying the film in exchange for keeping the photos. With this $50 investment I was in business.

A few days later I went into the agency, near tears, with my pictures. I had to do my own hair and makeup, I didn't know how, and the effect was disastrous. I was expecting to look like a worldly sophisticated goddess of high-end retail. The base I used was the wrong color and I didn't blend it well either so it looked like a carnival mask. I tried to straighten my hair, but I had a mix of textures worthy of a patchwork quilt. None of these flaws showed up in the mirror the way they did on film. On film every flaw glares at you. When I showed the pictures to Frances Grill, I thought I was washed up then and there. Frances puffed away on a cigarette in a long holder and was thrilled: "These aren't the best pictures," she squawked in a thick New York accent, "but people can see you can photograph. It's enough to get you started." I became a believer.

Starting off as a model is nothing but leg work. I was riding the subways all day long wearing cocktail dresses and pumps bought at thrift shops, with the odd accessory of a big, black-vinyl portfolio sticking to me in the summer heat. This process of traveling around is called a go-c. I'd have to go see someone at a catalog house or a photographer. Lots of times the line of models would stretch from the front door all the way back to the elevator. Everybody on these go-c's was a nobody. None of us had worked yet with a magazine or a photographer that would make us "somebody" in the eyes of the fashion industry.

The atmosphere among the girls was always very competitive and uneasy. If we had longer legs, or better hair, or clearer skin we all knew that would make us more likely to get picked for the job. Standing on lines or sitting in the waiting rooms could be a snake pit of insecurity with everyone comparing themselves to each other. It tends to bring out the worst in people.

A few times I fell prey to some dirty tricks. Another hopeful beginner would tell me "My friend was here yesterday, and she looks a lot like you. They sent her away, because she wasn't the type they wanted. You should just go to your next go-c and not waste your time." And I was dumb enough to leave the first time it happened. But it wasn't just catty models that took advantage of my inexperience, the clients did it too.

I went on an appointment for a showroom job, modeling clothes in an office, for boutique and department store buyers. I tried on a cheap little sportswear ensemble and came out of the dressing room. The showroom owner had a buyer there, so he asked me to try on about six outfits. I was doing my best, and felt sure I was going to get hired for this marvelous $350 an hour gig. I ran back to the agency bursting with pride when I was through, and asked if they had called to hire me. When I told my booker what had happened and she picked up the phone, I wasn't hired. Then she got furious and demanded payment for what I had done. She turned to me and explained I was only there to be seen by the client. It was a job to *show* people clothes. To spend an hour trying on five outfits counted as work. I didn't want Gretchen to pursue the matter. I thought it would upset the client and hurt my chances of ever getting hired there. The hesitation I had was that I wanted to be *liked.* I didn't want to be perceived as a troublemaker. It didn't occur to me that there was no use in considering the client's feelings who had used me. Gretchen and I argued back and forth over what to do, and in the end I never got paid. I'd already done the job for free.

Most of the time appointments felt like a total waste. Whoever it was who had the power over hiring would flip through my book of color xeroxes made from slides, snap it shut, and put it back in my hands without a word. Going home after days like that I'd sit on the subway in a daze wondering what was wrong with me and *when* something was going to happen.

Luckily, it didn't take long. A month later I went to Agnès B., a French designer who was new to America. She liked the way I looked and hired me to model for the press kit for her boutiques that were opening in the states. We shot in her boutique in SoHo, a familiar stomping ground for me, and the clothes were chic and sporty. It wasn't like I was trying to pull off wearing an expensive couture garment that I had never touched before or seen anyone wearing in real life. A hairdresser and a makeup artist were there, who knew what they were doing, and finally, I got some results out of a photo shoot that made me feel good!

Once those pictures went into circulation I started really working. I did *Seventeen* magazine, which meant a lot to me since I had barely graduated from reading it. And then I got the bounce I needed and an entrée into the places I really wanted to be going. I had an appointment to see Bruce Weber, the photographer who did the original Calvin Klein underwear ads. He was hotter than fire in the fashion business. I was an hour late getting there because I got lost on my way to his loft way downtown in the bowels of TriBeCa. When I walked in there he was as sweet and jovial as Santa Claus, with rosy cheeks, a big round belly, and a fluffy white beard. I apologized for being late, and he just laughed and said, "I'm glad you could make it, honey." He looked at my book and his agent/companion Nan Bush poured me a glass of water. Bruce flipped through my book quickly with Nan standing behind him studying every page over his shoulder. Bruce snapped my book shut and I expected to hear "Thanks, but no thanks." Bruce busted a big smile and told me right there I had the job.

I was booked on my first professional trip. I joined a group of about ten models Bruce had installed in his Bellport, Long Island, beach house. I'd never been in this environment before with a lot of models I'd seen in magazines already. I did the smart thing. I knew how to shut up and listen. I shared a room with another model named Allison, who said she planned on being an astrophysicist as she was contorting herself in the mirror. I told her I thought that was "def, but what the fuck are you doing in front of the mirror now?" "Practicing modeling," she said, like it was the most natural thing in the world. My brain was on scramble for a minute. She explained that it was good to watch yourself in the mirror so you'd know what you look like in front of the camera and it gave you a chance to come up with some new poses. She'd just dropped a jewel on me. I waited for a respectable interval to pass, so she

Bruce Weber

My shoot with Bruce Weber for French Connection.

wouldn't think I was copying her, and I locked myself in the bathroom and started practicing. I performed well on that shoot. Word got out and the agency got calls from all the big magazines. Things were really looking up in 1984.

STEPPING UP TO THE PLATE

Everything was going so good now. The agency called on Friday with the news that *Mademoiselle* had booked me for a week of shoots, one of which was lingerie, which terrified me, and "cover tries," which I was elated about. I'd have to be ready to go to Los Angeles in two weeks. If the pictures made the grade, I'd officially be a big-league player. More often than not magazines reject shoots—they don't like the photographer's work, or how the location looks or the model. And the same clothes just get reshot on someone else. I've learned from years of experience whatever goes wrong on a shoot the model will get blamed. It's never the light was bad, the hairdresser was inexperienced, or the clothes were a mess. The final word is always "Veronica looked bad." I was ready to step up to the plate.

I felt sick all weekend. I'd wake up nauseated. Then I'd be starving and eat something and vomit. This went on for four days, and finally I took myself to the emergency room. I was given an IV to rehydrate my body; the attending physician came back and told me I'd be just fine. And I was pregnant. I just crumpled up into a ball on the examining table and started to cry. I was broke, just living from check to check. My relationship was very strained at this point, because my work took me away from it. I'd caused this problem myself. I was irresponsible with the birth control, thinking I was so special the laws of nature didn't apply to me. I got myself in a position where I had to make a harsh choice. I made a selfish decision, I wanted my freedom and my career.

I had to borrow money and withdraw my entire savings from the bank in order to pay for the abortion. While I got the money together and looked for a clinic for the service, I watched helplessly as I lost control of my body. My breasts swelled, my skin got blotchy, and my thighs and ass got bigger. I was forced to cancel my booking for *Mademoiselle*. I made up some lie to tell the agency and they lost confidence in me, because you did not cancel a job this big unless you were dead. And then the day came when the anesthesiologist clamped the mask down on my face in the clinic. Tears were streaming down my face as I went under. I was feeling bitter and guilty. I remember mumbling to the surgical team, "I know it's not a falafel and then a baby. It's a baby and I'm sorry."

A few hours later I came to in a recovery room. There must have been sixty women lying on surgical gurneys who had just had the same procedure. It reminded me of an army hospital out of a World War II movie.

A nurse gave me a cup of hot cocoa, and I started crying again and didn't stop crying for three days. I never told anybody the truth about why I canceled my first big booking.

For months my career floundered. The phone didn't ring; the agency couldn't be pushing me after I hadn't shown up and they'd put their reputation on the line for me. But I did get another chance. American *Vogue*, the ultimate legitimizer of commercial success, wanted to see me. I wanted a new haircut for the occasion. One of my friends sent me to her friend who was a hot studio hairdresser who worked with all the big photographers. I sat back and let him do his thing. I put on my best outfit and walked into *Vogue*, only to have the model booker for the magazine call the agency—in front of me—and tell them I had *the* worst hair she had ever seen and what were they doing sending me there? I had salon shock—I'd been given a high maintenance asymmetric haircut that only looked good straight. It was August. I'm black and my hair is nappy by nature. I looked at that white lady with stick straight hair that looked like it was put on earth to bounce and behave, listened to her crisp Yankee accent and said to myself I really don't think I can explain this to her. I kept my game face on as I walked out of the offices. I couldn't even react, I was so frustrated by the encounter because I didn't have the power to control my looks. On the way home I reasoned that being a model for hire is not too different from being a rent-a-car. Like Hertz or Avis, the agencies dispatch their fleet for the customer's approval. If you rent a car and it's not pristine and exactly to your liking you give it back and get another one—there are always more cars.

Styles were changing, Jean Paul Gaultier was the wunderkind of fashion in 1984 when he brought his show to town. Gaultier was the antithesis of the designers who ruled Seventh Avenue in that era, Bill Blass and Oscar de la Renta were elegant middle-aged courtiers serving the Jackie O. society-type clientele. Calvin Klein was a monster success too. His whole vibe was about the impossibly cool, urbane, and beautiful jet set, and I didn't have the polish it took to walk his runway yet. There were other designers like Willi Smith and Steven Sprouse who were coming up but Gaultier hit it just right for the sexually ambiguous, fringe-culture-youth zeitgeist. Gaultier was seeing models in the offices of Bergdorf Goodman. There were a lot of young, distinctly European, gender-bending club-type kids running around in the offices chirping in French, smoking cigarettes, tacking sketches of the clothes on the wall with Polaroids of the models that had been chosen to wear them for the show. All the colors and the characters were so miraculously cool and studied I felt like I had been transposed into an eighties version of the movie *Funny Face*. I asked this young kid in a sailor shirt with a bleached blond crew cut and ears that stuck out like a chimpanzee where I could find Gaultier. Laughing, he stuck his hand out and said, "It iz me. I am Jean Paul." We both started laughing. As soon as I tried some clothes on, he told me I was booked for the show, then he said I should consider coming to Paris, because I'd be able to do a lot there. As I was leaving, Jean Paul pulled me to the side and said before you come to Paris "you will be needing ze right underwear." I was still wearing Carter's, you know the underwear your mom buys you for school every year, the cotton ones that come three in a pack. He thought they were "charming for real life, very Lolita," but under a clingy dress they "looked like diapers." I'd make $700 for the show, he said, so now would be a good time to invest in a G-string.

The show was on and it was proclaimed by the fashion press as "the event of the season." I showed up at the big circus tent pitched in the shadow of the World Trade Center. Every big model was in the show, which had a live gospel choir providing the music. It was a fierce hallelujah scene, the hardcore fashion kids in the audience were so moved by the mix of couture and old-time religion a lot of them were in tears. The clothes were inspired by *Gone with the Wind* for the men and the women were dressed as African goddesses. I walked out behind Iman, who was dressed in some sort of Afrocentric "Nutcracker" hoop skirt which Gaultier had a little boy pop out from underneath. I stopped at the end runway. Thousands of camera lenses floated in the air like soap bubbles. Flashbulbs popped. I realized that they were pointed at me. Instantly, I was hooked on the feeling of being in the limelight. Gaultier was a big break for me because I got exposure to the international fashion press, out there on the runway. I got a lot more exposure when I got back into the dressing room. I was standing there in my brand new G-string, changing into my street clothes, when the flaps of the tent flew up. Kids I recognized from the East Village club scene rushed the dressing area. No one was interested in seeing naked models—they had come to steal Gaultier's pricey creations. It was total pandemonium. Security guards, New York police officers, and Gaultier's assistants chased these kids around and people engaged in brutal games of tug-of-war with the clothes. It was straight out of the Keystone Cops.

After the Gaultier show I got the fever for France. Every time I'd go into the agency there'd be someone going to Paris or coming back from Paris. I'd been in the game for about seven or eight months and hadn't really made much money, about $3,000 in total. I'd done magazines, and a few catalog jobs that paid well, but I was barely eking out a living. I was working toward my goal everyday—which was making a solid living in the business, but like any business when you're starting out, it's a heavy investment of time and money. You have to pay for things like composite cards, New York City rent, clothes for appointments, trips to the hairdresser, leg waxing, manicures, transport, and even though the agency was telling me "you're going to be a big star someday" I kept wondering *when* it was going to happen or if I'd even be able to survive until it did. You know how hard it is when you compare yourself to other people. Being a model you compare yourself to other women all the time, and it causes a lot of jealousy and inferiority, because being just as attractive, if not more so than the next person determines whether or not you can put food on your table or a roof over your head. But no matter, I was determined to get to Paris, another city that fueled my fantasies, and get there before I became obsolete waiting for my turn to really shine.

I got my agency to hook me up with an agent in France. I filled a tiny plaid suitcase I'd inherited from my aunt when she died, with three pairs of pants, three sweaters, a T-shirt, and three pairs of shoes. I had no idea what was about to happen. My limited French consisted of a few phrases. "*Comment-allez vous?*" and of course the famous line from the Patti LaBelle song, "Lady Marmalade": "*Voulez-vous couchez avec moi ce soir, uh-huh.*"

I boarded the plane for the overnight flight to Paris with $100 and a one-way ticket.

························
CITY OF LIGHT
························

On my mother's birthday, November 9, 1984, I touched down at Paris's Charles de Gaulle airport. It was seven-thirty A.M. Riding over the wide cobblestoned deserted Boulevard de Champs Elysées, in a rattling diesel-powered Peugeot taxi, I gasped at a fire-red sunrise positioned perfectly in the center of the Arc de Triomphe. My gasps scared the bejesus out of the taxi driver and he slammed on the brakes, jerking us both forward. He turned around and hurled some insults at me, but mercifully, I couldn't understand. There I was at my destination, my new agency on the Rue Washington, a few doors in from the Champs Elysées. I was so happy—until I read the meter on the taxi—215 francs. I told the driver in English that I was not paying "two hundred fifteen franc dollars for this!" Suddenly his English flew into gear, he called me a dumb, rude, stingy American, got out and threw my suitcase in the gutter. I was just standing there in shock, holding my 1,000 francs in my hand. He snatched at my little wad of cash and took what was due him, threw his burning cigarette butt at my feet, and drove off. I thought to myself, "Vive la France," 'cause I ain't leaving till I conquer this motherfucker!

France is like another planet. My agency was in an eighteenth-century building, with a door that looked like the gates of a medieval village. It was about twenty-five feet high and had an elaborate latch and a tiny little door cut into it that wasn't even tall enough for me to walk through without stooping. It took me about twenty minutes of fiddling with the door before I made it through into this marvelous interior courtyard. The agency, called Fam, was on the bottom floor of an apartment building with huge windows and balconies. The edifice was so ornate with its curli-cue carvings, that it struck me as being the visual candy of French architecture. From then on I walked around Paris with my neck stretched up in the air. Every sight was stunning. It felt like I was walking around on top of a wedding cake.

That first morning at Fam, my measurements were taken and translated into metrics. Test photos of me were run off in black-and-white, and an agency sticker was affixed to each one. This would function as my composite card for the time being. I was nineteen, but the agency said it would better if I told people I was fifteen. "No way would my parents let me be here at fifteen all alone, I can't embarrass my parents like that. I'm proud to be nineteen. I just want to be my age." Everyone in the room rolled their eyes and let it go. Then came the next question about my heritage. "I'm black," was my answer. I was advised that it would thrill clients and help me get more bookings if I told people I was "something more exotic." I knew they weren't going to like the honest answer. "I look the way I do because I come from the polluted gene pool that resulted from slavery." I was sure that truth would be too confrontational for the people whom I'd be meeting for jobs. The room went silent and we let that one go too. Finally the bookers wanted to know if Veronica Webb was my real name. Yes it was, my older sisters had named me after a character in *Archie*, their favorite comic book. There was some discussion about changing my name for a minute, but that little anecdote went over well, and I was sent on my way with the same age, race, and name I'd come in with.

64 rue de Rennes was my new address. It was a "model apartment," on one of the

In the courtyard of Karl Lagerfeld's house. Credit: Andre Leon Talley choicest corners of the city, that belonged to the owner of my agency. There were five other girls from around the world already installed in the big, airy, classic six-bedroom French apartment. As the newcomer, I was awarded the smallest and noisiest bedroom. I came in that first cold rainy afternoon with my little plaid suitcase. My new roommates showed a sort of cursory interest in who I was, that was until everyone retreated to their rooms. We were all in our late teens and early twenties, all foreigners to Paris. I was the only American. We had no adult supervision to speak of, except for a Moroccan housekeeper who came in every other day to make sure we hadn't burned the house down. Otherwise it was anything goes. We were all in various stages of our careers, ranging from ingenue, to rising star, to burnout. We were all watching each other's progress with trepidation and envy. We never got very close, and one of the girls told me that it was better that way because you never knew how long people were going to last in the business, and we were all competing anyway.

Paris was no picnic. I'm a language-dependent person. Not speaking French robbed me of my most reliable skill. In effect I was at the level of a five-year-old, and felt like a total imbecile. Simple things like using a pay phone, navigating the subway, grocery shopping, or asking directions were like the labors of Hercules. It was a horrible way to live, like taking an untethered space walk.

All I wanted was to work, be proud of myself, make friends, be loved, and have a good time. It's what I looked for everywhere. For the first time in my life I was genuinely on my own. I had no friends in Paris, no social circle, no language skills, no markers, and no bearings. I grew a lot closer to my family during this time. The phone on rue de Rennes was rigged so no international calls could be placed from the house—none of us had the money to pay for those phone bills. If I wanted to call someone I knew back home in the States I'd have to go to the phone booth with a bucket of change and talk for a few minutes before my francs ran out. My mother and my sisters and I began to write one another almost daily, and I still have all the letters. They're the first indication I had that I was becoming my mother's and sisters' equal. I was starting to become a woman.

Just before things took off career wise, I made this entry into my diary.

11/25/84 Heartsick softness in Paris. Quiet, solitude, alienation. Alone and forgotten. I wish my parents would call. I miss them so much. I'm sitting in my room on rue de Rennes, looking out at nothing, wondering about everything. My heart aches for anything familiar. A smile, a genuine word, a familiar place, a familiar bed. Paris is a city of high anxiety and tears. A bottle of wine, another sleepless night. I'm not sure if I'm happy, but then again I never am. Things are going well at work. A lot of tentatives with the big photographers. I hate rue de Rennes. I feel like I just pay rent here. One of my roommates is so impossible, one day she's nice to me, I don't know why or what she wants. Her niceness is phony. I know I'm not wanted here or welcome in the little social situations in a genuine way. I don't even want to be near anyone. Why should I set myself up accepting false hospitality? I can't have another psychotic nightmare day. I want darkness now. I'm lonely and tired.

I had nothing except my goal of being a successful model. It was deep winter in Paris, and I was lost and freezing everyday trying to get to appointments and hold back my tears. I felt so vulnerable and disoriented from putting myself out for approval all the time—not to mention being dead broke. In the evenings I'd come home and make myself something to eat in my bedroom and stand in front of the mirror and examine myself naked and then in a series of outfits and look for flaws. I'd try on outfits I'd planned to wear on go-c's. And then I'd screw around with makeup and practice modeling, praying for

a chance to get a booking where I could show people I
deserved to be in the business.

Four days after that entry in my journal, I got the break that
would make my career take off once again. I was booked for a
spread in Italian *Vogue* with the most sought after photographer in Paris, Peter Lindbergh. I recorded it as: 11/29/84 "I
wonder every day if I'm getting to know myself better. I worked
with Peter Lindbergh today and got four great pages for myself
in Italian *Vogue*. I can't express my relief at finally doing something I feel good about. I've felt so wimpy and feckless since I
left New York. I feel as though
I've lost my edge. It takes a long
time to get an edge in New
York—but I had it. Now I have
hope that I can regain it here in
Paris. I'm lonely and I just wish
I had my boyfriend, someone to
hold me until it comes back. I
feel so urgent."

I was so elated that night I
slept in my makeup. I wanted
to look just as perfect the next
day when I went on another
appointment. Once the word
was out that I'd been photographed by Lindbergh, everything changed. Clients treated
me differently on go-c's, suddenly there was a level of
respect toward me. People
smiled and called me by name.

Peter Lindbergh

The smiles had nothing to do with them liking me personally. I
had become a hot commodity—if I was good enough for
Lindbergh I was good enough for them.

I started getting lots of jobs, doing layouts for Italian, French, and English magazines. After taxes and commissions I was making about $33 a day. This is how it works: I did the job, the agency did the billing, and the money would take anywhere from sixty to 120 days to reach its bank account and then be transferred to my hands. I had no legal papers (and never did for about ten years) to work in France, so all my earnings were given to me and kept in cash. After my rent and the cost of buying the magazines I appeared in, and the printing of composite cards, and the cash advances my agency gave me so I'd have some walk-around money, and the 33 percent taxes I paid to the French government were tallied up, I was always in debt. Luckily for me there was the perception that I was heading toward stardom so I could take as much cash in advance as I needed. Little did I know that this put me in the position of an indentured servant. I'd be beholden to stay at that agency until I worked off the galloping debt I was creating.

I had tons of pictures on the newsstands in Europe. Everyone in the business was telling me "you're a star." And even though that was true on some small level, I was a broke star. It wasn't easy for me to make money because all the high-paying catalog and advertising jobs were almost the exclusive province of white girls. My booker had told me: "You're a black girl, so it's not going to be so easy to reach that dream." I'd hear it again and again over the years. I'd be submitted for high paying jobs and the booker would tell me "they don't want any black girls." Eventually I got immune to the hurt, but the rage at being categorically excluded burned like a nasty frostbite.

Trying to become a success was wreaking havoc on my personal life. My boyfriend Darius called the day before he came to Paris and said that he'd been sleeping with someone else because he thought I was fooling around too. We'd had problems like this in the past, but this time I wasn't at fault. Then the other shoe dropped. I'd left enough money behind to cover my expenses for some time on the apartment we shared in New York. Darius told me rent checks were bouncing. I was devastated, and thrown off balance. Darius was counting the money he thought I was making and wanted to force me into a position where I'd have to support him. This wouldn't be the last time I'd find myself in a situation like this. One thing that comes with even a promise of financial success is worrying about people using you.

12/2/84 My spirit feels so faulty. I can't believe the week is starting again. I don't feel good about it. I wonder if I'm thinking clearly about relationships. About men. About life in general. I know I'm thinking clearly about my career, because it's more rational in a sense that it proceeds in a linear fashion. There's another girl here in the apartment who's successful, she has covers and flies around all the time and is gone for endless days on trips. I wonder if I'll ever be in that position. It's already not easy to have a relationship, and getting to the big time is only going to make it worse. I'm really mad that all the money at home got fucked-up. I came here with $100, because I left the rest of the money my mother gave me for the trip in New York to cover my expenses. Somewhere $1,000 was wasted but where? But I can't dwell on the money thing. I wish I was the sort of person whose feelings and perceptions slapped them in the face. I'm always willing to wait and see, I always think things will pass, days will get better. I only make moves in extreme cases. Right now, I'm so nervous I'm eating to the point of no return. All I'm doing is trying to create a problem that I can solve. It's a very petty feeling of control.

It's Christmastime in Paris. I'm feeling so strange, so bad. I'm losing myself. I can't rest my head, it's so full of names, places, personalities, ideas, wants, and bad feelings. I have no money, no phone, no home to call my own. I have none of the comforts of success. I'm full of conflict.

My life was sinking but my career was getting better.

I spent Christmas breaking up with my boyfriend, after my booker told me he had been asking where he could get drugs in Paris. That's where all the money had been going for the rent in New York. Things had to change. Like they say, you can never be too rich or too thin. The one thing I had immediate control over was my weight, being skinny was a means of getting rich. So I took out my frustrations by starving myself, to the point of fainting, for my first job after the holidays. Lindbergh booked me again to shoot the haute couture for *Vogue*, a prestigious sitting. If those pictures were published it would take me to the next level, giving me a more sophisticated image and placing me in the big earning leagues for fashion shows and affording me a chance to get a designer campaign.

What I really needed was to escape my relationship. It was like a chess game. My first move was to find another relationship. I left my boyfriend behind in the model apartment, which meant that he would eventually get kicked out since he had no business being there without me. I moved in with a much older man, a wickedly funny English photographer. It raised a lot of eyebrows in the business—no one could figure out what I was in it for. We were ill-suited; he was too old for me and I was too young for him and the combination didn't jibe well with my image-conscious job. At work, people were not shy about questioning me or offering opinions on this new relationship. I was too full of pride and fear to trust anyone enough to talk about the financial and emotional trouble I was in with my boyfriend from New York. I was really unhappy inside. I was lucky to be booked everyday, prancing, preening, and smiling on cue in a photo studio, but the work only exacerbated my confusion.

I was on a sharp learning curve and having a stimulating time despite my growing pains. Modeling opened up the world to me like a storybook. Like Cinderella, I had the foot that fit the glass slipper and I had officially been invited to the opulent masquerade ball that the fashion world is. It was a ball that would last twelve years, but unlike Cinderella I didn't get a Prince Charming to partner me while I was dancing. I was going to castles in the south of France, jumping out of helicopters in Norway onto polar glaciers, visiting ancient monasteries in Italy, swinging in London, hanging out with the Rolling Stones in the recording studio, driving through the middle of the African desert in Morocco at midnight dressed up like a Bedouin nomad, and then I was off to Hollywood. This was all in just one ten-day period. My life had become a weird, wild whirlwind.

By the time I appeared in the lobby of the Shangri La hotel in Santa Monica on Monday morning, July 8, 1985, I had frostbite in one toe, a bladder infection, a skin rash, dysentery, and a chronic cold as a result of the constant traveling. I showed up wrinkled, tired, and covered with dog hair for some reason and with a bottle of cranberry juice under my arm. I had landed in Los Angeles to do a spread for an Italian magazine with a new photographer called Herb Ritts, who everybody said was "going to be a big star." At that point I was considered a big star in Europe, my agent provided evidence of that fact by telling me the Italian magazine had held their presses

Herb Ritts

waiting for Herb's pictures of me. Herb expected a lot of me. It was blazing hot and we were working outside, I was wearing black leather and rubber clothes, a black monkey fur wig and standing on a black backdrop painted with tar. I was steaming, stinking, and suffering. Herb wanted me to do some nudes, he needed me to stand still longer than my body wanted me to, and I just felt bad that I wasn't really cut out for this modeling thing. My resolve and passion for modeling was beginning to fray. I got back to my room that night, with heat rash added to my list of ailments, and wrote in my journal: "I've decided I'd like to be a writer. At the moment I don't have any skill, maybe not even the talent for it, but I'd like to try. If not for the glory of it then just for myself." It would be another four years of struggling with self-doubt and the seduction of modeling before I got up the nerve to try and get published.

October 1985 featured my first runway season in Milan. My agent, David Brown, at Richardo Gay Agency had secured ten shows at a stellar fee of $1,000, which is like getting $25,000 a show today and I'd never made that much money in a week. I got the star treatment, the agency had agreed to cover all my expenses including my phone bill. I was also warned by David Brown, that under no circumstances should I tell anyone the terms of my engagement or about my $1,000 fee. I was excited. My expectations and my agent's expectations were for me to be a runway star right out the box.

I got to Milan and was installed in the Hotel Fierra, a kind of Holiday Inn convention center hotel across from the Fierra, an arena where you'd go to see the boat or auto show. The only difference is that this arena had runways and display booths for designer wares. All the A-list models were in the Fierra and we were all assigned an agent or a driver who'd take us individually on about fifteen go-c's a day. The runway business is competitive. The majority of models who make their living in the business don't support themselves by doing print work—they do it on the runway. It's a hard gig too—you're responsible for flying yourself in, covering hotel expenses, and if you're lucky enough to work, it's 16 hours a day, seven days a week, for four weeks in four different countries. It's like being a glamorous migrant worker.

The first day out on appointments I got picked up on a motorcycle. I had so many designers to see, scheduled from ten A.M. to midnight, there wasn't time to drive in a car from place to place. I felt like I was in some cool Fellini movie, getting whisked around by this long-haired, olive-skinned Italian boy, through the streets of Milan, which looks a lot different from Paris. The buildings are like Paris, but more earthy because they're not white stone, they have this particular color scheme of mustard, rust, and moss. The effect of the architecture strikes people in different ways—I find it comforting, a lot of people find it depressing.

At my first appointment I took off the motorcycle helmet thinking I was going to shake my hair out and stand resplendent like Botticelli's *Venus* transported into an Italian car commercial. It didn't quite work that way—there was an angry look of dismay on the designer's face. A staccato conversation in Italian was taking place between Luca, my chaperon/chauffeur, and the designer. When I looked in the mirror I started to get the drift as to what they were talking about. I'd straightened my hair, and half of it had reverted to fuzz and stuck to my head in the shape of a helmet, and the makeup I put on had started to run. I looked like a Barbie doll a cat had played with, not a four-figure runway model. As we walked down the stairs Luca told me the designer had said I looked too heavy in the hips for his clothes. It was ten-fifteen A.M. What a rude awakening.

I was disturbed by the event. Luca and I went back to the agency to request a car so I could arrive fresh to appointments the rest of the day. We got a car and I fared a little better but not great. I was disillusioned to the point of hostility. I thought I had been promised a wonderful present, and I opened it up and there was dog shit inside. I'll bet the designers felt the same way about me.

I didn't know how to handle this new arena of competition. I was inexperienced, and so oversensitive that I couldn't look at myself and see what I was doing wrong, so I blamed my inexperience on the designers being stuck up. It's really immature to want something and then when you don't get it, criticize it. My insecurity bred an attitude of anger and sullen defiance, which was just me being defensive about being really scared and feeling inadequate. I did a couple of shows and I didn't perform well. I hadn't developed the body confidence needed to walk a runway. And I'd also been eating way too much, because I was exhausted by the demands. But, there was something else behind the overeating. I was disappointed, and looking for a way to stuff down hurt feelings and get some comfort and satisfaction. I ended up gaining about five pounds in as many days. The phone rang early one morning in Milan. It was David telling me, "Don't worry about your bookings for today, we want to bring you in and talk to you." David came to fetch me personally and took me to the agency.

David led me past the busy booking tables where the phones were ringing off the hook during the hectic show season and into the office of Richardo, the agency's owner. Richardo had been an agent longer than anyone else except Eileen Ford. He has a keen eye and a sort of paternal manner that can turn blunt and unfeeling in an instant. I sat down in the fancy high-tech Italian-design office, it was all dark and modern. "Veronica," he began in his baritone voice, "the designers are complaining that you can't walk and you're too heavy for the clothes. I'm losing money. They don't want to pay. You've done three shows and I'll pay you for those, and the hotel bill you have now and the phone. You should go back to Paris."

I came back to the hotel from the agency dejected, and in the lobby, I bumped into an English model I'd worked with on shoots. She asked me how much I was making per show. She told me that she was making $300 after being a steady performer booking twenty shows a season for the last five years. I told her it wasn't going very well for me and I was told to keep my price to myself. She begged me to tell her, because she felt she and some of the other girls weren't being treated fairly, and the only way for that to end was if "all us models stick together and help each other." I relented and told her how much I was being paid, trusting that this was an act of solidarity. I also asked her to wait until I had gotten paid and left town with my wages before taking the issue up with the agency. I went up into my room and started packing. Five minutes later I got a call from David and Richardo; the two of them were furious. Word had spread like wildfire in the last five minutes about how much money I was making, and a group of models were demanding more money before they would finish the season. And who would pay the consequences for trusting people? Me. Richardo was now responsible for getting the models who were proven earners more cash if he wanted to hold on to them. Out of concern for his bottom line and in order to teach me a lesson too, he reneged on covering my expenses. I decided to leave the agency at that point because even though I didn't perform well, a guarantee is a guarantee and the whole thing just turned out to be a big mess. I went home with next to nothing and the sense that I'd never be able to be in league to earn that kind of money again.

After the horrible showing I made in Milan my first season, I wanted to be able to compete in the business and regain my pride. Luckily for me, Rei Kawakubo, the designer of Commes des Garçons, an avant-garde Japanese company, latched on to the way I looked and made me the star of her show that season and for many seasons to come. It was a whole different world from the rest of the design establishment. The clothes were like these delicate pieces of origami, more intellectual than sensual. Her presentation was unique too. There were no high heels—

ever—and we were instructed, through interpreters for Mrs. Kawakubo, to "walk as though we were on the street. No turns, no smiling, just go straight down to the end of the runway and walk back."

Commes des Garçons ran their shows like a paramilitary camp. The call time was always six A.M. and you had to arrive right on time, because the staff took a count at the door. There were no mirrors, so that we couldn't see how the outfits looked on us. We had to go through strict rehearsals, two before the show where a lot of the clothes and the models got weeded out, and two more at six A.M. on the actual day of the show. I have to thank the people at Commes des Garçons for two things, one, giving me the chance to get up the confidence that I needed to become a "showgirl." And two, I met Marpessa, who has become one of the truest friends of my life, backstage my first season there.

It was early in the morning and Marpessa was perched on the makeup counter, wearing a leather jacket hanging open with not a stitch on underneath, reading *Women's Wear Daily*. Her hair was picked out into this big sandy brown Afro. She had the exact proportions of a Barbie doll. I really liked her when she started talking. She'd just read something in the paper that obviously offended her and blurted out, "They are saying here that this new model, however you pronounce her name, is supposed to be an African princess. So what is she doing with two tons of relaxer in her hair." Marpessa wasn't talking to anyone in particular, she just had something to say, balancing a Camel with a long ash between her lips. I looked at her and thought, she's tough, she's grounded, she's cool. This is the friend for me. I scooted over to her and introduced myself. We got along right away, and to this day we're like alter egos. She's adventurous where I'm cautious, I'm studious where she's cavalier. She takes no shit off of anybody, where I tend to suck it up and accept it. Marpessa is constantly struggling to keep weight on her perfect figure by eating luxurious liverwurst sandwiches and I'm struggling to stay thin guzzling protein drinks. Marpessa was a star in every area of the business. She was a top earner and performer on the runways in the European and American markets, and a strong presence in magazines. She gave me the gift of taking me under her wing and helped to make me a player in the business.

Marpessa and I spent hours upon hours trying on clothes. It was an exercise that would look absurd to anyone else. We would go over to each other's apartments in Paris and spend the day mixing and matching everything in the closets. Every shirt had to be tried on with each pair of pants; every bag, shoe, and belt, had to be tried on with everything. It wasn't unusual for us to spend two hours in the house on a hot summer day trying on coats. We were playing dress up, using ourselves like dolls, which is the basis of fashion. When we exhausted the possibilities we'd make lists of new clothes we needed and take off on Marpessa's moped, whizzing around Paris in search of style. Marpessa knew every nook and cranny of the city, she'd already been there for four years, her French (not to mention English) was perfect and unaccented. She has a facility for languages, because she's a Dutch girl and no one can understand a word of that language. Her competence inspired me to take control of my life and maximize my time in the city.

I was looking for an outlet, trying to get inspired and fulfilled creatively. I had been a dancer and an art student and I missed that release. Ironically, it came when I discovered the way designers think and work. Marpessa had been Karl Lagerfeld's pet model and muse since he took over at Chanel like a merchant king, remaking the legendary label in his own image. It was Marpessa who brought me into the fold. Being hired at Chanel flung open a door to a world I had never seen before. Karl Lagerfeld's persona is drawn from the great classical traditions of European royalty and letters. His whole carriage and lifestyle personifies the expression "to the manor born." He dresses like a modernized dandy from the court of Louis XIV, in perfect three-piece suits, jeweled cufflinks and tie pins. His shock of thick white hair pulled into a flawless ponytail made me think of the powdered wigs of French monarchy. Karl has a heavy German accent that flows from language to language effortlessly, he has a gift for puns which come easily to him because he's like an encyclopedia of world knowledge. Marpessa showed me this official-looking book, fatter than an unabridged dictionary, before

Frits Berends

we went over there the first time. The book was called the *Tombe de la Noblesse*, which means *Register of the Nobility*, and among the names of families from centuries ago Karl's name was listed. We went to the offices of Chanel on the rue Cambon behind the famous Ritz Hotel. The place didn't reek, it stank of old money. Sitting behind his desk with all his titled assistants, Karl embodied every notion of cultured extraordinary wealth, except he was hot and fresh and randy at the same time. It's a seductive combination in one person.

Lagerfeld was the first designer I got to watch up close. The process of how designers worked excited my imagination. I loved the way Karl made drawings and then summoned teams of seamstresses with pins and bolts of fabrics to make the sketches into clothing. Best of all, Karl solicited and respected our opinions. We'd learn a lot from Karl. Marpessa was very close to him and was always invited to dinners and parties at his country chateau, or out on the town in Monte Carlo. Marpessa would come back and report on what the really rich and glamorous people were doing. She described how the tables would be set for a twelve-course meal, with as many forks to use. She'd show me the drill with the forks. Marpessa had figured it out by watching Princess Caroline of Monaco, who was seated at the same table. In case you're wondering, you start from the outside and work your way in with the forks and knives. The big spoon at the top of the plate is for dessert and the little one is for stirring coffee. It wouldn't be long before I'd find myself at a fancy dinner and I was thankful for the lesson. At one point, Marpessa and I talked about going to finishing school in Switzerland, but then decided against it because modeling was on-the-job training.

It was an exciting time in fashion, it was the eighties, and Wall Street was roaring with riches, oil money was pouring in to the coffers of every company selling luxury products. People wanted clothes that reflected glamour and excess. Pouf skirts were in, the new labels to worship weren't on Calvin Klein jeans any more. If you had money for a Chanel suit or the body for Azzedine, that meant you'd arrived.

I did my first Chanel show and Karl trusted me and Marpessa with some of the best creations he was showing that season. I couldn't walk in heels yet, so Karl generously made the concession to let me wear flat shoes with all my outfits. I did have to wear heels with one spectacular checkered Chanel suit and I was terrified at the fitting in Karl's studio. I took Marpessa aside, freaking out about what I was going to do. She came up with a solution, she asked Karl if we could walk out together on the runway since our outfits were similar for that passage in the show. Marpesssa convinced Karl, leaving out the real reason, which I'm sure he knew. When the day of the show came she threw aside the strut she was famous for to walk slowly arm and arm with me so I wouldn't fall flat on my face on the runway. At last I'd performed well in a show that was the standard of glamour for the industry. The only correction I got from Karl's longtime assistant Gilles Du Four is that I was "too shy on the runway and disappeared into the other girls" when they reviewed the videotape of the show. I wasn't daunted by the comment, in fact it liberated me to develop a comic persona on the runway. I'd have some great moments during the years I was invited to walk the runways at Chanel.

The other thing that Karl did for me and Marpessa was to put us in the advertising for K.L., the label he did under his own name. It was really hard if not impossible to be black or a person of color and get an advertising job in those days and it's just about as difficult now over a decade later. I don't know exactly what the logic was on the part of the people who did the hiring, but outside of fashion shows it was hard for "dark girls" to make real money. For us to be taken to places like Monte Carlo, the south of France, and put in the most expensive luxury clothes in the world and held up as the standard bearers of wealth and beauty was no small gesture on Karl's part. It would be few and far between jobs like that for me and I was grateful to be endorsed by Karl in that capacity and still am to this day, because no matter how hard you work at something it takes a believer with plenty of power to help you get to the next level.

Azzedine Alaia, the African designer from Tunisia, was a designer with whom I'd have the most profound relationship of my career. It was 1985 when Azzedine summoned me to his studio in Paris. I was intimidated by the request. At that time Azzedine's clothes had started a revolution in the fashion world. Everyone was working out in gyms and people wanted to show off their new bodies. Azzedine made his reputation cutting the most body-conscious clothes the world had ever seen. His approach to dressing women is all straight sex and glamour, which is part of the reason I was intimidated. Grace Jones used to wear his clothes all the time and even walk the runways for Azzedine. Tina Turner is a big client of Azzedine's too; that tells that the clothes are not for shrinking violets. The most famous image of his clothes is that quintessentially eighties Robert Palmer video "I Didn't Mean to Turn You On." You know, the one with the models in tight black dresses and red lipstick, playing instruments, pretending to be the band. If you could walk the runway for Azzedine, not only did it mean you had one

Karl Lagerfeld

of the best bodies in the business, but it put you in league with women like Grace Jones and Tina Turner.

Photographs of Azzedine's clothes dominated the magazine pages, because no matter how you moved in the garment every angle was perfect for the model as well as the photographer. Azzedine was also on the cutting edge in every other way—his house was designed by Andrée Puttman, the predecessor of Phillipe Starck, his friends were all the great living painters, singers, and movie stars. Both the legendary and the ingenues flocked to Azzedine to get his magic touch.

Azzedine's one of those people who you can't have a neutral reaction to—his personality's too big. At the time I met Azzedine he was in that mysterious part of life where you don't ask people their age, because they look youthful and asking them how old they are just undermines all the work it takes to keep up the appearance of youth. He stands about 5 feet 3 inches tall and always wears a humble uniform of black cotton Chinese pajamas. Azzedine has a wry smile coupled with a biting, combative sense of humor. In '85 when we first met there was a lot of terrorist activity in Paris, including bombs going off in subways and shopping centers, which made the atmosphere very tense. Azzedine would do things like hide old-fashioned alarm clocks in his employees' lunch boxes set to go off at the time they'd be taking the subways home, which caused one of the seamstresses to be detained by the police. Azzedine kept "secret dossiers" under his desk of the worst photographs and stupidest quotes from people in the business. I have a file in there that he pulls out every once in a while just to let me know he's watching. Azzedine is also an excellent mimic—it's not unusual for him to turn on a Prince or Tina Turner CD, put on some heels, and re-create a number word for word, step by step. Azzedine is as willing to make you laugh as he is to make you cry—if he feels you've crossed him. Once a famous actress came in to have some clothes made for her. Because he felt that she was not being considerate enough of the seamstress, Azzedine just opened the front door of the boutique and physically pushed her out onto the sidewalk.

Azzedine's house was a very special place. The top floor was Azzedine's studio where he did everything himself. The room was overflowing with fabrics, magazines, and half-made garments, everything was organized so no one else could find anything except him. The floors below were hives of activity where the seamstresses would be sewing away and the shipping people would be sending out orders all over the world. The ground floor was the boutique. At lunch time every day the entire staff, including the accountant, the seamstress, and the custodian, sat down in his long basement kitchen, that in some other century was the wine cellar, and ate together. The chef Soumarie was from Senegal, and he made the most delicate French food for the staff. He and Azzedine would often have these acerbic, but jovial running arguments at mealtime, which would amuse everyone to no end. I liked it there, there was a sense of family that I'd really been missing since I'd left Detroit.

I ended up spending all my free time over at Azzedine's house watching him make clothes, sketch outfits, make the patterns, and do the draping in muslin to sew the prototype of clothes he was going to put on the runway. He's a perfectionist and incapable of delegating work. I'd sit in the studio with Azzedine and his assistants in the late afternoons. All kinds of people came by to visit and talk, the setup was like a Parisian salon—artists and musicians and models talking about their feelings, and what made their worlds revolve.

Eventually, I started doing fittings for Azzedine. It could take as many as one hundred hours over a period of weeks to get one jacket just right. We'd work till late in the night watching TV, accompanied by Azzedine's evil Yorkshire terrier Patapouf, who bit me at least two dozen times. My French grew by leaps and bounds hanging out with Azzedine, who was rapidly becoming a father figure to me. I had a little notebook and I'd jot down every new word I learned. Then at home I'd listen to the Radio Montmartre, the nationwide talk-radio station, and repeat what I heard while I watched myself in the mirror. Azzedine was proud of me for learning French, but his mischievous side couldn't be contained. I was going to an important job one day and Azzedine gave me a primer of French phrases that would be useful in the studio. He pointed to articles of clothing telling me the names in French. He told me the argot for pants was *"kakette,"* pants were called *"chatonette,"* and if you really liked something you were supposed to say *"cette grosse rouge* ____ " and fill in the blank. I went off to the studio the next morning, and throughout the day I used my new French to talk about how wonderful I thought the clothes were that were being shot on me. Well, by lunch time the editor Betty Bertrand was red-faced and on the phone to my agent asking in French, "What is wrong with this girl! Does she have Tourette's syndrome or something?" My agent got on the phone and asked me what the hell was going on. I said I was using the new French that Azzedine had taught me the night before. I was told to get Azzedine on the phone right away. What I came to find out was that he had taught me the most graphic sexual slang in the place of the real names of the clothes, so every time I was saying a pair of pants looked or felt nice, I was saying "I really like this big red cock!" Or if I thought we should try and shoot the clothes this way or that way Azzedine had tricked me into saying "I think this big red pussy would look better this way." It was like I was going on about some explicit sexual fantasy. It turned out to be an endearing joke at the end of the day, but still . . .

Azzedine helped me tremendously. He didn't just teach me to speak French, but he let me live in his house when I came back and forth to Paris and he pushed me like mad with photographers. But I think what he most keyed into about me was that I was always writing and drawing, even before I knew what

Backstage at Azzedine.

I wanted to do with it he encouraged me. He was also aware of my flaws, one of which was always getting myself into a relationship with a guy who was no good for me. I was sailing toward success at that time, but lots of times I was depressed, or moody, which is no good when you're supposed to be free and easy and show up with a smile at work every day. Azzedine would tell me over and over, "This is the one time in your life when you can do what you're doing now. If you're not with someone who is making your life easier then you don't need to be with them. In your case, I think you'd be better off alone, because you don't choose well." His words made sense, but they stung too, because they were so true. It would take me another seven years to understand why I put myself in situations that were mentally abusive and to learn to have the strength to pull myself out of bad relationships.

I had been dating an English drummer named Astin for a while. He had real Jekyll and Hyde personalities, all sweetness and charm until there was something that took me away from him. We'd be riding through London and he'd think that I was looking out the car window at some guy on the street, and he'd blow up. And then he'd accuse me of looking at other men, then call me a liar when I said I was just looking out the window at a part of London I'd never seen before. Then the car would become a weapon. He'd start to speed, and then jerk to a stop throwing me around in the seat. He'd run red lights screaming at the top of his lungs all the way to the destination. I'd be scared out of my wits, shaking when I got out of the car. Once we got to where we were going he'd apologize if there were going to be other people there, and then give me threatening looks for the rest of the night, sometimes even pulling me aside and warning me that if I didn't look happy in front of people there'd be hell to pay once we got home. He also threatened to hit me a lot. He never went through with it, because that was the one moment where I had absolutely no fear. I wasn't scared because I'd caught a lot of ass whoopings as a kid, and was trained by my father not to show emotion or fear when I was getting hit—because that would just make me get another punishment. A violent man only wants to feel your fear, and have total control over your being. It's like they get some evil pleasure that I can't understand.

One thing that doesn't go away too easily is mental abuse and you can't do anything about it in the aftermath—there's no calling the cops to come rescue you, and it's hard to make it hold up in court. This scenario went on for about a year between the two of us, and my performance on the job started sliding quickly downward. I'd gain weight and be withdrawn, my confidence badly shaken by the part of my life that should have been giving me pleasure. Finally after about a year of this we went to see this movie *Sweet Dreams*, the Patsy Cline story starring Jessica Lange. In the story she has a crazy jealous husband who was making her feel lower than a run-over snake all the time and then she gets on a plane after a horrible argument with her husband and the plane crashes. And she's dead.

I sat there in the theater sobbing and I thought, "You know what, this could be my life—living with this asshole who makes me feel bad and reaches into my pockets all the time and belittles me every chance he gets and I'm on a plane and I could end up dead having wasted time, getting my feelings hurt and die broken and unhappy. FUCK THAT! I'm outta here!" I got on the plane the next day and left London, with no explanation, and never ever, ever, ever missed him again for even a second. He called for about a week but I'd just hang up the phone. He tried to apologize and win me back by talking to my friends, but I never told the stories to anyone so they didn't know what I'd gone through with him.

You wonder why someone in my position would put up with that kind of shit? I wasn't married to the guy. I certainly didn't need financial support—it was the other way around. We didn't have a child. There was nothing to trap me into the situation. The sex was really good—which will always hold you. But that wasn't the heart of the reason why I stayed . . . I can tell you why, but it took me a long time of making mistakes and repeating the same relationship to various degrees. When the abuse started happening I couldn't believe it, I would think that everyone has fights and that this too will pass. Then I would think it must have been something *I* did the next time it happened, and once I started thinking it was my fault I was on a greased pole to a hell of humiliation and self-doubt. When it happened again, I thought I could fix it, but my wanting to fix it had more to do with my ego than helping the guy I was with, and that's really important to understand. My father, God bless his soul, could be very cold, cruel, and critical of me. I felt like he never really accepted me, and I'd be in these relationships trying to make

Daddy love me. But you see, you only get one chance per person, you can't substitute someone for someone else. The only people in life you have to accept unconditionally are your family because there is no escaping your flesh and blood. You can't choose your family, but you can choose your friends and your lovers,

no one has the right to ever mistreat you. For people who abuse people it's not even personal. They'd do the same to anyone else who was with them, because they're not doing it *to* you they're doing it *at* you.

The movie *Star '80* is a chilling portrait of the

My first photo shoot for Interview Magazine

kind of relationship I was in, escalated to the nth degree. I was never physically damaged by a man, but my spirit was made to feel faint a lot. Like Dorothy Stratten, a lot of girls who leave home for the big city are prone to nightmare relationships because they're on unfamiliar turf without their family nearby and it makes them easy targets. The only way you can fix a relationship like that is to GET OUT.

After that episode I went back to my parents' house in Detroit and changed my name to Lie Low for a little while. I had wanted my parents to come visit me in Paris but my father's health was poor at the time. He'd pretty much had health problems all my life. He was in his sixties when I was born, and his heart and kidneys were failing slowly. My mother always said, "We've got our passports, as soon as Daddy gets a little bit better we'll come and see you." I wanted them to come to Paris, take them out and show them the city, treat them to a holiday on my success. The passports would never get stamped. My mother had made a commitment to my father for better or for worse, in sickness and in health, and she stuck by his side at every minute until they were parted by death. I'd go home a lot and bring gifts for everyone and tell stories—but there's nothing like having your family there to see what you've done. After this last sick relationship ended, I got the fever for America again. I missed my country and I missed my culture. Plus I wanted to be close to home in case anything happened to Daddy, so I moved back to New York.

When I first came back to New York, Azzedine brought me with him to translate conversations between him and Madonna, who had summoned Azzedine to make the costumes for her world tour. I remembered seeing Madonna around Danceteria the first summer I'd come to New York back in '82. She'd grown into a legitimate superstar by '87, and both Azzedine and I were excited to meet her. She came exactly on time to Morgan's Hotel where Azzedine and I were holed up in a series of chic high-tech hotel suites. When I picked up the phone and heard Madonna's famous voice say she was in the lobby with her publicist Liz Rosenberg, I got a rush like I was on a roller coaster. I'll never forget when she walked into the room—it was like time stopped for a minute. See, she wasn't merely famous, and she wasn't a legend, she was a phenomenon. Just coming off the cover of *Time*, the movie *Desperately Seeking Susan,* and a series of bubble-gum tunes with provocative sexual images and lyrics, she became a hub of pop culture. No matter where I went in the world Madonna was there in some way, her every move heavily anticipated. She was tiny, but slightly stocky, and really strong, which made her seem invincible. Her hair was bleached white and like a delicate mass of cropped cotton candy meringue gelled into a polite punk-rock hairdo. She was in black from head to toe, ballet slippers, leggings, and a T-shirt with a black leather jacket on top. The only flourish was, a coat of red lipstick that made me think of Marilyn Monroe. What was most alluring about her was the way she radiated power and control.

We said our hellos and I told Madonna that I was from Detroit like her. Her face registered surprise and she said "Get the fuck outta here," sounding exactly like Joe Pesci in *GoodFellas*, and then she and Azzedine started talking about what she wanted for her tour. I translated back and forth between the two of them. In between every sentence I relayed to Azzedine, Madonna and her publicist were discussing the details of her day. When it was time for Madonna to answer she did without missing a beat. Azzedine took her measurements, which I jotted down on a piece of paper, and then, to my horror, she spotted an ostrich leather coat that Azzedine and I had been working on for about seventy hours over the last two months. She loved the coat, it was exquisite, any girl would have coveted the thing. He had brought it to show her as a sample, but it was supposed to be mine to keep. Well, that's not the

way it went. Azzedine gave it to Madonna and she walked out
with it on her back. I was devastated, I felt like a preteen on
Christmas and my dad had given my present to the neighbor's
child who he valued more than me because she was the lead
majorette and I was just a cheerleader. Come to think of it
that's probably why I was a good model—I was capable of being
emotional about clothes. Azzedine promised to make me
another one (I'm still waiting) and we went on that night to see
Madonna at Lincoln Center in the David Mamet play *Goose
and Tom Tom*, that she was starring in with her then husband
Sean Penn. It was a funny night. Azzedine couldn't understand
English so I was whispering the lines in his ear in French during the performance—we were asked to leave the theater by
the usher and somehow managed not to get kicked out, staying
till the end in uncomfortable silence surrounded by pissed-off
theater patrons.

Afterward there was a party at Sardi's, the famous Broadway
eatery with the caricatures of luminaries of the Great White Way
like Barrymore and Coward hanging on the walls. Everyone in
the world was there. It was the first time I'd experienced the
bright lights and crush of the paparazzi. I have to tell you I liked
the bright lights, and it wasn't even aimed at me.

Madonna showed me and Azzedine to our table, she sat me
down between Andy Warhol and Warren Beatty. Azzedine sat
next to Warhol and the painter Julian Schnabel. Conversations
between these men were so raucous, talking about art, idioms,
and isms, that I started to feel like I was doing karaoke. Most
of the time I didn't really know what I was translating, and was
a little too tipsy to care, but I liked the way it sounded. Warren
Beatty kept trying to engage me in a tête-à-tête but I was too
shy to respond. I wasn't afraid of Andy at all because he was
one of my heroes. I wanted to know all about the Factory in
the sixties and what made people famous pop stars. Andy said,
"You have to wear a recognizable uniform." When you're at a

table of famous people at a public event there's never any real continuity to dialogue because too many people want to meet them, or say hello, and the interruptions are constant, the greatest of which is the famous person switching back and forth between public and private personas with a turn of their head. While Andy and Warren were talking about something else I noticed that Madonna had done something really ill—she'd hung the precious Azzedine coat over a radiator! Ugh! I popped out of my chair and told her she couldn't leave something that special languishing over an inferno! Madonna looked at me like I was a crackhead trying to tell her what do, and then I think she was amused and told someone to go hang the coat up for her. Azzedine witnessed the exchange from the table. I told him what went on and he still laughs about it to this day. The thing I was most happy about was that I got to meet Andy and I wasn't disappointed—but most important he liked me enough to put me in *Interview* magazine as "a person to watch." It was a long way from sitting in Food, the sandwich joint in SoHo, three years earlier hoping that Warhol might show up one day and notice me. The next morning the phone rang in the hotel and Madonna told me, "Warren has a crush on you." I was confused and I asked her why, and then I asked if she was making it up. "Why do you think?" she said, kind of exasperated, and she assured me she didn't "go around calling people with some made-up shit." In my head it just didn't fit, Madonna spent a minute trying to school me on what it meant to have a rich famous Hollywood legend come courting you. I didn't get it, so she gave up and we got off the phone.

Those were my first two days back in New York and I started to get the feeling things were going to be different now than before I'd left. And they were. The next thing I knew I was an interview subject for reporters. Andy had me shot for *Interview* and they wrote a little story on me. On the heels of that piece I ended up in a full-page story in *The New York Times*, written by the veteran fashion reporter Bernadine Morris. Bernadine wrote I was "one of fashion's bright new models and can change from a gamine to sultry sophisticate in a matter of seconds winking as she does." There were quotes from Calvin Klein: "She's funny and exciting and has a great sense of style," and Karl Lagerfeld went on record calling me "a hard worker and a quick study." It was a lucky break for me, that story in the *Times*. It's like getting stamped by the U.S. mint as being the legit article, and it gave my face "a name," helping to set me up for the coming supermodel phenomenon.

At the same time I was getting recognition as a model, I really started to want to do other things besides model. I felt locked out of the upper echelons of earning like contracts and ad campaigns, because traditionally those jobs were never assigned to black girls, and because I'd come to New York to try and do something personal and creative.

The late eighties were such a great time in New York. There was a strong black arts renaissance going on in the city. Spike Lee was making these little independent films like *She's Gotta Have It*, that were making big shakes around the globe. The Hudlin Brothers started the Black Film Makers Foundation, and would soon follow that up with movies like *House Party* and *Boomerang*. A whole new crop of black voices like Nelson George and Greg Tate were in the press and hip-hop culture was coming up off the streets growing into the dominant form of pop culture.

Russell Simmons, the owner and founder of Rush Communications, was the mastermind behind hip-hop music. On any given night I'd see him in the clubs or the hot restaurants. The first time I met Russell was at a party rapper KRS-1 gave for his Stop the Violence Movement, inspired by the tragic homicide of his partner, dee-jay Scott La Rock. Russell was sitting at the bar in the club with a drink in his hand, a Newport dangling between his lips, windbreaker on his back, Adidas on his feet, he still dresses the same way. My agent Bethann introduced us. Russell was loud and brash, it took him a couple of beats to get around to saying hello to me, because he was holding court with a crowd of pretty girls and young boys from around the way. One of those young boys was Andre Harrell, Russell's protégé who started uptown records and would go on to become the CEO of Motown records. Russell said "Hi" and looked me over. I had my old-school gear on: Chicago Bulls warm-up jacket, long-sleeve jersey, black leather medallion with a puffy red, yellow, and green map of Africa in the middle, Adidas Lycra running tights with two stripes up the side with a tennis skirt over them, and some Nike Delta Force high-top sneakers. Once Russell took it in he said, "I don't know why kids like you from Connecticut hear one or two rap records and then try to pose like you down with hip-hop." "Umph," I thought to myself, "he's really not giving a fuck about what he says to anybody." At first I was offended and then I thought well, if he's willing to say anything without editing himself at least he's someone you can count on for an honest opinion, even if it is presumptuous. I rolled my eyes and said very politely, "Fuck you, I'm from the east side of Detroit. I just wanted to come by and say hi, you know, let you know I admire you is all." I could see that gave Russell pause, he smiled and told me he thought I was all right. From then on we've been friends. Being around all these entrepreneurial young black people just made me thirsty for more success, to do something more than just "work for," to want to "do for me."

During the years Bethann represented me she invested a lot of time, care, and love into my development. I lived in her house with her for a few months, and cried on her shoulder a lot, I had pangs of guilt when I told her I wanted to take the month of February off and just see what else I could do with my life. Bethann warned me against it, even a month off would make my clients think that I was unreliable. I didn't listen. One thing you have to realize when you're modeling is that there aren't going to be a lot of people around with an unselfish interest in you. I spent a month not really knowing what to do because I had no idea how to manage my own time. Everyday when you wake up you call into the agency and say, "What's my day?" Your agent gives you an hourly breakdown of places to go. The days when there's time off in between jobs are spent getting waxed, manicures, pedicures, going to the gym, being at the ready for the next booking. It caused a lot of anxiety in me for the first time in my life to be in control of my schedule, because before that my time had been regulated by parents, school, or work. I looked around for acting classes, I thought that might be a good route to follow and I started work on a novel that's so horrendous, to this day I won't let anyone read it. At the time I had a friend who was an actor named Al Payne, and he and a friend who was a playwright named Reggie Rock Bythewood, had two plays ready to go and I decided to bankroll the enterprise and be the producer. We started a little theater group called the Tribe. We installed ourselves in the Harlem Y on 135th street and Malcolm X Boulevard and started doing issue-oriented youth theater. I had no experience as a producer, but energy, optimism, and money can go pretty far toward anything you're trying to accomplish. We set the run for four weeks, we had a good two weeks and then attendance fell off to nothing. The venture was a financial disaster for me, but I learned the way you have to look at things like that—most of the time you pay for your education.

Turning my sights on acting I found my way into William Esper Studios in New York. The acting studio's been around since the late fifties. I stayed in the program for two years, going three nights a week. My teacher, Maggie Flannigan, a red-headed atomic pixie, ran the class like a boot camp. It felt good to get into an academic environment again. It made me feel as if I had more control over my life than I did as a model.

(Little did I know the acting world is a thousand times harsher than the fashion world.) I had all types of insecurities going in. I wondered if I was going to be accepted by the other students being that I was this horrible cliché of a model-turning-actress. But, that was not the case with the other pupils.

Acting class is a wild place because everyone in there is living out their emotions in the context of acting exercises and scene studies. It takes about six or seven weeks before you start to see everyone's emotional and social issues surfacing. You've got man-haters and misogynists, racists, victims of sexual abuse, closeted sexuality, the painfully shy or people emotionally damaged in some way that puts up a barrier and makes it nearly impossible for them to play a certain character. Sometimes people would lose control and get violent. I found out that it was nearly impossible for me to show vulnerability, especially doing something like Ibsen's A Doll's House where the wife is prey to her husband's domination. I'd go through those scenes like a robot. Our teacher used to say, "the best place for an actor to be is in therapy." I couldn't understand why until we really got into scene studies and heavily sublimated feelings would come up and I'd feel strangely emotionally out of control for days at a time. It's easy to go crazy as an actor. I struggled a lot with my lessons, because acting makes you bump up against all the shitty stuff in your personality, like excessive pride, vanity, and defensiveness. As strange as this might sound, I really liked doing the work. My teachers thought that I could have a shot in the business, which encouraged me to think that just maybe I could.

Missing classes was cause for expulsion and I took that condition very seriously. You can't make money as a model if you're not available to hop on a plane at any given moment and go wherever for any length of time. My modeling career suffered tremendously. In the space of one year my financial situation changed so drastically I went from living in a duplex penthouse apartment on the Hudson River with a swimming pool, to a basement studio apartment in the East Village. I have a strict rule about managing money: You have to live within your income. For me I divide my money into quarters, 25 percent taxes, 25 percent for rent/household, 25 percent reinvested in my business, and 25 percent tucked away in a savings account only to be touched in case of disaster or for a serious investment like buying a house.

I could do little modeling jobs around New York, so I wasn't starving. But, at the same time, I chose to give up all the prestige trips for magazines that keep a model's image top-notch, and going to Europe to do the collections, which keeps your pockets full, in hopes of becoming a paid actress one day. No matter how established you are in a profession, if you're not available your agent will put someone in the slot you're not filling and your clients will move on. It was a scary period for me.

I hate not having money, I really do. I have no romantic bohemian notions about poverty, especially where women are concerned. It's very difficult to protect yourself if you don't have money of your own. The one thing I will say for that period of financial hardship is that it hardened my drive to succeed all over again, making the courage to get my writing career going a necessity.

Getting published happened by a lucky accident. *Paper* magazine, which is often described as a "downtown bible of cool," ran a cover story on me and Fab Five Freddy in the summer of 1990. A month or so later the publishers Kim Hastreiter and David Hershkovits called and asked me, along with some other celebrities, to contribute a restaurant review to the magazine. I was so thrilled to be writing something for publication in New York that I slaved over my six paragraphs for weeks on end. When my review came out in print, the feedback at the magazine was really good. Kim and David called me and said something I'd never heard before: "You have a voice, we'd like you to write for us." There was nothing in the world I wanted more! At that time *Paper* was still in its infancy, and couldn't afford to pay the writers—but I didn't care. I wanted to write so badly that I was willing to work for free. I started doing interviews. In the early days, and even now, when people hear my name as the writer the PR people or subjects say "Veronica Webb the model?" The reaction cuts both ways. People are either curious to meet me or veto the idea because they don't think models can write. My very first interview was with the Hudlin Brothers, who'd just directed the movie *House Party*. They cancelled the appointment five times before we finally met, but that turned out to be the least of my problems. One thing not normally associated with writing is stage fright, but in the middle of the interview with the Hudlins I just froze. The tape recorder was going, I had my carefully researched notes in front of me, and all of a sudden, I started pouring sweat. My mind went completely blank. I couldn't speak, it wasn't that anything dramatic happened. I just got overwhelmed by the fact that I was actually doing it. Sitting in the room in the role of a reporter! Reggie Hudlin registered my distress and took pity. He agreed to meet me again when I got myself together. Had Reggie not helped me out, and had I failed on my first assignment, you might not have this book in your hands right now.

I had other obstacles to deal with as a cub reporter: I couldn't type and I hadn't had any writing instruction since high school. I was just coming at it raw, you know, just trying stuff until it worked. I dedicated most every night to writing and in six months had published about twelve articles. Slowly, but surely, things were building, and then my big break came. Glenn O'Brien, the author of Madonna's *Sex*, who was an editor at *Interview* magazine, gave me an assignment to write about Denzel Washington for their cover. Denzel had just won an Oscar for his performance as the Civil War soldier in *Glory*. Writing a cover story meant as much to me as being on the cover of *Vogue*. Once that story hit the stands it made more people associate my name with writing. I got work at *Elle*, *Details*, *The Source*. I reached another one of my goals—I was getting paid to write.

Summer of 1990, I finished my first year of acting classes, and made the cut for the second year of the program. It was time to get my modeling career back on track. I missed the thrill of the phone ringing with people wanting to pay me to do things and the charge I get being around the high-strung creativity of the fashion industry. I was in Paris staying with Azzedine again, and things were going better than expected. *Elle* magazine took me to Morocco for a cover shoot. I'd never had the cover of an American magazine, the

hardest won page of a fashion magazine in the business. And finally after six years I had a chance. We were staying in the Hotel Mamounia in Marrakesh. I'd never really seen a place like this before. With its elaborate Islamic decor it looked like a palace out of *Ali Baba and the Forty Thieves*. The five-star hotel was hexagonal with an open center court and terraced floors all the way up to the domed ceiling. Every surface was decorated with lacy woodwork and pointed arches, inlaid

Todd Eberle

tiles, pillows, and carpets. When I got to my room it was more lush and exotic than the lobby, I hopped into bed and dreamed I was a genie in a bottle. The next morning I was up at 2:45 A.M. in time to eat and be alert enough for the 4:00 A.M. call time for the cover shoot. Hair and makeup started at 3:30 and we had to be at our location in the desert by the time the sun rose. I am not a morning person. But, I was thankful for the early start because that meant I wouldn't be in the heavy sweaters and coats I was modeling for the fall September issue during the unbearable heat of the noonday sun. So there I was with the heat of the sand burning through the soles of my shoes at nine-thirty in the morning and smiling like a horny bride at the thought of having a cover that my mother could go buy at the grocery store. By noon we were done taking pictures and went into town.

OPPORTUNITY RINGS

When I got back to Paris, I had a message on my answering machine in New York that would change my life dramatically. It was the famous director Spike Lee saying he wanted to audition me for his new movie *Jungle Fever*. The next message was from David Schiff, my theatrical agent, saying that Spike's office would be calling me. I'd have to get on the plane right away and come to New York for the casting. I was overjoyed and terrified at the same time, elated by the opportunity, but scared I might fail. David was representing me informally until I booked something. I felt that if I didn't get this he might lose faith, an unnecessary pressure I invented for myself. Little did I imagine how treacherous it would be to step through this looking glass into yet another wonderland.

I left Paris for New York the next day. I did a little shoot for

Vogue in my apartment about young writers starting out. In the middle of the session my phone rang. It was Spike. They were putting auditions on tape and he wanted me to come over *right away*. I couldn't because I was working and wouldn't be available for the next four or five hours. But, before I could say that Spike said, "You don't have anything to do, so get over here." I explained what I was doing, and he said I was lying. I couldn't believe how rude and dismissive he was, considering that I wasn't being unreasonable, not to mention the fact that we'd never spoken before. But like a lot of young powerful men Spike had a case of "kingitis" where the world revolves around their every wish and whatever's in the way of their wishes is a complete and utterly unworthy lump of shit as far as they're concerned.

This would be a ruling factor for the rest of the time I'd be involved with him. I went through a series of auditions that you'll read about in one of the essays in this book, but what isn't in that piece is what was going on with me emotionally behind the scenes. And you can't read it between the lines of that article either. I was too compromised at the time to tell the whole story.

JUMPING THROUGH HOOPS

I had really grandiose notions of what would happen once someone let me be in a movie. It's embarrassing now to read this entry from my journal, my naivete, arrogance, and ambition were a recipe for a fall.

7/5/90 I wrote this month's cover story for *Interview* on Denzel. I have my own column in *Paper* magazine. My career is back on track better than ever. I have damn near half the issue of American *Elle* coming out in September.

Best photographers, best fashion, and a good relationship with Gilles Bensimone, the magazine's star photographer, and the publisher, Regis Pangiez. I've just been cast in *Jungle Fever*, Spike Lee's next film. I am the ingenue. The star about to happen. My daily rotation of calls is star-studded, Robert De Niro, Warren Beatty, Isaac Mizrahi. I

am independent. I have every reason to be proud of myself and I am. The only thing that's demoralizing me is that I'm constantly in the throes of sexual controversy. People say I've slept with everyone I've worked with. It's just so insulting because I sit down and do my work, and it reduces everything to having to defend myself against accusations that aren't true. It's like hazing. Spike is putting sexual pressure on me. I don't like it. I hate it. Tomorrow he wants me to go to Martha's Vineyard with him. The guy just won't take no for an answer. I told him I didn't want to get myself into a situation that might perpetuate the idea that we could be sleeping together. Spike asked me why? Because I've worked too long and too hard to get where I am on my own two feet! I will not be swallowed up as a sexual object or in the shadow of a famous man whose desires are based probably more on conquest and power than on love. He says his "desire is foremost to make a great film." I will play opposite him and give the performance of a lifetime. This is my first, it may be my last . . . Whatever it is, when *Jungle Fever* comes into art and film schools for study and dissertation they are going to notice me. People will cry when I cry. I'll raise my arms and keep the audience laughing into eternity. Film is forever. Once I flicker across the screen I am an immortal. In the meantime the industry is a wretched purgatory filled with twisted shabby thorny paths. My feet will no doubt blister and bleed. At best it will benefit my spirit. I've decided to isolate myself and spend time alone. To read. To watch people act. I wanted this role bad! I got it. Now, I need to run with it. I must be the best. It will take everything I've got. Already I feel a little Hitchcock and Tippi Hedren. David Schiff, my brilliant and loving agent at Intertalent, has put all the details of salary, billing, and comfort to rest in a bed of roses. Now, he said, the snag I can look forward to is psychological abuse. Already I'm praying to God that avoiding a relationship with Spike will not cost me the film, and gain me an adversary. No matter what happens I'm going to be called a bitch and no doubt treated like one. I feel good about myself in my heart, but bad in my skin. Life can be made rough. Rough by the callous and insensitive desires of others.

My friend Terry MacElroy is a brilliant painter who is perhaps too existential to let the world discover his existence. He said to me, "Beauty is power, a power [I] don't realize." This is true. He told me that I'm "easy to fall in love with. You can't hate a person for having those feelings." Terry's not given to hyperbole, it's more that he sees everything from the outside looking in. He said, "Spike hand picked you. You have a part in the movie. In a Spike Lee movie. This is outrageous! It's abstract, it's like saying I have a million dollars, or a billion. Those sums exist, they are real but their possession and power are abstract." I'm getting what I want, so live with it. I've got to decipher how to keep my happiness in easy reach.

Today I'm nothing but a strong body and a weeping eye. People are turning on me. I'm turning to Bob now for friendship. I hope my judgement isn't wrong.

7/6/90 My day began in tears. The phone rang twice in the half-sleeping dreaming time of the morning. The first call was from an agent that I'd left some years earlier saying she'd spotted me on the street and that I was moving fast and she'd send me a note full of thoughts. (It turned out to be one of the meanest letters I ever got.) Bob called soon after and that's when the tears turned on like a faucet. Spike had invited me to Martha's Vineyard for the weekend. When I implied that it wasn't at all Catholic, and would cause unneeded sexual innuendo, he intimated that I might lose my part if I didn't comply with his wishes. I was surprised that Bob was right there for me. He told me, "You've played ball every step of the way. You came back from Europe at his request. It's not fair that he hold it over your head before you start to do the part. As an actor it's hard to get work. As a black actress it's impossible. I would hate to see you lose the part over this. He's young, and doesn't know maybe, but those things should never be mixed. Maybe if he wants to do something once the movie starts or afterward then that's more acceptable. If it does come down to that and you lose your part you have to go public with it. You're very intelligent and articulate. The world will believe you." I cried. "Look, tell him you can't go. You have work to do. You're at your mother's for the weekend. Leave the machine on. I can't promise you I won't take him aside and say something. It's just not right. You know what to do. It's going to be okay, don't worry. I have to go now. I have two readings. I'll call you later. Are you all right? I'll call you later. Bye bye." By the time he told me the "world would believe me" I straightened up.

The Bob I was writing about in my journal was Robert De Niro, whom I'd been madly in love with some years earlier. When he ended the affair it was the first and only time in my life I was brokenhearted. And that's all I'll ever say about him— so don't ask.

Call waiting gave its muffled clicking sound. It was Alexa Jones, Spike's girlfriend, and my agent's sister. Alexa was the person that gave Spike my home number in the first place trying to help me and her brother out with my career. Alexa told me that she and Spike had broken up last night on the phone. She'd broken up with him, and he'd confirmed it this morning. It was only nine-thirty. My life had become, with a cruel sudden twist, a horror story. How could I be caught in the middle of this? The day went on. There was the gym in the morning. Pain. I almost didn't notice the difficulty of the exercises intended to burn fat off my thighs. Instead, I put my full concentration on weaseling out, plotting how to avoid the 4:25 P.M. plane that afternoon from La Guardia to Martha's Vineyard. Dinah Washington was on the Walkman, "A Slick Chick on the Mellow Side." I found solace in the lyrics. I let the time pass leisurely. Everything took longer than expected. That was the explanation for the man expecting me in the Vineyard. I went to the pool for a dip. Read a few pages of *The Mambo Kings*, couldn't concentrate. I was outraged, fearful, angry at being sexually objectified once again. The world seemed to be a freak show. The thought that I might lose my part was a monster that I could not reckon with.

> Two-thirty, starving, hungry. Dying for a cigarette. Immobilized by fear. I left the gym for a fitting at Isaac Mizrahi, full of anger. Stopped at Donald Sacks's, got a sandwich and a coffee. Cursed the world. Arrived at Isaac's and told him the story. He seems to think that I should date Spike. He has some kind of chocolate Woody Allen fantasy that he's projecting on me. Measurements were taken for

the wardrobe Isaac was designing for my character in the film. My hips rang in at 38¼". Oh.

Called 40 Acres and a Mule [Spike's company] at three-fifty-five to get Ruthie Carter's number. She's the costume designer on Spike's films. I also made it sound urgent that they find Spike for me. I stayed rooted to my chair until five. The plane left. My part may have flown away with it, but not my soul. That was firmly rooted to my heart in Manhattan. Spike left a message, "I guess you changed your mind. No problem." I felt relieved somehow. I didn't believe I had lost my part. I'd just announced I was doing the movie to some society reporter at *WWD*. I came home and made dinner plans with John Lurie. We ate a fish meal. I drank wine and took a load off my mind. I talked about my part. We talked about John's script. We tried to see a movie. This summer was slim pickins—*Robo Cop 2* or *Days of Thunder*. John had a harmonica and he played the blues as we walked to nowhere. Found park benches. Chatted until the chatter wore out. Went to the Bottom Line. Saw the Frank Morgan Quartet. Thought about *Mo' Better Blues* watching the musicians. Thought the piano player was Wesley Snipes at first. I'm just trippin'. Went home and melted. Seemed like ten years passed in 24 hrs. And I ain't seen nothin' yet.

The Spike chronicles continued. He kept calling with more demands. He wanted me to write an article on his sister, the actress Joie Lee, for an issue of *Spin* he was guest editing. My agent advised me to play ball, and write the piece, I had zero interest in her as a subject and I knew that if it wasn't lavishly favorable I'd reduce my chances of getting the part.

Finally when I finished the piece, which was like passing a kidney stone, it was time to hand it in to Spike and he insisted I do it in person. The "only" time he had was over dinner. I said I'd meet him at the Pizzeria Uno on my corner. I was truly in a frenzy. Why did things have to be so difficult? What was he going to ask of me next? Whatever the next twist of fate would be I was going to get it on tape. I took the little tape recorder I used for interviews and strapped it to my ribs with a roll of duct tape. I hadn't spent my youth watching spy movies for nothing. The problem was no matter what I put on the silhouette of the tape recorder was visible. When in doubt for a big meeting, Chanel is always the answer. I took a Chanel bag that Karl Lagerfeld had given me as a present the last time I was in Paris after one of the shows and hid the tape recorder inside under an Hermès scarf. I tested the sound and could hear myself just fine—even over the noise of my TV set. At the appointed time I set out for the pizzeria with the article. Spike was at the pizzeria waiting for me in a booth. He ordered a pizza and a banana split, happily sucking it up while I sat there nervous and sweating like an informant wearing a wire in a sting operation. Spike asked me why I was so cold toward him and nervous. "Truthfully," I said, "I can't tell you." Finally he got to the point. He wanted to give me a copy of the script. I breathed a major sigh of relief and ran home laughing at myself. A few months later, *People* magazine published an article on sexual harassment in the film industry, the actress Halle Berry, who was also in *Jungle Fever*, was quoted in the piece. She said that she'd been sexually harassed by an unnamed director during a film and had simply told her aggressor to call her "during business hours." I wished I had had her savvy and confidence. I was struggling to build self-esteem into my character, and I'd get knocked around emotionally a lot more before I was strong enough to put an end to being treated badly by people I thought had power over me.

Spike continued pursuing me during the preproduction of the film. It's funny the reactions people have toward you when you start to become successful. In general, and I hate to say this but it's true, most people aren't happy for you. They smile in your face and *tell* you they're happy for you, but in reality they're not. Every time I turned my head after I got this little part in the movie someone had some kind of negative gossip to report. There's always going to be someone there who you think is your friend to tell you every mean evil thing people are whispering behind your back. They're not telling you to let you know to watch your back, they're telling you because they get pleasure out of making you squirm. Between the movie, the *Elle* cover, and the direction my writing career was going in, I found that I increasingly became a target for speculation and envy.

I just wanted to do my work and take it to the highest level possible, make money and get fame—no shame in that. But it was hard to concentrate between all this "he said, she said" that was going on around me. Spike was there and he was powerful and he wasn't going away.

Eventually, I thought that he could protect me, provide some kind of shield and that maybe he somewhere might really genuinely be able to love me. So, I played my hand. I played it the wrong way. Going out with Spike snowballed into an avalanche of problems. I wasn't ready for what would happen. I didn't think anybody would care enough to make an issue out of it, that the world would just have to leave me alone for fear of offending him. The opposite was true. I'd wake up and read in the New York papers that we were living together. We were not. I was spending time with him at his place in Brooklyn, but I kept my apartment in the city where I spent most of my time. A waiter at Time Café where I used to eat lunch all the time lived on Spike's block, and fed the story to the papers. Random people would stop me on the street and launch into some issue they had with his work, cursing him out to filth, using me like I was his stand-in for a scene from a movie. It wasn't long before people were telling me gangsters uptown were thinking about kidnapping me, and I was getting death threats from white supremacy groups. Spike straightened out the waiter, he wasn't worried about the death threats—because he said he wasn't the one who was getting the letters—and as for the kidnapping rumors he said, "Black people don't kidnap each other."

Spike was really supportive of my writing, though. He bought me my first computer for Christmas, and a printer for my birthday. Our best times together were sitting at home writing. Spike was writing the script for *Malcolm X* by hand (he never learned to type) and I'd work on various articles. I had my own idea for a movie. My friend Lance Yates and I had optioned the rights to the book *Everything and Nothing; The Dorothy Dandridge Story*. Dorothy Dandridge was the first black actress to be nominated for an Oscar for Best Actress in the 1953 movie *Carmen Jones*. She was an unbelievable talent, but she couldn't get the kind of work she wanted in segregated America and she ended up committing suicide ten years after the movie. I thought I would develop the movie to star in it

myself. A delusional, lofty ambition considering I only had a year of acting class, and I couldn't sing. Spike suggested that I try to write the screenplay, because I wasn't ready to star in a movie by a long shot. Instead of taking that as constructive criticism—which it was—I took it as a damning insult. It was the same advice author Terry MacMillan gave me a year earlier. I'd just read her book *Disappearing Acts* and was moved enough to track her down. I'd read in an article she had a teaching job at a university in Arizona. I got hold of her through the dean's office. She came on the phone and I tried to maintain my composure while I explained that I was a huge fan and begged her to write the Dandridge screenplay. Terry was jovial and flattered, but she was scrambling to finish her new novel *Waiting to Exhale*. I was shocked when she told me that she had read a few of my articles and said she thought I had what it took to write a screenplay. She told me to stay in touch and went back to her work.

In the end, nothing happened with the project, because I didn't know how to write a screenplay either, and the rights reverted back to the publishing company.

It's very hard to be in a relationship with someone as famous as Spike who symbolizes as much as he does. Everything has a hundred times more magnitude than it does when you're just two private citizens trying to make your love happen. Everything you do echoes through the press long after you think the issue is solved at home. In an issue of *Vanity Fair*, the writer asked Spike if we were a couple. He said that he "saw a lot of different women." This stung because at the time he was interviewed for the article it was my understanding that we were in an exclusive relationship. The week before it was published I had taken Spike home to meet my parents. When my mother got on the phone and asked me, "Doesn't this fellow have any integrity as far as you're concerned?" I was too shaken to answer. He treated our relationship the same way when he made an appearance on the *Arsenio Hall Show*. Arsenio said he heard that during rehearsals for the movie Spike and I were playing around and that he'd pretended to propose to me. And now that we had become a couple in real life, he should get down on his knees and propose to me right there in front of the studio audience. I watched the show at home on TV and it made me wince. The position Arsenio had put Spike in was really embarrassing. Spike said to Arsenio, "Why don't you do it, you have as much reason as I would." I'd never met Arsenio Hall. The two of them threw my name and my feelings around like a football for about ten more seconds—it seemed like an hour. I didn't blow up at him or give him an ultimatum. I just began to quietly withdraw emotionally. Those were minor incidents compared to the incident that signaled the beginning of the end of our relationship.

The filming of *Jungle Fever* ended and I had written the piece for *Elle* about my experience of filming the movie. Just as the magazine was about to go to press my editor called me in a panic. The office had got an anonymous call saying that I had "been completely cut out of the movie." *Elle* couldn't run the story if that was the case, it was a long piece and a headline was planned for the cover: "Veronica Webb on Spike Lee—The Making of *Jungle Fever.*" I called Spike at the editing room where he was cutting the film. He wouldn't come to the phone until I said it was an emergency. I was calm when I told him about the call and I needed to know so that the magazine could go to press. Spike exploded, "What is this, I'm not making my movies for the *New York Post* or anybody else in the press. I'm sick of this shit!" I knew Spike was under pressure but I didn't think it was too much to ask as someone who worked on the film and was adding some good publicity, not to mention the fact that I was his girlfriend, he could at least just say yes or no. Instead, he slammed the phone down. I called back and he yelled down the phone that he wasn't talking to the press about what he was doing. He reminded me that he had told me when I was writing the piece to put a sentence in about not knowing if all my scenes would be in the final version of the film or what my performance would be like. And that was that, he hung up the phone on me again. I called my editor and said Spike wouldn't tell me, but we had the line in the piece about not knowing what the outcome would be, and could he and the rest of the editors see if they thought we could go ahead on the strength of that. An agonizing hour went by before *Elle* called me back with the decision to run the piece.

A few weeks later part of the cast of *Jungle Fever* went to the Cannes Film Festival. Wesley Snipes, Anthony Quinn, and Stevie Wonder were there to do publicity for the film. We stayed in the Ritz Carlton on the Croisette. Isaac, Azzedine, and Karl had all lavished me with dresses for the big week to wear to the premieres, parties, and press junkets. It should have been the time of my life, but I was nervous to the point of distraction. I didn't know what I was there to celebrate or promote. Spike still hadn't told me what was going on. The second day we had to do a press conference. I was told where to go and when and if anybody asked me a question I was supposed to say "I haven't seen the film yet." Wesley and Mr. Quinn had seen the film, but I was not invited to the advance screening. I was supposed to wait and see it with the general population at the premiere. I sat in the theater in the dark and waited for myself to come on the screen. I was *in* the movie but my part had gone from eight whole scenes to like eight lines. . . . I just felt shocked, because I'd had such a torturous wait. I wasn't good or bad in the movie, just a bland incidental character, performing the standard function of women in movies: asking the male characters expositional questions and having sex with them. I kept thinking, all that time and emotion for this? I was nauseous as the final credits rolled. At the film festival after the credits, spotlights blast the row of seats for the cast and director, and you're meant to stand up while the audience claps for you. I could barely make it to my feet, because my instinct was to hit the floor and crawl on my hands and knees all the way back to my momma's house in Detroit.

The house lights went up. The next step in the protocol is to walk the red carpet down the grand staircase, pose for a hundred million paparazzi shots and go out to dinner with the cast and crew. When the heavy door of the limo swung shut—Spike and I were riding with some other people, but I can't remember who—Godzilla could have been in the car breathing fire for all I knew. I managed to croak out congratulations to my director. We went back to the room to change out of black tie for dinner. I was silent, just trying to maintain myself and get through the rest of the evening. Spike asked me what was wrong. I gave him some snippy response that it'd be better to talk about it later. I'd picked a fight, and Spike got annoyed. He accused me of being "really selfish," because I didn't congratulate him on the film until "we were in the car." I couldn't believe what I was hearing! I lost it. I picked up the big gaudy gilded Louis XIV lamp and swung it at him. I missed. Spike started struggling with me until I gave up and locked myself in the bathroom crying. Spike got dressed and left for dinner.

A few minutes later someone was knocking on the door of the suite—I was still in tears. I was totally dejected; my ego was shattered into a hundred million bits. I'd really set myself up: I wanted to be a star so badly, and thought the minute I got on screen the world would be at my feet. But right then, I didn't want to face anyone. The knocking continued and I realized it was at the bathroom door. Spike had come back upstairs to calm me down and coax me to the dinner table. I just stood there in my bathrobe staring at him, his words not even registering. Another knock came at the door and it was a woman from the publicity department at Universal, in a tizzy saying that we'd better get down there because

Arthur Elgort

Tom Pollack, the chairman of the studio, was sitting at an empty table waiting for the director. She looked at my face and realized I was the cause of the problem. She offered to wait with me as long as it took for me to get ready and come to dinner. And then in an effort to cheer me up she said, "You were very pretty in the movie." That was the last thing in the world I wanted to hear, that I was "pretty." I shook my head and gave up and got dressed. I went into the dining room.

Mr. Quinn was at the table next to us. I'd interviewed him before and he had been really sweet to me. I spent most of the dinner in a sad silence. Mr. Quinn leaned over and said to me quietly, "It's only a picture. There'll be others, honey." After dinner there was a party at a disco for the movie and Stevie Wonder was playing the songs he'd written for the sound track. I went for five minutes and got back to the room alone to make plans to get the hell out of there. De Niro was in town for a movie he was promoting and I called him up crying like I've done so many times before. Bob sympathized with me, and offered me a ride home on the jet he had on loan from the film company.

The next day I got up and held myself together by some strange glue during eight hours of interviews, responding to questions by rote, toeing the company line, and then I left on the jet with Bob. The best thing that came out of going to Cannes was that I made two new friends, Jane Rosenthal, who's Bob's partner in Tribeca Films, and Melissa Maxwell, a young screen writer who had worked with John Singleton on *Boyz in the Hood*. From then on those two women would become touchstones in my life.

Back in New York I didn't know what to say to my friends about my performance in the movie. I started to sink into a depression. I told Spike I thought it would be better if we didn't see each other anymore. I felt he'd betrayed me. I was nurturing too much animosity. For us to have a trusting relationship with each other seemed as futile as rearranging the deck chairs on the *Titanic*. Surprisingly, Spike agreed easily, he only wanted one concession—that neither of us would tell anyone we'd broken up because he didn't want people thinking we had "been together just for the film." I reasoned he was probably right, and it would be easier to just act like nothing happened because all it would do was cause negative publicity, and more social bullshit to contend with.

Spike is a clever operator. He tried everything to mend the hurt feelings, he brought me a cactus (a fitting symbol of his love) when he came to pick me up for the New York premiere of *Jungle Fever*. On a few days he even suggested we get married. I was really unhappy and I couldn't see much future in that. We stayed together for a while longer until I woke up one morning and thought, "I never want to wake up in Brooklyn again."

Spike was filming *Malcolm X* at the time and he was gleeful that day because he was about to direct the largest, most expensive scene of his career. All that morning people were asking me if I was going to the set to watch the crowd scene being filmed at the train station up in Harlem. Other writers and actors who were friends of Spike's had been invited and it was an honor and event to go. I hadn't been invited. Spike called me that afternoon to check in and see how I was doing—after a little more than a year of being together I really had no emotion left when I told him that we weren't going to see each other anymore. We weren't contributing to each other's happiness enough to make it worthwhile. It was over.

Spike called me a lot, but I didn't return his calls. I had nothing left to say. You can't date someone with as much power as he has and escape repercussions when it ends—especially if you're the one who leaves. I was ostracized by the people who were loyal to his camp. I was even treated harshly by people who wanted to win Spike's favor. There was nothing I could do about it. When you're in a situation like that you only have one choice—you have to get your shit together and excel.

I went back to Paris again and picked up the pieces. I'd ignored and alienated most of my clients by assuming I was going to have instantaneous success as an actress and I wouldn't need their support anymore. I was really wrong. But at least no one rubbed it in my face. The only repercussion I had to deal with was from Karl Lagerfeld, who had his assistant Gilles Du Four tell me, justifiably, that he "didn't trust me anymore because I had canceled on him too many times while filming the movie so why should he trust me now?" Once again it was Marpessa to the rescue, convincing Karl to let me back on the runways at Chanel. I had to suck up the fact that the show was already fully booked and there was no more money left in the budget to pay the models. If I wanted to do the show I'd be doing it for free. I got one dress to wear in the couture show in July '91, in my heyday I would have been given at least five outfits to model. I was grateful to Karl once again for his generosity. I'd learned my lesson: Always remember who started you and never abuse their faith when you start getting a little leverage off the platform they risked giving you.

I hadn't been in Paris for a week when I got a call from David Schiff. Spike was offering me a part in *Malcolm X*. It was a déjà vu from *Jungle Fever*, only this time I was cynical. I didn't want to do it—but David said I'd only be cutting off my nose to spite my face. It was one scene with Denzel Washington, it'd only take half a day and I didn't have to audition. I finished my couture shows and left for New York. It was strange to walk onto the set again, after everything that had transpired between me and Spike. I felt like I had grown up a lot when I walked onto the set in Queens, because I wasn't enchanted and emotional like I was before, I had come to do a job and leave. In my scene I was playing a pregnant Muslim woman, Sister Lucille, the mother of The Honorable Elijah Mohammed's illegitimate children. I was warning Brother

Malcolm that he would be murdered by his mentor. I had to wear a pregnancy suit. It's a body suit padded with latex breasts and a belly that you put on under your clothes. Denzel and I did our scene seated at the dining room table—his resemblance to Malcolm is not as strong in person as it comes across on film. A three-year-old and a five-year-old were playing my other two kids in the scene. The three-year-old was fidgety and we had to do the scene over and over because it was hard for him to concentrate. Denzel found the solution, he

took off his ring and gave it to the kid to play with while we said our lines. I was out of there in about five hours. Spike and I were polite with each other but that was it. I thanked him for thinking of me for the part. I meant it because *Malcolm X* is a film I'm really proud to be part of. Like *Roots*, it represents a cultural milestone.

PICK UP THE PIECES

I needed a change. I thought for a while that I would sell every-thing I had and join a traveling theater company to try and get my chops up as an actor. That plan was too drastic. Instead, I moved to Los Angeles that fall to try and get auditions out there. I sublet this little place in Los Feliz, a neighborhood in East L.A. I wasn't there but three weeks before I got robbed, joined a gun club, and failed at every audition. I decided acting came at too high a price and I left L.A. for Paris, retreating into the safe and welcoming arms of the fashion world.

SUPERMODEL

Things were good in Paris when I threw myself back into model-ing full-time. During the year or so I was away things had changed a lot. The term supermodel had been invented to describe highly paid, high-profile models. The reason I think the word came into being in the first place was that there was more media than ever before and fashion was ready made to feed the media machine. Everyone can relate to getting dressed and wanting to look their best. Suddenly the collections turned into a huge tool of self-pro-motion. When I started out in the mid-eighties there was only Elsa Klensch with CNN's *Style* stationed in the tents with a camera crew. By the early nineties there were no less than 200 reporters backstage at any major show waving microphones, cameras, and tape recorders. Every morning during the collections it was like *Meet the Press!* I'd wake up in the wee hours of the morning at Marpessa's house in Paris or at the Ritz and get dressed like I was going to a fancy cocktail party or a concert because by ten A.M. I would have done at least twenty on-camera interviews. Journalists asked the models everything—what the fashion forecast was to why models date rock stars. One hot topic, championed in

Andrew MacPherson

the press by Naomi Campbell, was the historical exclusion of black models and other models of color from cosmetics contracts. It didn't make sense that cosmetics companies were ignoring that segment of their consumer base. The 1990 U.S. census had projected by the year 2000 the majority of the American population would be people of color. *Time* magazine ran a cover story based on the census report called the "Browning of America." The piece addressed how society might change to include greater ethnic representation in school curriculums, to altering images and ideals of beauty in the media. There was great speculation in the fashion industry as to who would be the first company to take the leap and put a black model under contract or if that barrier would ever be broken. Personally, I felt insulted that no major cosmetics company, not to mention a lot of fashion houses, weren't aggressively competing for my dollars with their advertising images.

I was sitting in my apartment in New York on a summer day trying to write, I'd been frustrated with the slow pace and isolation of writing. The phone rang and I was relieved to have some contact with the outside world. "Hello?" A cheery, sultry voice belonging to my friend Elizabeth Saltzman, who was editor at large at *Mademoiselle* was calling me up with an unbelievable opportunity. Elizabeth was an associate of Ronald O. Perelman, chairman of the board at Mac Andrews Forbes and the fifth richest man in America. Elizabeth explained to me that among the holdings of the company was the cosmetics giant Revlon. Mr. Perelman was looking for a spokes-model for Colorstyle, a new line of cosmetics formulated specifically for black women, and the chairman had personally supervised the hiring of Cindy Crawford and Claudia Schiffer, who were under contract at the company.

"You mean a cosmetics contract?" I asked Elizabeth in disbelief. That's exactly what she was talking about. Elizabeth said if I'd be interested, Mr. Perelman's office was expecting my call. *Interested* wasn't the word! I would've gone to war to win a cosmetics contract! There are two glass ceilings in the fashion industry, one is age: I was twenty-six at the time, pushing the limit for viability as a model. (I've been told by editors that when women over thirty are featured in the magazines the readers write and complain.) The other one is race. No black model had ever gotten an exclusive cosmetics contract, the highest commercial achievement in the industry, and I wanted to crack it. I called the number Elizabeth gave me and set up an appointment.

I rode my bike to the G.M. building, across from the Plaza Hotel, and took the elevator up to the top floor. I wasn't expecting what I encountered. There was a heavy security detail, big guys in dark suits wearing ear pieces, obviously carrying guns. I could tell by the way their suits were hanging under their left arms. The secretary ushered me down a long hallway, decorated with framed mirrors and murals, to a waiting room that looked like a library in a Ralph Lauren ad. I settled down in a tufted-leather wing chair. I was amazed when a maid appeared dressed in a French uniform complete with white gloves, and asked me in a heavy Eastern European accent if I wanted something to drink. I asked for a glass of water. Within thirty seconds a butler entered another door carrying a thick sterling silver tray with water in a Baccarat crystal glass. Before I could finish, the butler returned to lead me into the conference room. The conference room consisted of a long shiny wooden table, with about thirty leather chairs tucked underneath with a neat row of blotters lined up in front of them. Framed photos of Cindy Crawford from her *Playboy* pictorial hung on the walls between other photographs. I was in the room alone and I didn't know where to sit. This was all new to me. I opted to stand and look out of the window until Mr. Perelman came in. I didn't want to risk offending him by sitting in his favorite chair. The door swung open and there he was, about 5 feet 5 inches tall, a bald pate, trim body, rosy cheeks, and a big smile with a cigar stuck in the middle of it—the man who might pay me a million dollars. Mr. Perelman moved across the room with a healthy gait, stuck his hand out, told me to call him "Ron" and complimented the Jimi Hendrix T-shirt I was wearing. He wanted to know about me as a person and asked for a brief history of my life. I ran through the highlights of my career and asked him what I could do for him. He needed a spokesmodel and wanted to know what I'd do with the job. I knew a lot about the company, some of it was negative. In the mid '70's I remembered the boycott of Revlon, caused by one of their former executives being quoted in *Essence* magazine that the reason there was no direct marketing to black consumers was because the products made by black companies were so inferior to what was produced on the general market that blacks would just buy Revlon products without any extra encouragement. At black churches all across the country women took their Revlon products and dumped them in coffins indicating that any relationship with the company was dead. The boycott died down when Iman was featured in advertising for a line called Polished Ambers and Revlon sponsored a traveling exhibit of African art in conjunction with the new image.

Iman, sadly, was never put under contract, even though some twenty years later a lot of consumers still identify her with Revlon. I appreciated that Revlon was going forward with a new line that was specifically formulated for black women. The chemists that made the line were African-American and had seniority in the company. The challenge in my mind was making consumers feel comfortable by letting them know that this was not a publicity stunt and that the cosmetics they were getting were the best the company had to offer, not just something that was being dumped into the community for a quick buck. I had to go through the process of seeing it for myself before I could think about staking my name and reputation, not to mention signing away my time and more of my anonymity and privacy to be part of the venture. By the time I finished the meeting with Mr. Perelman I had nearly talked my way out of a position as a spokesmodel. Mr. Perelman thought I might be of better use to the company sitting in an office as an advisor on the project. Well, an office job wasn't really my first choice. But whatever, it might be a job with Ron Perelman and I wanted to play ball in that league.

Mr. Perelman's office set up meetings with the advertising department and the publicity department, which stretched on for the next six months. The nature of the job changed several times in Ron's mind. Finally we settled on the idea that spokesmodel would be the best position for me. Mr. Perelman wanted to close the deal principal to principal; he actually wanted to negotiate the terms of the contract with me personally. I thought it over. It took about two seconds before I knew that I was no match for him. I wanted to bring in Monique Pillard, who was then representing me at Elite Models. The deal fell apart once I got Elite involved. I asked Monique what the problem was and she couldn't rightly tell me. That happens sometimes, the client just stonewalls the agent when they've moved on to someone else. All Monique could tell me was that Revlon didn't want to do it anymore. I said I'd get Mr. Perelman on the phone or one of his advisors. When I finished reeling off names of people I'd met in the advertising and executive branches of the company, Monique said, "Could you introduce me? I would love to meet those people." Right then I knew I'd be better off trying to bring this thing to a close another way, because what was going on here wasn't working for me.

Days of worrying turned into weeks. I called friends in the movie and music businesses for advice. It was the first time I'd mentioned to anyone that some sort of deal was in the works. I got a lot of good advice, but none of it really clicked. And then, duh, one midnight it occurred to me to do the obvious thing—I called Cindy Crawford. Cindy had been in the business longer than I had and I'd worked with her at fashion shows and been a guest on MTV's *House of Style*. Cindy has always been friendly and supportive even though we don't hang out, but she firmly believes that most models get messed around in the business because we don't help each other out. Cindy was not bothered by my calling her after midnight on a weekday. She told me to call her lawyer and business manager, Bernard Wincig. He could handle it for me. Cindy was helpful, but I could detect in her voice that she was annoyed. I asked her why, and she said it just bothered her that everybody didn't have legal counsel. She got adamant expressing her disgust about how often models sign contracts that lawyers haven't looked over, and that protection shouldn't just be for models who were smart enough to know, because "everyone should have a lawyer because it's fair." I was totally relieved and thankful to Cindy that she had given me a tool to fight my way back into the deal.

I called the offices of Wincig & Wincig in Manhattan. My call went right through to the senior Mr. Wincig. Cindy had called ahead to introduce me, smoothing the way. Bernie Wincig had this great tenor voice with all the classic notes of a New York cab driver's accent. His paternal manner, developed over decades of representing talent, put me at ease right away.

After a few minutes of talking to him I was happy to let him do the driving. He got my information and the details of what was going on for me at Revlon and in three short weeks we put the deal to bed. It was far and away not what I expected to get financially. We made a deal for three months or ten days work—whatever came first—and I'd be paid a total of $65,000. It's a lot of money in the workaday world, but in the world of cosmetics it's less than what white models get for a single day's work. I could have gotten depressed about it, but depression wasn't going to serve me. I could've made a stink about it in the press but that wasn't to my advantage either. What was going to help me was having the faith to gamble on myself.

I knew I had an entry-level deal, but once I got in the door I'd prove I was worth top dollar. What I was betting on was the attention the venture would get in the press because no black woman had ever had an exclusive contract. Revlon only required one day's shooting for the first campaign. I reasoned the remaining nine contract days would be eaten up in no time fulfilling media obligations. The worst thing that could have happened in my wager is that I was wrong. Being wrong would have meant I would've done a Revlon ad, gotten $65,000, and a lot of press that would only add to my worth as model in the overall market. The key thing though was that once I was identified as the first black model with an exclusive contract and identified with the product it would be harder for Revlon to get rid of me.

Once Mr. Wincig closed the deal and cooked up a plan to extend the deal, I asked Monique at Elite if we could go out to lunch. I told Monique that the deal was done and I'd like to pay her 5 percent to administrate it. Monique was shocked that I had acted on my own behalf, telling me she could not have models handling their own affairs. I felt Monique had to understand it was better for me and the agency to have this deal than not to have it and no one had to know that she wasn't the one who closed it. She said that she would talk to John Casablancas, the legendary owner of Elite, about my offer and let me know. I explained to Monique the deal would probably grow quickly and that I wanted to keep her happy and John happy because I wanted to work with them. No sooner had I walked the two blocks back to my house, and put the key in the lock than the phone was ringing. It was my new lawyer Mr. Wincig on the phone telling me that Monique's lawyer had called him threatening to take legal action. What could they do? Nothing really. I got enraged. I couldn't believe that I was trying to pay her for work she didn't do; I brought the deal back from the dead and was dealing with her in good faith and now this was her return gesture. Bernie told me to calm down, he would call her personally and find out what the problem was. Monique claimed to have nothing to do with the lawyer calling up making threats, he "just happened to be walking past her office when she came back from lunch and made the call on his own." I thought that was really strange. Normally, a lawyer doesn't start making calls on his own on a client's behalf, because it costs the client money. I told Bernard that we were going shopping for a new agency. We'd use the new prestige of the Revlon contract as leverage to help cut a better deal percentage-wise with my new representation. So, there I was with a place in fashion history, a shot at getting a couple million dollars just around the corner and no modeling agency. I never pictured myself in that scenario.

I thought of all the agencies in town. I'd been with Click and I'd been with Bethann, but I liked the access and power of being with a big agency. Just the brand recognition of a name like Elite, or, voila, Ford would be good for me. I went to Ford and cut a deal. My percentage or commission to the agency was significantly lower than the 20 percent I paid elsewhere and I could pay a lower commission because of what I brought to the table after seven years in the business. I was happy to sign a deal with Eileen Ford and her family, because they were straight with me and they had been in the modeling business longer

Patrick Demarchelier

than any other agency. In fact, Eileen Ford is often credited with inventing the concept of the modeling agency. I just felt like I was banking with a white glove outfit, like the Morgan Guaranty Trust, because Ford really seemed above reproach.

Once I settled down with my duties at Revlon and into the relationship with Ford I wanted to repay Cindy for her help. Cindy had done me a great favor by introducing me to Mr. Wincig, and the way I could do a good turn by her was telling her about the commission structures that I had negotiated for myself. I assumed she had a similar commission arrangement because she's known to handle her business better than anyone in the industry and if she was already in that arrangement then I thought I'd thank her with flowers. Cindy was silent when I called to tell her about the commission structure I had set up for myself, which existed for most other models of our caliber. The silence was probably shock because she had been paying the standard rate at Elite. Cindy thanked me and hung up the phone to do what she had to do.

Months later I got a letter in the mail from John Casablancas on his personal stationery. I sent Elite a check for 5 percent on the Revlon contract. Their lawyer had asked for it and I cut the check just to shut them up. The letter said that 5 percent was not the rate that Elite charged their models, and words to the effect that my contract was a joke and Elite was happy not to be part of it. I couldn't stop laughing at this smug tone when I was reading the letter because the joke was on him. I'd just finished signing a three-year deal with Revlon for seven figures. All I was picturing, while I filed the letter away in a box marked *Mail I've Loved*, was John Casablancas's concerned face for his bottom line on that dark day when Cindy called to lower her commission.

The years I spent at Revlon were a mixed blessing. The work brought a whole new level of financial freedom and public recognition into my life, but there were frustrations too. I realized that I had pretty much topped out in terms of where I could go in my career. Over the three years I was there the focus on Colorstyle was dwindling. I tried and tried to find out why I was increasingly out of the loop as far as shoots, personal appearances, and corporate-sponsored events were concerned. It took me about a year to get some kind of answer. The head of marketing took a short meeting with me, where I was informed that the line was slated to be discontinued about a year after I'd been put under contract. The new market research indicated ethnic consumers wanted to see themselves not as "separate but equal," but integrated into general advertising with whites, and see the same packaging on the same display with classic Revlon. And that the head of marketing would be my point person to help me to maximize my time at the company as a spokesmodel. After that meeting I never heard from her again. It took a long time for it to dawn on me that once Colorstyle was discontinued, I wouldn't have a job anymore.

Two years and eight months into the Revlon deal, I started hearing rumors that I was getting fired. I hadn't really done anything wrong to make me paranoid. But everything seemed status quo to me, I was anxiously waiting to hear if I was going to be renewed. No one at Revlon would get on the phone with any of my representation to say yea or nay. The talent coordinator put in a call to Ford to book me for Revlon's annual charity event in Los Angeles for breast cancer. The event was to take place six months after the terms of my contract expired so I'd assumed that meant they were renewing. A few days later I had to make a personal appearance for Revlon, the company was being honored by first lady Hillary Clinton at a gala event at the Pierre Hotel in New York. The reason Mrs. Clinton was showing up to honor Revlon was for the work we'd done in the fight against breast cancer. For the first year I was under contract I'd crossed the states on a whistle stop tour of drug stores to help raise the 250,000 signatures needed to declare breast cancer an official epidemic. Doctors Susan Love and Dennis Slamon at the U.C.L.A. Breast Cancer Research Center coached Daisy Fuentes, Lauren Hutton, and me on the message to send out to the public. Revlon is a huge underwriter of the program and it was the company's way of giving back to the consumer. The way it worked was I would go to a city, do all the local media, talking to people about breast cancer detection and prevention. At the end of whatever interview I was doing I'd ask the audience to come out to a drugstore where I'd be trading an eight-by-ten autographed photo in return for their signing the petition that would be forwarded to the White House. The experience of meeting people who cared about or had been affected by the disease was very moving. The most tragic thing about breast cancer—which affects one out of eight American women in their lifetime—is that the disease is hereditary. It was not unusual to meet a woman who'd lost her mother and aunts to the disease. Hearing the stories of survivors gave me new respect for my health (it made me quit smoking), and it also lent a greater sense of purpose and satisfaction to selling makeup.

After a year of being on the road collecting signatures Daisy, Lauren, and I found ourselves in the White House receiving a personal thank you from the Clintons along with other members of the National Breast Cancer Coalition. This evening at the Pierre Hotel in New York was another fund-raiser in the fight against breast cancer which is a long, long way from being over. I was excited because the PR department had arranged for me to be photographed with Hillary Clinton and have a short two-minute audience with her. I was in my house getting my hair and makeup done and getting ready to put on a wonderful evening gown I'd had especially made for the event. A friend called me on the phone, who I had gotten to know while I was at Revlon. I can't remember why she was calling me, because I was staggered by what she had to say next: "I heard about the contract today. If there's anything I can do let me know." I didn't know what she was talking about, and then it dawned on me she was talking about *my* contract. She was the only one at the company who had the good graces and the consideration to tell me what everyone else knew—that I had been terminated and Halle Berry had been hired. I can tell you honestly that when I hung up that phone I cried like a baby with a safety pin stuck in her eye. I liked my job a lot and I sure as hell loved the money. I just wished that it didn't have to end this way. It's so cliché to get on the phone and cry to your lawyer when "they don't want me anymore," like some pathetic has-been starlet like Norma Desmond in *Sunset Boulevard*, but that was me. I thought it was the end of the world. A few minutes later the PR department at Revlon called offering their condolences. I was so strongly identified with the brand that they felt that it would be confusing to the audience to use my image to represent a new approach.

It didn't help either that I was scheduled to make a public appearance just two hours after I got the official kiss-off, where I had to meet and be photographed with first lady Hillary Clinton at a black-tie dinner with about seven hundred people in attendance. You know when they say "the show must go on," this is just what it means. No matter how rejected or depressed you feel—you have to meet your obligations. The job has since passed on to actress Halle Berry, and I'm happy Revlon has continued to hire black models and reach out to the black consumers directly.

After I was terminated at Revlon I felt like a failure. Revlon tends to have really long-term relationships with talent—Cindy Crawford had been with the company for over a decade and Lauren Hutton has been employed by the company on and off for the last twenty years. Maybe it was just bad luck or the fact that I wasn't concentrating on modeling and maintaining my image as a symbol of fashion and beauty as much as I was burning the midnight oil on the computer.

At the very beginning of my contract I'd been picked up by Sherry Berman, an agent at N.S. Bienstalk in New York, one of the best broadcasting agencies in the country. Sherry had read my columns in *Paper* magazine and thought I would make a good journalist. Things went well from the beginning, I went out for a job on Channel One, the news service that's in the schools, but got rejected in part because of my Revlon contract. There was a lot of controversy over showing commercials to kids in schools and having a reporter who was a spokesperson for a major advertiser was considered a problem. The same problem came up when I was up for the *Jane* show, which everyone has come to know as *Ricki Lake* over the last five years. I got very close to becoming the host of the show. There were only three other people under consideration. Thinking about fitting my image into daytime TV was a funny thing. It was hard for people to see me as a person the daytime audience could relate to. I really didn't personify the struggles of most of the viewers. And once I signed the Revlon contract, which happened on the final day of meetings with the producers, it really knocked me out of the game. It wasn't easy to get me on TV. Sherry Berman had to contend with the age-old prejudices that plague models, like models can't talk, can't think, are hard to relate to, and can't be trusted to show up on time. Well, I was only guilty of one of those things once in my career. I didn't show up on time for *Good Morning America* and it cost me my job.

I got my first job in broadcast journalism doing a show called *Oh La La* which was a knockoff of *House of Style*. Then I moved on to contributing spots on Fox's *Front Page*, and then to *Last Call,* a short-lived late night show on CBS. No matter what I was doing I always covered fashion, as that was my pedigree and most producers thought I didn't have credibility in any other area. I was glad to be working but frustrated by the limitations imposed on me by being a model. I don't mean to slight the career that's given me the exposure and means to do almost everything else I've wanted to do professionally—including writing this book—but I just couldn't figure out how to overcome the obstacle of being a model without destroying the blessings that come with it. For most of my career I'd been on the fence about whether or not to maximize the fame and the notoriety that can come with being a successful model. As a black model you really can't make it unless you have a lot of other dimensions to your career. It's not enough just to be a beauty. By the late eighties I had decided that there was a glass ceiling based on race in the fashion industry and I resigned myself to treating modeling like a waitressing job, as the thing I did on the side to support my writing. I can't say that my writing ever suffered as a result of modeling. The contrary is true, but my work as a model was certainly secondary to my desire to write. I headed in the direction of broadcast journalism because it allowed me to use every part of myself, my ability to write and my love of being on camera. It took me three years to land a job in broadcasting where I could stretch out. I don't remember the exact twists and turns of how Sherry landed me this job, but it was called *The Sunday Show*, an early afternoon show in Great Britain, which was a very irreverent take on pop culture and celebrity. The biggest interview I booked was with the Artist Formerly Known as Prince, getting him to agree to an interview was another crazy coincidence of luck and opportunism on my part.

I'd flown over to London in January of 1995 to do some publicity for *The Sunday Show*, which was debuting in about ten days. I was having dinner with my friend Michael White who produces movies, Broadway plays, and West End shows, most famously *The Rocky Horror Picture Show*. Michael's in his mid-sixties, and still likes to go out and party with the best of them. Michael coaxed me out to this party for Madonna at Brown's nightclub even though I was dead tired. The Brit Awards ceremony (the English Grammys) had just ended and record producer Nellee Hooper, who'd produced *Bedtime Stories* for Madonna, was giving her a party at the club. I'd never been to Brown's before. It's tucked away on a quiet street in the West End of London. It looks like a bank from the outside, and the inside is an intimate high-tech triplex done up eighties style in chrome and leather. I was shocked that the dance floor was completely empty. The second floor was loaded with stars. Madonna, the guest of honor, was holding court on the couches in the back corner; Lenox Lewis, the English heavyweight champ, was holed up on the back staircase with his crew; English rockers like Blur and Jamiroquai were tumbling around the room making merry. Everybody was getting loaded and chatting about sex and work. Michael and I went to the bar to get a drink and wandered over to say hello to Madonna. I hadn't seen her since the time I'd met her years ago with Azzedine. Madonna looked amazing that night in a silver Versace floor-length gown, it fit like a slick of poured mercury. A shock of white-blond straight hair to her waist that would have made any mermaid proud set her whole look off. I went to say hello and congratulate her on the trophies she'd taken home that night from the "Brits." It took her a minute to scan her memory and place who I was. Just as she located me in her mental files, my girlfriend Karen Binns came over with a security guard and interrupted our conversation. "Prince is looking for you," Karen said, breathless and excited. My eyes lit up like Karen had said an armored car full of unmarked bills had turned over and she had two shovels. I'm a hardcore Prince fan, always have been. Freshman year of high school I was so enamored of his music and persona that I wore purple every day down to my under-wear in tribute to his musical genius. Madonna looked at me like "ick," and said half-jokingly, "Don't even go there." I wasn't try-ing to hear that, it would have taken the four horsemen of the apocalypse to drag me away from that invitation. Prince's body-guard, Aaron, led me over to where "the Boss," as his employees addressed him, had put down stakes. Prince was sitting all alone in a little alcove with a bodyguard in the opposite end of the room from Madonna. He was dressed like a lyric out of his song "Arrogance" from the album ♀, decked out in a custom-cut electric blue suit with Cuban heels to match, accessorized with a "pimp rag tootsie pop and a cane."

He asked me to sit down next to him. I was so nervous about making a memorable impression. I did the normal thing and introduced myself. It made him laugh, because he said he knew who I was. Then I made the huge faux pas of calling him Prince, and like a testy spoiled child he kicked me softly in the shin with his pointy little boot. It wasn't exactly the perfect ice breaker, but celebrity has its privileges and we started laughing and talking. He asked me what I was doing in London. I told him I'd come over to do publicity for my new show that was airing next week. He asked for some details of the show but I didn't have any really because it hadn't been on the air yet. So, I just made it up, I said the show was watched by five million people every week, which would have been true if I had said I hope five million people would be watching. Prince said he'd like to help me, and he'd appear live on the show's premiere, he had a bunch of new songs and he'd send me a tape to listen to and I could pick the song he'd perform on the show. I told him what would help me more than anything was if he would give me an interview. Since he hadn't given a TV interview in ten years, it could be the coup that could make my career. He asked me where I was staying and told me that he'd call me tomorrow to set up the details of the show. He got up to go to the bathroom and I left. I was on the other side of the room talking to Nellee Hooper for a minute and then the Artist Formerly Known as Prince's security guard came huffing over asking why I'd left. The boss wanted to say good night. I walked into the hallway where he was supposed to be standing and another bodyguard popped out of nowhere with a walkie-talkie. Prince was radioing in from his limo and the guard said, "Listen to this." The car stereo blasted a tune through the walkie-talkie and Prince said, "I'll send you some more music tomorrow." The walkie-talkie went dead as he sped off. Elated, I handed the walkie-talkie back to the bodyguard and floated back into the party. I'd met one of my idols and hadn't been disappointed. By this time it was four in the morning and I had to do a spot on the *Big Breakfast*, the morning show in London that goes out live at six A.M. By the time I arrived at the studio the British press was on to the fact that I'd been hanging out with Prince at the club. The Artist Formerly Known as Prince was starting a national tour with his band, the New Power Generation, in England in about two weeks so the media machine was on his butt full-time. I took the chance of announcing that not only had he said he was going to play *The Sunday Show* but he had consented to an interview as well. I didn't have anything on paper. I hoped that our conversation wouldn't amount to silly club talk and nothing would come through in the end, which would have been really embarrassing. Instinct told me that he was a person of his word—especially when it came to women. After all this is the man who put women way out front in his band: Wendy and Lisa, Sheila E., and other protégés like Vanity and Mayte. I wasn't wrong. As per our conversation, Prince did the song and interview. Not only did Prince play but he did it live from Wembly stadium, where I and the crew of *The Sunday Show* were the only people in the audience. The song he played was the world premiere of "Billy Jack Bitch." There we were on stage with an elaborate three-tiered bedroom apparatus called the endorphine machine, with $175,000 worth of live-feed equipment on hand to broadcast the event and me out front with the mike, in charge of extracting an interview with this most elusive of personalities.

The song went off without a hitch and then as my producer was counting down into the interview after the break things started getting really wacky. A week before the interview, Prince and I had been on the phone and he was setting conditions for the interview. He wanted me to call him "Torra Torra" when referring to his current contractual and artistic disputes with Warner Brothers, which is why he had the word "slave" painted on his cheek. "Prince" when we were talking about any music he had done under that name, and not be referred to at all when asking him a direct question or anything pertaining to music he had done under the title of ♀. It took a few conversations to convince him that would be way too much information for the viewers to sort out. So, I shouldn't have been surprised when Prince slipped out from the wings and asked me, "Do you mind if I wear a mask?" The question threw me, it seemed like a kinky request for an interview, so I asked him what kind of mask. "Lace," he said without a trace of irony or hesitation. It's my job as a journalist to make the subject comfortable so I said okay. I didn't have time to argue with him, we were counting in from ten on live TV and we were halfway through at this point. I glanced over at my producer who now had four fingers in the air which he was rapidly folding down into a fist, and Prince had one more request—he wanted an "interpreter" for the interview! I almost fainted. I didn't know what he was up to. He spoke English . . . I shouted out to Murray my producer the words Prince was whispering in my ear. "Murray, he wants an interpreter or he won't do the story . . . Mayte is going to answer the questions after I address them to him." Just as I finished the words Murray's hand had folded into a fist, his index finger was pointed at me and time was up. We had to go with the mask and Mayte, Prince's fiancée, and the New Power Generation dancer as the interpreter. Not the best of circumstances by any stretch of the imagination.

The first question out of my mouth was, "Why are you giving an interview and refusing to speak?" to which he had Mayte reply, "He has to sing tonight," which was a cute fib. When I asked how he expected people to understand his situation if he wasn't going to speak, he had Mayte answer "Next question." I had to question the mask, which Mayte said was to cover up for his "ugliness." The Artist Formerly Known as Prince said he was boycotting America until 1999 because he had been under "hypnosis for the last ten years" but he wouldn't say by whom or to what end he had been hypnotized. The reason he gave for changing his name was "his spirit told him to." The band was almost as cagey as their leader, kind but skipping on eggshells in order not to offend their boss. Finally

I had to say that people were thinking that they were "nuts," between the wacky behavior and the name changes. Morris, the organ player, gave the most accessible answer that they "just want to get a concept across to people that's fun." The interview was good and bizarre. I'm not sure who was making a monkey out of whom in this situation. As the minutes ticked on it got more and more farcical. Prince was asking me questions through Mayte. The interview went on for some ten minutes with the band answering questions—unfortunately no one was interested in the band. I thought some flattery might make him more candid with me. I told him I thought he had created a whole universe of music akin to what Duke Ellington had done in his lifetime and that somewhere along the line I'm sure he felt like he wasn't getting his props. And maybe, a more mature styling and move away from eccentric behavior might make people take him more seriously. His quick and caustic retort was, "Who does your hair?" and then he and his future wife got up and left.

The interview was cut short for the live broadcast. I was upset I hadn't come away with the air time it could have had, and it certainly wasn't the coup I expected as a reporter. The BBC held the piece that we filmed at Wembley at the beginning of March for an April Fool's Day special, which would have been my dream if I was pursuing a career as a comic instead of a journalist. When the piece aired in its entirety the phone lines lit up at the TV station. People wanted to know if the show was a hoax, if it really was "the real Prince" wearing the black-and-silver lamé lace mask who sat silently through an extended national interview. Even though it wasn't exactly what I hoped for I was stunned at the time that I was even able to pull it off, and I had a kind of postpartum depression because I couldn't imagine where I could go from there. It wasn't long before I was hired and fired at *Good Morning America*.

The good thing about losing my job on *Good Morning*

America is that I stopped distracting myself from writing. I always imagined myself as a writer. I love doing it so much I thought that God might punish me and make me starve to death if I tried to do it for a living. Everything else I've done more or less was a way to hedge my bets. There's nothing wrong with hedging your bets, but there's no service to yourself hiding from something you believe you're meant to do. I'm lucky like a cat, every time I fail I seem to land on my feet. Luck is nothing to be proud of, just thankful for. I've tried a lot of things in my life, most of them haven't worked out to my expectations. More often than not I'll set up my move to the basket and then bounce off the rim, but what matters is that I'm in the game. I have a joke I tell myself when things look bad: "I've managed to fail my way to success." That's what everyone does who makes anything of themselves. Not everything is perfectly executed in the game of life, but everything you do adds up to the few plays that win.

It took me a long time to make the leap of faith to try and make a living as writer. The basic reason was fear, an emotion that's never helped me unless I was dealing with physical danger, otherwise it just makes me angry. But there were other reasons too, I had the perfect safety net as a model. I was making a lot of money, traveling the world, taking in experiences faster than I could process them for the most part. For a dozen years my life was a blur of airports and outfits. Every day was something new, and all I had to do was stay in gear, move ahead and go with the flow. For all its perks modeling has a cruel irony to it, the better you get at it the less use there is for you. It takes time to develop as a model. Time means years. Years mean age. Age means obsolescence. It's something you have to accept gracefully. After all I would never have had a chance if someone else hadn't become obsolete and made room for me in the industry. It's hard though to feel that rush of privilege and excitement ebb away as the phone stops ringing on the hour with agents passing on requests for your presence in some exotic locale for a large amount of money.

Looking in the rearview mirror at the road I've traveled the one thing that is mine, that I have ownership of is my writing. What I have to offer you on these pages is not a blueprint for living. It's insights and experiences I went through growing from a girl to a woman, being successful in a profession that pushed me into the limelight, laid a magic carpet under my feet, and put a deceiving veneer over my life. I struggled through my twenties trying to find a philosophy for living. I went through a lot of agonizing uncertainty thinking that if I wasn't married by the time I was thirty that I'd disappear on a scrap heap of unwanted women, or that if I wasn't a world-renowned historical icon that the sands would run out of the hourglass. The morning I woke up and I was thirty years old, I was shocked to find the world was turning on its axis as it had the day before: I wasn't in love or married, there was no child in my womb or rocking quietly in a cradle, and I hadn't reached the lofty professional goals that I had set for myself, so I decided to relax. There is no set timetable for anything. I've made my worst mistakes trying to rush circumstances, the most concrete outcome of rushing is creating problems. Iman once told me that "most of the problems we have we create ourselves," and I've proven those words true on many occasions. I've learned not to look outside of myself and compare my life to the lives of other people who are more successful at love or money than I am. It's hard not to succumb to the downward spiral of wishing I was more successful in life, but when those feelings come on I remember the advice Barry White gave me: the most dangerous question you can ask yourself as an artist is "*When* will I . . . ?" You can only succeed by asking "*How* can I . . . ?" And most important, there really is no such thing as "making it." You're not done doing the work God put you here to do until you're in your grave, which means you have to get up and "make it" everyday.

Some of the following essays are snapshots of certain events and moods, and others deal more with universal struggles like love, family, politics, and race. This book is not intended to be a manifesto, or a definitive social tract. It's just the way I saw the world as I was growing up. These are the same stories I might tell you if we met at a cocktail party.

WOMEN

Patrick McMullen

A Bitch Is a Bitch
a Dog Is a Dog

Don't call me bitch, you bastard—and other thoughts on the battle of the sexes.

Why do I have to be your doormat? And why is bitch the dirty word you rub across my back?

"Bitch, noun. The female of the dog or other carnivorous mammals/a spiteful or malicious woman/a sexually promiscuous woman." Noah Webster

"Life ain't nothin' but bitches and money." N.W.A.

T he word "bitch" seems to be making a spectacularly successful comeback in urban American English. There I am, waiting at a stoplight perched quietly on the seat of my Raleigh one-speed, when some knucklehead takes it upon himself to say, "I sure would like to get some of that ass." My stomach flips in embarrassment and my lip curls in response. The light turns green and I ride off. The man shouts after me, in lowly coda to the gross proposition, "Bitch!"

I don't mind that people want to speak out. In fact, I've always been an advocate of public greeting and discourse. But, when language becomes so much dirty psychic laundry, and individuals use one another randomly to vent their frustrations, it's time to shut up, stay off the street, or take a good hard look.

Language is at once a great liberator and a fierce incarcerator. Certain words are like little prison bars, they hold so much meaning behind them. A man calling me a bitch is the equivalent of a white calling a black a nigger in the old South. As a woman, if you're not willing to take your life in your hands, it's a stinging daily abuse that women, nine times out of ten, are obliged to suffer in prudent reticence. There is no word that is the male counterpart to bitch. Bastard, perhaps, but I have yet to see a man wearing a pair of shorts on a hot summer day flustered to the point of tears, suffering from the "b" word assault on the street all day. Most of us are no longer able to find solace in our homes from the open bustfest that is Manhattan. Men whom I deeply admire and respect, my close friend for one, an enormously talented actor, and on general principle, a deep and insightful thinker, lets the word trip off his lips with shocking and casual regularity. It seems to be a common term for women now, a staple in an era of dwindling vocabulary, sexual paranoia, and the acceptable absence of respect. One of my favorite performers in the world of hip-hop, the hands-down reigning sex symbol of rap, Big Daddy Kane, has to refer to my sisters like that, and Ice-T, the breathtakingly articulate grand orator of ghetto life in modern America, uses the disappointing and abrasive terminology. As descriptions of "bitches" slide through my eardrums and into my mind like twin earwigs, I'm enraged by the feeling of helplessness and alienation I get from the artists who I look to for information, inspiration, and identification. These are my male counterparts, my contemporaries, making their way in the world on their own, same as me. I wonder, if they saw me on the street, is that what I would be reduced to, in their minds. I don't know if I should turn the music off. I flounder, wondering how to respond, how to defend myself. I take the word personally. Always. Usually I'm resigned to a half-hearted dismissal of the bad stuff, and take cues from the good stuff, but a feeling of self-doubt and cowardice lingers long after the music has stopped. The dichotomy between Afro-centric pride and black-on-black love, intended to rally support in this time of crisis in black America, is too often diluted, in some cases annulled, by the negative lyrics concerning women. Sexually active women, who let me remind you, are not acting alone, are often betrayed by their lovers as "hoes," "bitches," etc. Let me pull your coat fellas, the ladies aren't doing anything you're not. It's a war between men and women out there, and it's worse than it's ever been before. Trying to get to the root of the problem is as complex as unraveling the Arab-Jewish conflict.

Verbal abuse built up its ugly profile through mass media and all forms of popular culture in the eighties, and now in the nineties, it seems to be turning on us full face. Andrew Dice Clay is case in point—it's funny to be ugly. It's a tool of manhood, even. The more parables and metaphors he can find to reduce and humiliate the species, the more money he makes. The deeper the objectification and rejection of women, minorities, and gays, the harder America laughs. But in reality the suffering goes deeper, becoming commonplace on the urban sidewalks, on the hot new records, and even on the lips of our loved ones. When "just" calling a woman a bitch, or using the term casually, loses its shock value, the level of insult is logically bound to escalate. For the time being, all I can say is put on your aural armor, don your thinking cap, and above all, put a bug in the car of your brother, your cousin, your lover, father, your best friend. The dignity you save may be your own.

—New York, July 1990

IT'S MY RIGHT

No, You Can't Take That
Away from Me

When I came into womanhood, I never questioned that it was my right as an adult to choose to live as I pleased. There would be obstacles in achieving sexual and social freedom, yes, but not as many as the generation of women before me. There were new laws put in place by freedom riders and flower children. My generation rode the upside of the civil rights movement and the sexual revolution. This era is remembered by many Americans as Camelot, a shining moment when citizen warriors took to the streets to fight the dragon of social ills, and won. It was my right to go to school alongside white America, eat in its restaurants, sit side by side in a public restroom, and take a dump next to it. I could work in the marketplace of white America and there were laws that would put the theories of integration into practice; that's affirmative action, ya'll. In my lifetime, this was the new constitution. Gone was the constitution that kept blacks and women from voting, the constitution upon which this country was founded and which proclaimed "a Negro was three-fifths of a man." These victories were won before my time, but I thought this was the deal for my lifetime, at least.

I also reaped the benefits of the sexual revolution. When I matured sexually, I had the privileged birthright of the liberated woman. I was meant to vote, to control my sexuality in a newly uninhibited set of social mores, not to be harassed or discriminated against in the workplace on the basis of my gender. This was coupled with the timely emergence of Planned Parenthood, to administer the birth control pill, the diaphragm, and uncensored reproductive counseling in their clinics, including information on abortion.

A woman's control over her reproductive system is an integral part of entering society. That's fundamental. Teen pregnancies inhibit the educational process of the mother by nearly guaranteeing she will not enter the marketplace at full intellectual and earning capacity. Having a child without a support system in this economy can be the kiss of death for a decent future.

The rights to birth control and abortion also were hard won. Growing up, I never questioned these things as my inalienable rights. In the last eight years, since the grotesque Reagan/Bush sideshow of constitutional abuse, I have come to question the stability of any right currently allotted me under the Bill of Rights. Affirmative action got the Humpty Dumpty by the Supreme Court some summers ago. Another fairy tale of equality. *Roe* v. *Wade* is teetering precariously on that same wall this summer. If she is to fall, who will put the Constitution back together again?

Roe v. *Wade* is a right to freedom under attack. The attempts of right-to-life groups to take away abortion rights and call it a religious issue (or "Operation Rescue") is ludicrous. In a nation devoid of health care, day care, and an effective school system, these actions, if they continue to succeed, only stand to increase the ranks and the suffering of the underclass. In effect, they enslave the men, women, and children denied these rights. The debate over abortion at the Supreme Court, the Catholic Church, and other tax-exempt political parties decides the shared fate of individuals who do not share the same wealth, beliefs, or social advantages as the above and smacks of despotism. After all, was it not the same faux piety and self-righteous fire of this government's religious zealots that created the original conditions of slavery upon which our nation was founded? Sounds like the birth of a nation to me.

It is a rare person who has a neutral reaction to abortion when personally confronted with the issue. The political reality and the social ramifications are one thing; the individual reality is quite another. I've never met anyone who really wanted to have an abortion. It's a terrible moment of necessity and sorrow. In my own experience abortion is not the best of moral choices I have made. My decision has made me uneasy over the years; it haunts me in the naive hugs of my nieces and nephews, one of whom is the age of the fetus I chose to terminate. It echoes in their laughter. A dream deferred. When I think about the abortion, I try to come to terms with the feeling that I chose suicide for another person. The popularity of the abortion option in this country and the runaway sales of *Final Exit*, Derek Humphry's manual on methods of suicide for the terminally ill, drive that notion home. It bespeaks an image of people faced with gravely inadequate health care and grisly standards of living, who find suicide a viable and preferable option to life in these United States.

I ask my oldest sister, a doctor with a profound and credible faith in God, her opinion on the controversy. She has these words: "I've been in a lab when the specimens come in. All the fetuses have to be submitted. I used to believe that they were just globs of tissue, until I saw them. I haven't seen it for five years, but it comes into my mind once a week. The hands and palms are fully formed. The children have looks on their faces. I'm one of the faithful, but I can't tell anybody what to do. You can't teach people through terrorism; God does not teach that way. You have to help. That's why I'm going to adopt somebody as soon as I can." The core of the abortion issue is not the right to birth; it is the right to life.

—Washington, D.C., April 1992

It's Exam Time

What I Don't Know Will Hurt Me

So here I am in the gynecologist's office. I go every six months like clockwork. It's a familiar ritual to most women, staring up at the ceiling during the primary exam, trying to muster the nonchalance to behave like it's the most natural of situations. Making a little polite conversation with the doctor, pretending as if we're just a couple of girlfriends catching up with each other over a cup of coffee. I've learned to tolerate the awkwardness of the exercise, but what continues to make me squeamish is the moment when the doctor performs the breast exam. I have an automatic reflex to a physician's hands probing my breasts: I exhale strongly, turn my head to the side, and let the lyrics from "Make the World Go Away" scroll across my memory. This is part of the reality of being a woman I just don't want to deal with. It has nothing to do with being embarrassed by the physical contact, it's the dread that there might be some news.

Slyly, I use my peripheral vision to survey the doctor's expression. Her eyes register no change. The doctor asks me if I'm doing my exams regularly. Bracing myself against the spasm of guilt her question pushes through my body, I halfheartedly tell her, "Yes—when I remember." The exam is over now. She shuts the door to the room, leaving me alone. All I want to do is bolt out of there. Back out into the world where you never "see" the disease. I remind myself I should be doing the exam once a month, but the idea of it makes me wince. It's hard for me to admit why this instigates so many negative emotions. The answer: All I can think about is losing a breast, and my hair, were I ever to discover something—a lump, to be precise.

Around the time of my period, there tend to be little lumps, which I know are a common occurrence called fibrocystic breast disease, but I still hold my breath waiting for them to melt away—like the reaction I had to thoughts about the bogeyman under the bed when I was a kid. There's cognitive dissonance going on in that brain of mine that makes me think, "What I don't know won't hurt me." It's easy to think that in your twenties. Or so I thought until last year when the statistics on breast cancer were brought to my attention by the National Breast Cancer Coalition (NBCC) as part of a public awareness program Revlon is sponsoring. I couldn't imagine that every three minutes in this country a woman is diagnosed with breast cancer and every twelve minutes a woman loses her life to the very same disease in these United States. In real numbers that translates into 185,000 diagnoses and 46,000 deaths per year. These statistics are as alarming, if not more so, than those connected to the AIDS virus. (The latest numbers available from the Center for Disease Control's National AIDS Clearinghouse in Rockville, Maryland, are the following statistics: 31,671 adults diagnosed with AIDS in the first nine months of 1993. During the same period there were 16,927 deaths.)

In the past fifteen years, so much attention has been paid to research and prevention of either chronic or fatal sexually transmitted diseases that issues like breast and ovarian cancer, which impact women's health as directly and profoundly, have taken a backseat in the public consciousness. Sadly, 40 percent of all women with breast cancer will die within ten years of diagnosis.

One of the triumphs of touring with the NBCC was working on a petition drive that prompted President Clinton to declare breast cancer a national health epidemic on October 18, 1993. It was during those afternoons in drugstores and train stations that I came into contact with women who were struggling with the disease, survivors of breast or ovarian cancer and the families of people who had lost women to the disease. I had no clear image of what I would confront before I got there.

On a warm September afternoon in Boston, I met a woman named Beanie.° I remember her as quick-witted, fit, compact, and fashionable, with a glowing brown complexion. She was introduced to me on the petition drive by a college friend of my sister who lives in Boston. We three girls set off for some shopping before dinner, accompanied by their two young sons. Beanie compared notes with me about designer clothes and cities we'd visited. We sat down to dinner and I couldn't help but be impressed by the relationship between Beanie and her seven-year-old son, David. He was so attentive and respectful of his mother; they had the easy friendship of equals. David was also extraordinarily independent for a child his age. He read the menu by himself, ordered a steak and kept pace, more or less, with the adults' conversation, not demanding any special attention. When our meals came to the table, David asked his mother to help him cut his food. With a smile and an encouraging voice, Beanie told him he knew how, and she was going to leave soon, so he'd have to practice. I asked where she was going. "Well, I have breast cancer," she said. "I lost my mother,

°All names have been changed.

my aunt, and my grandmother and mine has spread to my head and neck." It was David who dealt with my shock and embarrassment. He shrugged his shoulders and said, "It's okay. Everybody feels that way the first time they hear it from someone they know."

One in three American women will be diagnosed with breast cancer during her lifetime.

Beanie and her son were the first people I met who put a face and a soul to the numbers.

—Atlanta, 1993

Don't Hate Me Because I'm Beautiful

Dressing for the Street
Has Never Been Harder

In these first few mixed-up months of the nineties I find myself more mystified and upset by sexuality than I was as a teenager. Constitutional as well as God-given rights concerning individual expression are becoming political footballs that are no longer goverened by the heart and mind giving orders to the hot seat of power, headquartered in my hot pants. I have an itching suspicion that I'm being dethroned.

As a child of the Nixon, Carter, Black Power, do your own thing, exteme sexual experimentation, punk-rock rebellion, equal rights, Cleopatra Jones, Billie Jean King seventies, I never thought that I would find myself as an adult part of the Reagan, Bush, right-to-life, Afro-centric, hip-hop, New Age,

Alt Rock, music, crack smoking, flag burning, right-wing, safe-sex '90s. As a kid, I was sure that the idea of the sexually and socially liberated woman was a concept that was not only long overdue, but part of the natural order of the social system that would forever be in place. I think I've been bamboozled.

On the most abstract and seemingly distant level, the mandate over what we do with our bodies is hashed out on Capitol Hill by Capitol Hillbillies like Jesse Helms. By the time they get through denying federally funded artists free expression Michelangelo's *David* will be wearing underpants. The remote and asexual David Souter, should he manage to defeat Faye Wattleton, the president of Planned Parenthood, will call into question all individual rights concerning reproduction. Every moment of every day the power struggle concerning female sexuality is in effect. In order to be a smooth operator operating correctly, I have to play by a set of rules that are not of my own making.

When the alarm goes off at seven A.M. the games begin: What do I wear to be safe on the subway? A lifetime of preparation goes behind my everyday dressing style, which is part James Brown, part James Bond, and geared toward international urban contact. My mother and father trained me to walk in a certain way, to cast my gaze at a certain level in order to avoid confrontation (i.e. male attention), to be ladylike and safe above all. To be ladylike was the ultimate key to street safety and happiness. Ladylike was a euphemism for being sexually uninviting. As repressive as that sounds (and is), it is also a safe and practical tool of survival. It seems that every moment is filled with split-second decisions designed to guard my honor and peace of mind from the cruel and oftentimes degrading judgments, not only of the hot shot passerby, but literally any man who wants to give me a look or phrase that will strip.

Every morning my thoughts are filled with what to wear in order to not be too provocative to the world outside, and how to be pleasing to myself and the one I'd like to please. Unless I walk out of the house in a gunnysack, I'm always slightly uncomfortable about what *level* of sexuality I'm giving off, not only to the men in the street but the men I have to deal with in the marketplace. For the past few years, having worked as a model on the international fashion circuit, I've found myself in a disturbing paradoxical position: revered on one hand; and on the other toppled from that pedestal as if beauty precluded humanity.

One morning on my way to the subway not 100 paces from my front door, the battle lines were clearly drawn. I put on a T-shirt, jacket, a pair of leggings, and wrapped a long sweater around my waist to cover my behind. In my disheveled leave-me-the-fuck-alone, eight A.M. sneaker mode, two cock strong randoms decided that I looked enticing enough to invite a little verbal harassment of the sexual variety. "Hey baby. Hey slim." (Sound effects, smooch, smooch.) "Could we walk with you?" Having reached my instantaneous boiling point on the subject I asked the two unappealing raggedy-ass, rough-around-the-edges fellows to "have some respect." One of them had the nerve to ask me why. Why! There are a hundred and one reasons why! I opted for the simple one-line, noncombative, nonphilosophical defense. Even though it wasn't true, I thought it would suffice. "I'm married." "Well, then," Mr. Let-me-jump-in-and-fuck-up-your-state-of-mind answered, "then you should dress accordingly." What! That comment turned my sense of self into a twenty-alarm blaze. "You asshole. I have the right to wear what I want, and walk where I want without being harassed by you or anyone else!" "Asshole . . . assshole," he kept muttering under his breath, turning to his buddy with a look of shock and wonderment that betrayed a sensitivity that made him almost human for a second. We parted on silent and hostile terms to our respective corners of Manhattan. I was outraged and puzzled that someone on the street would tell me to "dress accordingly." According to what? Where the hell was this guy getting this idea? Then I thought of David Souter's recent quote, "Public displays of general interest in sexuality indicate a receptiveness to sexual advances." It suddenly became apparent that this was simply a manifestation of the trickle-down theory—the institutional morals that have always existed on Capitol Hill, which appraise and set the boundaries for female sexuality oozing down and sliming the regular guy, and forcing the regular gal to walk a lifelong tightrope of fear and prudence. The sexually liberated woman may only be a figment of our imaginations. The last time I saw one was on film. And those moments are few and far between.

—Brooklyn, October 1992

DARE TO BE REAL

*"The Rejuvenation Will
Not Be Televised"*

W hen I woke up from a dream where I was wearing Birkenstocks and a long skirt, running alongside a stallion with total physical freedom, something inside me clicked. After five years of working the international glamour trade, I've come to the slow conclusion that women are being duped. Fashion is tyrannical in its dictates, especially when it comes to beauty, whose whims hold western women in exquisite bondage. The pages of the magazines and the hallowed halls of la mode worldwide have women scurrying in a mad race against the sands of time and the forces of Mother Nature to achieve some chemically enhanced Greek ideal of feminine beauty. Michelangelo arrived at an ideal after a lifetime of craftsmanship. His women with porcelain complexions, silky hair, aquiline features, devoid of unpleasant smells, flaws, and inability to change should be locked forever in stone as an object, rather than the model for their living, breathing, growing, lactating, menstruating, struggling, laughing human counterparts.

During fashion week in New York, being confronted with cooing faces at every turn—"You look marvelous, darling"—I wondered what people were reacting to: me or the makeup? Could anyone see or respect the little urchin princess from Detroit suffocating underneath? Is the real me that revolting that I need to undergo so thorough a transformation? Why am I sashaying about the runway trying to be something that I'm not? In traditional thinking, an hour under a blazing blow dryer, another half-hour in curlers, and an hour relinquishing my face to the brushes of some of the most talented makeup artists on the planet, would bring me to the ultimate fleeting metaphysical state known as fashion, a shining moment called "fabulous." To the contrary, I found myself racked with insecurities. Why blot out the toll living under a coat of foundation? Why melt down the spirals of ethnic heritage under the torturous winds of a blow dryer? Is it the right thing to sell the illusion that intensive camouflage is where it's at? Everything inside me cried out to be real! The heat of exertion will cause Mother Africa to snatch my hair back up toward heaven; moving through space and time causes liquids and powders carefully placed about the visage to melt and flake. At any moment I would turn into a shameful puddle of reality. In essence, I felt like a total fraud. A sort of traveling saleswoman for Ponce de León.

On my end, as a mannequin, the point of the sale is to convince a girl at fifteen she can look like a sophisticated twenty-five-year-old woman and the forty year-old woman she can be a perky fifteen-year-old all over again. And I'll tell two friends and they'll tell two friends and so on, and so on, and so on.

Two years ago I went through a bleak period where I believed if I added hair extensions, padded bras, false eyelashes—using all the artifice the market had to offer—I could compete on a higher level socially, sexually, emotionally, and commercially. Insanely I thought this would cure the cruel shortcomings of nature and fate, only to end up more miserable and uncertain of my self-image than I was to begin with. Every time I received a compliment, pangs of self-doubt registered in my abdomen. When are they going to find out I'm not real. Artifice and illusion have a way of sneaking up and snuffing you from behind. There is a grievous chasm for women between the perceived ideal of how we should look and how we are. The real challenge is to stand naked and alone, in front of the mirror, as you really are, and like it. To stand before your man and feel glorious in your real self. Simply put, chocolate will never be vanilla, vanilla will never be chocolate, and age will never be youth. The rejuvenation will not be publicized.

George Foreman's phenomenal performance in the title bout against the robotically developed Evander Holyfield is a case in point. Foreman proved to be at ease with himself and the impressions the years have imprinted on his body. I placed a bet on Foreman thinking "age before beauty"; my friend put his money on Holyfield, believing "youth must be served." Foreman served Holyfield up freshly. Foreman's triumph is that he became the populist hero. The sports media, like the fashion press, roots for the figure who fits the concept of the ideal. They had us duped into thinking that Holyfield was the one. There is a lesson to be learned from Foreman; his body slightly sagged and wiggled as a result of age was supported and mastered by instinct and intellect superbly conditioned by time. It is necessary—imperative—to work with nature, not against her. It is a fallacy to think that we can fight against time. There is no cream, salve, or machine that will bring back yesterday. If you dare to be real, you can go the distance. The rejuvenation will not be publicized. The answer comes from within.

—New York, May 1991

FASHION

Steven Meisel

MODELING

Breaking the Bounds of Beauty

I n the nine years I've posed under bright lights, in big cities, earning a living as a fashion model, I have witnessed two great changes in the business of modeling. The first applies to the diversity in the facial structure and racial types of my colleagues. When I started in the industry, the precincts of the beauty zone were just beginning to expand and its boundaries were guarded by friendly Valkyries, typified by Christy Brinkley and Iman. The easily racially identifiable faces of these goddesses were perfect configurations of aquiline features, unblemished by common twists of genetics. Whatever ethnicity a viewer could detect did not stray far from the Greek ideal.

"Ethnic" was the trend in the mid-eighties. Adding to the ranks were models occupying gray territory somewhere between African and Anglo-Saxon. Frances Grill, the president of Click model agency, built her reputation on aggressively selling this "ethnic" aesthetic to, as she puts it, "a market hungry for another dimension of beauty." Her aim was "to make classic beauties out of other kinds of beauties. Fashion is not a naturalistic business. It has a creative element that needs to be fueled by the new."

Change of season is identified as much by the permutations that designers make in silhouette as the crew of models they choose to represent their new vision. Fashion design had a moment of newness in the mid-eighties, with the appearance of Japanese designers Rei Kawakubo of Commes des Garçons and Yohji Yamamoto. Their concepts of construction and presentation defied the prevailing classicism of western fashions. As these designers stole the fashion world's attention, models of "ethnic" ilk, challenging the precepts of classic beauty, were instrumental tools.

Young women of all skin tones began flocking to the fashion capitals. The more exotic a young hopeful was, the better her chance of success. When I first arrived in Paris, the hot tip was to tell anyone considering you for work tales of mothers and fathers from far-flung corners of the globe. As a black American with the generational progeny of slavery with more blood lines than can be accounted for, I fitted the bill.

"The role of the black model was stimulated in the early seventies by the slogan 'Black is beautiful,' " Bethann Hardison, a former model who runs her own agency in New York, says. "Roughly ten years ago, another ground swell occurred, with support from magazines such as *Elle* and British *Vogue* helping to make stars out of black models Karen Alexander and Gail O'Neil. The trend culminated in the rise of Naomi Campbell, who has come to symbolize a black model for her generation."

The catwalk is now open to a whole new group of young women, and the second change I have seen in the industry widens the model agency's net further. The faces taken to represent conventional beauty in 1993 were not always considered to be so. The next keepers of the gate, Linda Evangelista and

Cindy Crawford, were a little more threatening than Brinkley and Iman, with their otherwise perfect faces punctuated by an odd nose or a mole. Evangelista struggled unnoticed for a long time. She once recounted, without pride, that she "started at the very bottom." At the outset, her equine nostrils were regarded as a handicap. Any reservations aside, the model marketed every move of her legendary career with the same brilliance as Madonna, destroying and reinventing her image season after season, too fast for imitators to catch up.

Publishing two covers in 1984, British *Vogue* reintroduced a slightly modified Crawford, identifying her as a star. On both occasions, an airbrush obliterated her mole. "I was considered risky in the beginning," she says. "I don't have blue eyes. I'm not the blondest blond. And I have a mole."

French designer Azzedine Alaia believes that a woman can always become beautiful. "Sometimes it's just a haircut, or the way a photographer sees a girl that can make the difference. But most of all, she must correspond with her time," he says.

Beautiful maybe but, in the generation preceding mine, few models were famous. Those who achieved recognition outside the fashion industry usually enjoyed a notoriety, which often piggy-backed the success of a more famous boyfriend: a rock star or sports figure. Public interest in models in those days concentrated on diet, exercise, and makeup tips. And, of course, the inevitable question: "Are you going to marry that famous boyfriend of yours?"

Media attention has reached near saturation point over the past several seasons. Backstage at fashion shows, the models and their attendant professionals are outnumbered by persistent paparazzi, and the crush of the press corps trying to catch the action. An integral part of professional modeling has become a readiness to meet the press. At eight A.M., a model in any sort of demand knows enough to apply a light coat of foundation and/or dark glasses.

"The ultimate accessory," Andre Leon Talley, the creative director of American *Vogue*, says, "is for a model to have her own camera crew."

What is all this media attention about? Why are people so interested? "People listen to models because they're beautiful and they make a lot of money," Alisa Bellettini, producer of MTV's bimonthly fashion special, *House of Style*, says.

Sandra Bernhard, who performed her one-woman show, *Giving Till It Hurts,* in London last year, is a fashion devotee. I asked her whether she thinks that all the attention to artifice, the dressing up to amplify feminine wiles is a backlash against the women's movement. "It's about projecting a certain femininity and sexuality. I'm talking about clothes that project power," she says. "The problem with the feminist movement is that women were told to demagnetize their sexual power. When a woman looks great she can manipulate a situation."

But why are models holding worldwide attention? "People always want to look to people who have style and self-containment. Models are dressed and coiffed and directed in their look. It makes sense. They seem to be the women with power at the moment," Bernhard says.

Whatever the motivation, worldwide media coverage gave new meaning to the term "supermodel." They were personified by a group, including Campbell and Evangelista, barely twentysomething and dripping in the power price tag uniforms of Chanel. "These girls carried themselves like queens," Elsa Klensch, host of CNN's weekly fashion news program *Style*, says. "They brought a kind of glamour to the business that had been missing for years."

Absolutely in step with the end of the go-go eighties, the supermodels were remote, untouchable and happy to let the public know how very, very well paid they were. The era, for me, is summed up perfectly by Evangelista's famous quote: "I don't get up for less than $10,000 a day." She had succeeded in turning herself into the most glamorous yuppie in the world.

There is something striking about that statement, despite its ostentation or any jealousy it might inspire. It is, perhaps, linked to the newest industry buzz word, "personality." No greater testament can be made to the cult of personality on the runway than the rotation of special guest stars invited by designers to join the models on the catwalk. A few seasons ago, it was Ivana Trump who symbolized the how-and-why of beauty just outside fashion's immediate family. This season, it's Sandra Bernhard.

Kristen McMenamy is another "personality." She is a very different kind of beauty. Reed-thin, she has no eyebrows at all, a ghost-white complexion, and a severely cropped, jet black pudding-basin hairdo. She slips into an eerie space between man and woman, human and "alien," as she is wont to describe herself. She is this year's thing. She is queen waif. "They also call me 'beast,'" she says, with another self-deprecating description that makes her laugh. McMenamy corresponds very much to our time. Her looks force the viewer to consider ambiguity and uncertainty. "I can't believe I don't get letters of protest from middle-America when I'm on a cover," she says. "I know the way I look is a trend. No matter how much I'm called a 'supermodel,' I'll never be Christy Brinkley."

Refreshingly, there is no bitterness in McMenamy's voice as she forecasts the trend that may spell the demise of her moment. "I don't know where the trend will go next. Probably the classically beautiful girl. Fashion just continues to repeat itself."

—Paris, 1990

BEAUTY: BUT IS IT?

Some call it witchcraft, but I call it addiction. For me, beauty is a contact high. I have hallucinations of experiencing and possessing what pleases my eye. Sometimes I stop and stare at a marvelous body passing me on the street or take time to consider from every angle an exquisitely crafted chair in a shop window. How satin the skin, how supple the leather, how good it would feel to be cradled in those arms. How happy I would be if only it or they were mine. Of course, it's much easier to be sure of a chair than a person. But in any case, what I hope for is a transfusion of the sensual comforts of the person or object into my soul.

Exposure to things or people that I find deeply appealing and that cannot or do not yet belong to my world stimulates my will to want. Initially, this type of relationship to beauty is an anonymous form of romance where I envision everything as being perfect for me. Beauty serves as a vessel for my fantasies. When the beauty is particularly striking, childish feelings that hibernate at my core awaken. I become hungry like a bear that's been asleep for the winter, with an appetite for an instantly perfect world where all desire is sated by sight and touch alone.

That world doesn't exist, but it is precisely this passionate, childish expectation that can breed contempt—my own and that of others. Often what I find beautiful I understand as a reflection of my sense of self, the thing that could possibly render me whole because it seems to represent parts of me that are missing. I know all this is not the way to understanding myself, Zen, or the zeitgeist, but I can't help it.

People do put faith in beauty. And if beauty does not conform to whatever virtue has been set for it, a believer can lose faith. Often beauty is overvalued as a cure-all and a catchall. In America, most of our daily diet of what is called beauty is fed to us through the media. The commercial world is dependent on formulas to make beauty "available" to everyone, of course helping along all the processes of acquisition—promising beautification and ultimately satisfaction. The formulas are based on the demystification of beauty. No need to get intimidated—just as they say in the restaurants, "enjoy." The formulas change every time you turn the page or squeeze the remote control.

I am especially vulnerable to depictions of opulently furnished homes, or to those Annie Leibovitz snapshots of happy, attractive celebrity couples. I look at these people and I think they must somehow be virtuous—even if I know they're assholes—because they obviously must have been determined to get where they are. (You can tell if someone is determined by the look on his or her face.) The more determined they are, the better looking they appear. And that goes for anybody, including Henry Kissinger, who was voted the sexiest man in America one year. Power becomes beautiful. But that's nothing a dose of tabloid TV can't cure. Tabloid TV is interesting because it idealizes the un-ideal. Murderers, for instance, become fully glamorized versions of stars—like roses with thorns. Thrilling to get a whiff, but you wouldn't want to handle them.

For a philosopher to say "the good and the beautiful are one" is infamy: if he goes on to add "also the true," one ought to thrash him. Truth is ugly. "We possess art lest we perish of the truth." This statement of Nietzsche's is provocative because it speaks to the assumptions that have equated goodness and beauty. If I see a beautiful chair, I assume the maker who produced such beauty is a good person. Just as illogical is modern anti-culture where adorable, beautiful people are assumed to be empty and not really contributing—as if what we find attractive is a trick. Sometimes cynicism eases the pain of not getting what you want.

When the TV, the magazines, the medicine cabinet, the shop windows, and all the readily available crushes are no longer enough, the pedestrian world of beauty loses its appeal. I have to make a trek to a temple of transcendence and transformation, like a museum. What luxury to go to these storehouses of coveted secrets, capable of transporting us. The most effective outings sway me even in my most ignorant and prejudicial moments, because what is in the museum far outstrips anything I own, or anyone I fantasize about. It's a chance to feel the greatness of civilization. It helps us to piece together the pieces of dreams, but even then there is no formula for making this experience of beauty last. Perhaps more than anything else, these places show us something profound about beauty. Real beauty is mysterious—there is no formula, only chemistry.

Keats once wrote, "Beauty is truth, truth beauty." But now we know that truth, like beauty, and beauty, like truth, are based on belief systems that are deeply subjective.

Why is beauty so captivating? Why does the pursuit of beauty play havoc with our emotions and burn holes in our pockets? Why do we as a culture keep score on the fifty most beautiful people? At the heart of every American, right next to the love of wealth, I think there's a belief in the advertising slogan "If you feel good, you look good." But then again, I think it depends on who's lookin'.

—East Hampton, 1993

SHOES

Stiletto After All These Years

I am in possession, by conservative estimate, of 150 pairs of shoes. I've put another 250 pairs to rest in a temperature-controlled storage space. They are uniformly stacked in clear plastic shoeboxes. Affixed to each box is a Polaroid of the pair, and on the white borders of the pictures are simple epitaphs, naming the designer of the shoe and which season the shoe came into being. It resembles Arlington National Cemetery, but this graveyard is dedicated to the footsoldiers of fashion.

The right pair of shoes can pull me out of a depression. And my optimal shoe, day or night, is a high heel.

The battle lines in footwear are drawn around comfort, attitude, impact, and edge. Of course, heels can be, well, difficult to wear. Many people are under the impression that a heel is too hard to negotiate, or that somehow it's a tool of feminist disempowerment. Wimps, all of you, I say! Actually, I've always felt more nimble in heels. The addition of height elongates the leg, lending me a sense of power and increasing my stride.

Heels give my feet a deceptively delicate appearance, like the hooves of a pig or a pony. But the best thing about a high heel is that it's like putting your ass on a pedestal.

Take a mental inventory of your shoe collection. Is there any romance associated with sneakers, comfy flats, or practical shoes for inclement weather? Hardly. For me, a well-crafted high heel is one of those household objects like a champagne glass—the mere presence holds the promise of magic. High heels, like champagne flutes, connote the best in life. Seduction. Dancing. Celebration. Both the champagne glass and the high heel are functional souvenirs. Ah, yes, I remember it well . . . that pair of fuzzy marabou mules I bought for our first night together. Those red patent leather Lucite heels for Valentine's Day. Those iron-maiden black leather stilettos I got to pierce your heart when you broke mine. The silver ones with lots of little straps when we got back together. A strappy shoe is one of those enduring and mysterious open structures like the Eiffel Tower, just pure romance. Then, of course, there is the basic killer black pump, that special agent, the 007 of the shoe department, always shined and at the ready. It's the high-level meeting shoe, the one that makes anyone say "yes" to anything. You can kill a man or a woman (figuratively speaking) with the right heel—spikes go straight to the brain.

Remember that dire fashion moment in the eighties when the working woman rejected the high heel? On Wall Street and in midtown Manhattan, women began pouring out of office buildings in skirt suits and sneakers. It still goes on all across America. Of course, there are very practical reasons for this attire, which like the shoes in question are too boring to detail. But the interesting and terrible thing about it is the idea that somehow dull shoes can be an equalizer of the sexes, that women need to become dowdy to be both safe and effective in the professional arena.

"The sound of heels is very sexy," says Dr. Valerie Steele,

professor at New York's Fashion Institute of Technology. "Both the fetishist and the regular guy have an equally deep response to many aspects of the heel."

There is no more amusing setting for male admiration of the heel than through the windows of Manolo Blahnik, just off Fifth Avenue in Manhattan. Under the guise of doing research for this column, I visited this chic cubbyhole boutique where shoes are displayed like fine jewels on pedestals. As I extended my bare legs and painted toes into pair after pair of shoes, I realized I was providing a peep show to the chauffeurs, businessmen, and tourists chancing by the store window. Two men in suits actually knocked on the window to give either a thumbs up or a thumbs down to my selections. I decided to venture outside and find out what they were thinking.

"Heels are something I could never have," offered gentleman number one. "I think women who wear them well have a tremendous amount of authority. I'm less inclined to believe that a woman in a heel is passive." Gentleman number two was more expressive. "I think that somehow heels give a woman identity," he said. I found these rather stunning revelations from two guys on their lunch hour who seemed unaffected by fashion.

The more we talked on the sidewalk the more I realized that these men had a very sophisticated view of women and saw heels as power tools akin to cuff links or an expensive watch on a man, that they, like me, viewed the use of this kind of shoe as an economic building block rather than an antiquated form of conspicuous consumption. I related our exchange to Dr. Steele. "Today the heel is the primo sartorial symbol of erotic womanhood," she told me. So, all you flat-footed doubters out there, get with the program. Or at least find another fetish.

—New York, May 1994

WHO NEEDS A THERAPIST WHEN YOU CAN SHOP?

I went to the opening of Barneys' uptown branch the other night. By now you've seen the snapshots and read the scoop about the store's blowout soirée. So I won't bore you with details about the captains of industry, fashion models, and style-making editors who were in attendance. Usually the movie premieres and AIDS benefits that have come to characterize the social life of this set are nothing more than very sophisticated office parties.

But this event was sort of wonderful—we had come together in the ballroom of the Pierre Hotel for the happiest of reasons. We all had a common link. Everyone who was in the room shops at Barneys. What a fantastic way, superficial though it may be, to feel connected. It felt like being in a room full of people who all go to the same therapist. Because, as you know, everyone does their best shopping when depressed. We had come to celebrate the cure.

You see, it was perfect that the party was held on the Tuesday after Labor Day. The reason being that human beings in this technological world are still atavistic and certain things are genetically encoded. Shopping at the change of the season is one of those things. I don't know what the Romans did, but I'm sure come September way back in B.C. they went out in search of new cashmere togas. Like squirrels gathering nuts for the winter, at the first chilly wind humans head to the stores in order to brace themselves for the short cold days to come.

In New York City, a squirrel has no truly compelling reason to bother to gather food for the winter. They could certainly feed off the tons of trash freshly deposited on the curbs of our great city. Anyone who's into fashion and buys clothes certainly has enough in their closets to last a lifetime. Squirrels, I am told, bury their nuts and oftentimes can't remember where they put them. Just like I might buy something and not remember why. Yet we continue to do it every season. So this is compelling reason enough.

Winter shopping is purely about creature comfort. In its own way, it's a metaphor for why we work—to keep the nastiness of life at bay and feel some softness against our skins. So let's just say from here on out anything I say is justified by the fact that shopping is therapy. In a recent example, I was emotionally broadsided by a series of losses. I did my aching and crying and praying—all the spiritual work necessary for recovery. But that doesn't amount to a hill of beans when you're trying to make an entrance.

So off I went with my sad-sack self in search of some glad rags. The size of the purchase, of course, corresponds to the size of the wound the shopper is suffering. If you've had a tow truck pull your guts out, it requires a huge Band-Aid.

Spurred on by the line "and miles to go before I sleep," I took a cab to Manolo Blahnik. Benjamin, my favorite salesclerk of all the fashion capitals of the world, swung open the heavy gold door of the shop and greeted me by name. Benjamin is always a wonderful sight. He is as beautiful, pulled-together, and classy as anyone could ever hope to be. His presence also has the peculiar effect of bringing to mind the classic Carole King tune "You've Got a Friend." I love the scent of new shoes, they have the same poignant and melancholy aroma as the smell of the air after a heavy rain. The poor sacrificial cows lined up on the shelves in their chic new shapes. Well, anyway, three pairs of shoes later, everything on my body that cracked was smiling.

A quick sweep through the Gap as a concession to thrift and the proletariat movement in fashion yielded a bunch of disposable accessories for an update on the classics. Which brings me to the subject of investment buying. In my darkest shopping hours, I find it is wisest to go for the best and the shiniest possessions—otherwise, mistakes are inevitable. I can't bother to fuss with a store that has more than two floors when I'm engaged in curative shopping. Too many ideas and opinions are represented in all the objects. I love the rarefied atmosphere of a good store. I find the order and precision very soothing to the nerves.

Enter the cool world of Hermès. Behind that door on East 57th Street are some of the finest handbags in the world. I thought of all the French women I know in their forties who carry Hermès bags handed down from their mothers that are still as chic today as the day they were made. This is the type of rationale I have to use on a major purchasing day. Twenty minutes and three grand later I was a proud owner. The price tag may sound obscene, but comfort doesn't come cheap. Walking down the street I explained to myself that the bag should last for thirty years. So for 65 cents a day, the price of a cup of coffee, I had made a great deal. Let's just hope I live that long.

—New York, September 1995

EATING OUT

Riding the Restaurant Cycle

Did you move to New York because you heard apartment living was so fabulous an experience it couldn't be missed? I didn't. Eight million of us (and counting) tolerate dwelling side by side, stacked one on top of another in tiny spaces, in order to seek a life rich in serendipity and opportunity beyond those apartment house walls. Restaurants function as surrogate living rooms in our predicament of limited space. I'm not alone when I attest to the common fact of having long-term friends in this city whose apartments I have never visited. On the rare occasions I have paid a visit, I can count on one hand, with a few fingers left over, the apartments in which I've dined.

On the wide avenues and narrow streets of the city, by conservative estimate at least 10,000 eateries of all descriptions are in operation. Dining in Manhattan is atmosphere driven. The food served is an experience secondary to decor, and to the menu. Think of how frequently, as a New Yorker, you do your entertaining in a restaurant. Whoever chooses the restaurant throws his group into relief against a backdrop of a shifting kaleidoscope of decoration. It's like planning a children's theme party—from the Zen of Japanese asceticism, to the Europhile (once removed), high-tech-nouvelle-design exercise so prevalent in our local dining halls. Since you know you can't escape being judged in New York City, choosing an establishment is the personal-tastes-and-standards review for a New Yorker. Whatever side of yourself you want to reveal to your dinner companion can be accommodated at a local eatery. Some choose the best because they feel they are the best. Others opt for thrift, as a sign of ingenuity. Choosing a restaurant is no mean feat. We've all been through it. The welcome phone call comes, "Where do you want to go tonight?" And then the clunker, "You choose the restaurant." The pressure's on. Living both sides of the experience you feel compelled, after soaking in pleasant atmosphere and downing fine food, to respond to the person who invited you as if they did the decorating and cooking themselves.

For many New Yorkers, "restauranting" begins with breakfast—a bagel and coffee in a brown sack from the deli. If you have an extended morning hour, a stack of flapjacks cooked in minutes on an open griddle in a diner might be the way to go. Your morning meal is being cooked in the same grease as the hamburger the guy in the booth to the left ordered after knocking off the midnight-to-eight shift or exiting a night spot.

At lunchtime too many of us order in and eat at our desks. We abuse mealtime to finish work or to make calls to the friends we never have time to see because we're just so busy. Others escape the confines of the workplace and play a game of beat the clock as they dash off to a lunch meeting in a cozy bistro or a quick get-together over a slice of pizza.

Work comes to a close. Making it through the moodiest hour

of the day, when the sun goes down and blood sugar levels drop, is cured by busying ourselves getting ready for a romantic rendezvous or business meeting in yet another restaurant.

With behinds plunked down on banquettes or shifting on creaking wooden chairs, diners are confronted with the Russian roulette of what kind of waiter or waitress they'll get. A hallmark of fine dining in this town is the recitation of the "specials." Specials are necessary to appease the habitual restaurant-goer—those people who eat in the same restaurant with such regularity that the restaurant would go out of business if the menu didn't change daily.

As the waiter or waitress spins the tale of "today's specials," I imagine they are in the same fix as Scheherazade fighting for survival. Around the table eyebrows knit as that tedious rendition of fishes and meats in pungent exotic sauces is delivered by your server. Almost without fail, your waiter is an out-of-work actor suffering the ultimate humiliation of reciting the "specials" instead of Shakespeare to a captive audience. "Do you have any questions about the 'specials'?" "Yes. What are they again?" Once served, forkfuls of this and that delicacy travel from plate to plate in a contest for who ordered the best entrée.

Check, please. Taxi home. Lights out. Sleep comes. Alarm rings. Pavlovian response. The restaurant cycle begins again.

Swinging open the refrigerator door of any given single dweller in Manhattan is to be confronted with a sorry sight. Brand-name water and a few good bottles of beer is all that is likely to be on the shelves. The other scenario is that it looks like a container convention, littered with Chinese food cartons and sweaty clear plastic lids covering the remnants of last night's takeout. I hear a lot of complaints of colds, stomach problems, and bloating from friends who keep these kinds of refrigerators. In my theory it comes from eating out too often, consuming food that passes through many hands, not knowing the full 411 on the ingredients, and digesting something not necessarily cooked with love. That's why I first started to cook for myself.

In the beginning it was not so easy. Most of the food I bought was wasted. The reason being I would buy too much, unable to eat it all before it went bad. Once I got the system down of shopping for one, I faced the problem of creating domestic bliss solo. I would spend the day rendering chicken soup from scratch and then be so tired of looking at—and smelling—my efforts I would go to a restaurant. Other times while cooking, my hunger would reach the point of desperation. The second the food was finished I would stand at the stove eating like a dog out of the dish, wiping the telltale scraps and stains from my chops, looking around the kitchen embarrassed, wondering if anyone had witnessed the lowly spectacle through the rear window from across the courtyard, and wondering if they'd judged me.

—New York, 1993

VEGAS, VERSACE, VERSAILLES

The Splendor of Splendor

We all need it. Freedom. Excitement. Abandon. Decadence. The promise of riches. Back in the stone age of social consciousness, when it was really interesting to be rich, people who had the wherewithal built monuments to these things. The palace of Versailles, for instance, was a theme park for the aristocracy. This tradition of excess continues today in democratic theme cities like Las Vegas and in the everyday theater of life, such as with fashion—take the work of couturier Gianni Versace. These examples of the art of adornment destroy our notions of scale and image and have given consumers an opportunity to respond to the promise of rising above the mundane and the mediocre.

The palace of Versailles was completed in 1789, shortly before the arrest and subsequent beheading of Louis XVI. It had a support staff of 10,000, 5,000 residents, 1,252 rooms with fireplaces, and over 600 more rooms without heat. The royal family divided its living quarters between some 152 rooms. From floor to ceiling, no surface was left untouched. Even if you stand on your head or turn a photograph of one of its rooms upside down, Versailles's beauty is not diminished. It's still possible for a person who visits the palace to believe that, like a god, she is the center of the universe.

Gianni Versace's fiendishly opulent work, as presented both in advertisements and on the runway, also blows apart ordinary ideas about image. Versace's vision of fashion erases boundaries, representing neither the slut nor the lady; nor are his clothes a class statement. A woman wearing one of his creations is an unknown equation.

The jackpot during the Middle Ages was to be born king. In the casinos of Vegas, hitting the jackpot is all about the possibility of living like a king. The possibility of spending a penny and winning a million dollars is a notion so untenable, it negates the concept of aristocracy. That's why it's so beautiful and thrilling.

Night in Vegas is the best backdrop for the giant, hot pink, undulating neon plume atop the Flamingo. A woman stepping out of a limousine in full Versace regalia is astonishing in the same way. And Versailles's especial beauty is ingrained in those palace walls. It is possible to copy Vegas, Versace, and Versailles, but not to reproduce them. The three are not tied into the forms of the times but lie outside the common idea of what a person is allowed and allotted. Vegas is for sanctioned exercise of vice. Versace is for joy. Versailles is a celebration of the sensual. And all are rawly unapologetic in their offer of escape to worlds of pleasure. They satisfy our hunger for irrational rewards by feeding us maximum artifice. The trick is in exaggerating both appearance and environment to the point of leading you and, perhaps, others to believe you are suddenly larger—more powerful—and more beautiful than you really are. Excess is the great liberator.

All people, no matter how unworldly they might be, dream of that one "fuck-you" moment when they look and feel like they have it all.

—Milan, 1993

POLITICS

THE "N" WORD

For black history month let's declare a national moratorium on using the word "nigger," not as a restriction of free speech, but as a time for reflection on the evolution of our cultural identity. Many of us say nigger because we're too young to have a visceral association to the true power of the word. For the affirmation-action generation and Generation X, calling one another nigger is something we are more familiar with in terms of entertainment from comedians Dick Gregory to Richard Pryor to rap artist Ice Cube. We've learned to laugh at the word, to desensitize ourselves to the word and ultimately adopt it as our title when conversing with our own kind. It's a way of being in the club. Calling each other nigger as a term of affection or affiliation is a grassroots kind of reverse psychology, where terms normally applied to our culture by outside cultures as a form of ridicule like "dope," "down," and "bad" are used as positive.

Simone de Beauvoir's *The Second Sex*,[1] deals with the second-class status of womanhood. There's one passage, when paraphrased, relates very well to why the word nigger passes

[1] *The Second Sex*, New York, Vintage Books, 1989.

through generations as both a curse and a vaccine: "The [child] is at once [their elders'] double and another person . . . Saddling [the] child with [their] own destiny is a way to proudly lay claim to [one's] own [blackness], and also a way of revenging [one's self] for it. The same process is found in drug addicts, [and] in all who at once take pride in belonging to a certain fraternity and feel humiliated by the association." Traditionally, to be called a nigger is a curse, a word designed to strip all peoples of African descent of their dignity and individual character, in order to deny us our rights to freedom and prosperity. On the same level incorporating the word into our own sense of blackness gives us possession of its meaning and inoculates us against the disease of racism.

Entertainers have made negritude in all its derivations available to the global village. When comedian Dick Gregory published his biography *Nigger*[2] in 1964, the title confronted Americans in the throes of Jim Crow, the civil rights struggle, and Black Power movement with their fears and self-loathing. Gregory's biography describes nigger status during his World War II childhood: starving, shining shoes and having his teeth kicked in by a white man for touching a white woman's ankle while plying his trade. The most touching part of the book is its dedication: "Dear Momma—Where you are, if you hear the word 'nigger' again, remember they are advertising my book." In my recollection that's the first declaration of the epithet as a self-utilized commodity.

At the same time the Last Poets were rapping to a natural bongo beat "niggers are afraid of revolution." Malcolm X was delivering the famous speech "Message to the Grass Roots," rallying Negroes to reject the word Negro and call themselves "black." He called for an understanding of the nature of revolution, and warned blacks not to shed blood in Korea. In 1967, Mohammed Ali committed the last gesture of true political sig-

[2] *Nigger*, New York, Washington Square Press, 1986.

nificance by a black sports figure. Ali refused to fight in Vietnam. "I got nothin' against no Viet Cong. No Vietnamese never called me a nigger,"[3] was Ali's economical and profound defense. The champ was stripped of his crown, tried by the U.S. Senate, and then, forsaking considerable riches at the height of his career, exiled himself to Africa. Ali would have starved rather than defend a country that considered him a nigger.

Ten years later America was integrated. The struggle for equality quieted down. I don't know if it was subversion or confessional relief but the racially based comedy of Richard Pryor made him a mainstream superstar. He was the first person who made me laugh when I heard him say nigger. Before Richard Pryor made the word funny it used to give me butterflies in my stomach, because when I heard it it meant that someone was coming to take away your respect or your life. My mother shook with rage every time she heard one of Pryor's routines. She lives with memories of an era which won't let her utter or laugh at the word "nigger."

However controversial Pryor was, his voice was loved in the 'hood. I remember people defending Pryor saying, using the words "takes the sting out of it." The irony of it is, it's like using a branding iron to heal a psychic wound. By inflicting pain on yourself, you don't flinch anymore when it comes from an external source, and there's so much scar tissue over the injury you can't see or remember its origin. But, everyone else sees it and identifies you by the ugly brand.

Richard Pryor's new autobiography, *Pryor Convictions*, details a trip to Africa in 1979, at the zenith of his popularity. What awed the superstar about Kenya was the country's black-run government. Black faces depicted on both currency and coins, and balanced images of black people in the national media. This experience of a society where blacks formed the dominant culture

[3] *I Am King*, New York, Penguin Books, 1975.

caused Pryor to have an "epiphany" in a hotel lobby in Nairobi. Pryor began saying to himself, "There are no niggers here. The people still have their self-respect, their pride." This revelation changed Pryor's point of view. He returned to the states wishing he had "never uttered the word nigger on stage or off . . ." He said "the word was misunderstood," even by himself.[4]

Once Pryor openly disavowed the word in his act he received death threats from fans and ridicule by his peers. Finally, he admitted his voice was not his own. "I wasn't Malcolm or Martin or anybody else." Just "a drug addicted, paranoid, frightened, lonely comedian who wanted to be liked, not hated." On a sad final note to the episode he writes, "I didn't want racial struggles. I walked too far out on the wing . . . and buckled under pressure."

The eighties roared in and many of the hard-won advances by black Americans started screeching toward a standstill. As usual in the face of adversity the culture invented a new idiom—hip-hop was born. The art form created an environment Chuck D., from the pioneering band Public Enemy, likened rap music to a "black CNN." Rappers write rhymes and young America graduated from chanting Mother Goose rhymes to rhymes about the predicament of black America. In the world of hip-hop nobody is shy about using the word "nigger." One of the most successful groups in rap's history is the now defunct Niggas Wit' Attitude. The band's name was shocking for sure, but it illustrated what was happening at street level, "free" blacks in the eighties were still catching hell, like niggers twenty years ago. One of their first hits was "F*** tha Police," a rebel tune which would prove itself to be a justified portrait of the treatment of black citizens by police. When the Rodney King case went down, L.A. police chief William Gates seemed only a heartbeat away from Bull Conner. Years later when tapes of L.A.P.D. officer Mark Fuhrman played in open court during

---

[4] *Pryor Convictions and Other Life Sentences*, New York, Pantheon Books, 1995.

the O.J. trial, officer Fuhrman used the word nigger so much I thought he was one. But, depending on how you interpret the word, where does it say you have to be black to be a nigger?

The most prominent figure to emerge from the rap scene is Russell Simmons, founder and CEO of Def Jam records, the most profitable black-owned entertainment company in the world. Some genres of rap have taken a lot of heat lately from the pulpits of Harlem to Capitol Hill for uses of profanity and subject matter.[5] Despite the pressures, Simmons, a proud defender, is still standing. For him the word nigger not only represents his livelihood but a way of life. "Twenty years ago when black people called each other nigger it was self-defeating, an affirmation of being second-class." According to Mr. Simmons, "When we say nigger now it's very positive. Now all white kids who buy into hip-hop culture call each other nigger —because they have no history with the word other than something positive. But, if their parents say it then they get offended." When I ask Mr. Simmons for a definition of what it means when young black kids say the word, he's quick to the draw. "When black kids call each other a 'real' nigger, or 'my' nigger, it means you walk a certain way . . . you have your own culture that you invent, so you don't have to buy into the U.S. culture that you're not really a part of. It means we're special, we have our own language." I have to concede that this logic is true. But then I remind him of the time he was infuriated during a negotiation with a white-owned conglomerate and said he got a "nigger deal." What exactly did the word "nigger" imply that day? "I speak two languages [black and white English] fluently. When a white person calls me nigger in a negative way it means zero—because of the way they interpret it. To them it means slave." For people like Russell Simmons, who's so self-defined, the word "nigger" can't render him a slave. Perhaps that is the definition the modern b-boy is rowing toward.

[5] Forbes List, 1995.

On the other hand, when I talk to everyday black people who don't have the will or fortune to be as fully self-possessed as Mr. Simmons, the common response is "Nigger is a good word when a black person says it. It's bad when a white person says it." When I ask the question, Why do you want to lay claim to a title that's not positive all the time? everybody's face goes blank. Including mine. Because the question really is, does using the word "nigger" to define ourselves really change the status quo?

—New York, December 1995

LET THEM EAT BULLETS

*Looking for the Smoking Gun
in the Children Killings*

Since July 1990, twenty-five children have been shot in New York. Twelve have died. Each of the shootings has been branded "accidental" and brought to us by the networks in deluxe technicolor, jump-cut and spliced up like a trailer for a horror movie. Live-action remote steady cam sucking up and spitting back landscapes of such outposts of Manhattan as East New York, the Bronx. This is American cinema verité—a nine-millimeter bullet through a black baby's brain.

This is internal warfare. The six o'clock news treats this phenomenon as if it were occurring in a location more remote than Karachi, Pakistan, where atrocities against innocents are explained as a fact of life, the predictable results of nondemocratic governments. The killing of children separates the civilized society from the uncivilized. In New York, it's a way of determining class lines. The current crisis in the Gulf rates higher on the scale of public outrage and personal sentiment than the deaths and injuries to children of color in New York; Detroit; Washington, D.C.; East L.A.; or Atlanta. When Saddam Hussein made a hostile invasion of the world's wealthiest nation, President Bush had a plan—double-quick in a hurry. Hostile invasion of territories is not acceptable to the Bush administration, innocent law-abiding nations of people should not suffer the whim of a dictator, or an unrecognized army. In America, people of the urban outposts are left to devise their own plan. In the aftermath of each shooting, the mothers of surviving children have no reinforcement; their only plan to defend themselves against hostile invaders is to keep their kids off the playgrounds, out of the courtyards of their residences, and in the house. Some parents who can afford the $400 buy bullet-proof vests and mittens for their offspring, a shrink-to-fit nightmare. For the moment, this is not a problem that directly affects parents with Wall Street salaries, or young singles with Village addresses. Many New Yorkers, although disturbed or shocked, feel immune, comforted even, that these "accidental" child shootings have not come across 110th Street or over the bridge. It seems that through language, geography, and policy, parts of the city are psychologically abandoned, because the state of lawlessness extends beyond general precepts of social reality. "Accidental" shootings? "Accidental" is a code word for routine, or expendable child shootings. The term "accidental" is callous and ridiculous when applied to the numbers: Twenty-five times in five months!

Remember when George and Barbara, Ron and Nancy, got really serious about America joining together to "Just Say No"? The farcical state of the union address where Bush had a secret service agent go into the park across from the White House and stage a buy of a dingy snowball-size rock of crack cocaine? After that, the war on drugs was priority number one. What's going to have to happen, who's going to have to die and how, before the president realizes that the routine killing of children is unacceptable and the first order of the nation's business?

What is it going to take to move the nation to such fervor? Will a Secret Service agent have to go into the park across from the White House, find a dead child of color, and display the bloody corpse for an ogling nation to realize just how serious this problem is? But that might not even work. We see it every night on the news; and it's just another chance to exploit a lurid visual of inner-city life. It's the cherry on top of what to many people is a chocolate mess. It's not a new problem. The mortality rate is higher because the weapons are more powerful. And each damn-near bankrupt, understaffed inner-city agency is left to deal with the "accidents."

Police Commissioner Brown has been able to institute a policy requiring gun distributors in the five boroughs to obtain written permission from the police department, accompanied by a ten-day waiting period, before they are allowed to receive shipments. Although it will not affect who is buying the weapons from the local shops, nor will it markedly reduce the flow of guns to the streets, it will serve from November on to give officials a more accurate idea of how many guns are legally in the city, for the remainder of the Dinkins administration. The city is out of control because guns are out of control. And that's no accident. It's American. It's constitutional. After twenty years of campaigns from gun-control lobbies, it has been impossible to enforce a national ten-day waiting period for private citizens wishing to purchase a handgun. The possession of a loaded illegal handgun now carries a 12-month mandatory sentence in New York State. Obviously the current law is not a deterrent. Members of the clergy in Harlem and parts of Brooklyn, where the shootings most often occur, have followed the mayor's lead in instituting an amnesty period for those wishing to turn in their guns, urging that weapons be surrendered at the altar and their owners possibly meet with Jesus at the same time.

As citizens, as voters, as humanitarians, we are responsible to ourselves, our children, our future, to do something about guns. There is only one use for a handgun or semiautomatic weapon—to shoot another person. Marksmanship perhaps, but the hunting of game is not one of a handgun's applications. Think about a bullet from a nine millimeter in a black baby's brain.

—New York, October 1991

CRIME SCENE

To Live and Die in L.A.

I'm a New Yorker. Have been for ten years. I like this town; it's a lot safer than the place I came from, that bad-ass, postindustrial monster known as Detroit, Michigan—Motown, the Murder City. Don't get me wrong. I love my hometown. I like the people—mostly Southern Negroes once removed—the art museums and the cultural history of the place. It's a great place to be from, but not the place where I want to end up. By the time I was five, I had made up my mind that New York was where I wanted to be, and when I arrived at sixteen years of age it was just like I pictured it—skyscrapers and everything. I fared a lot better than the character in the Stevie Wonder song "Living for the City."

My life and I found each other and we fell in love with this town, that tough love that we New Yorkers feel. The big town can be a real shit hole, but I like the smell of it. In New York I can walk the streets, live alone, and not be too afraid. I've been teargassed in Paris, woken up in the night by villains seizing my property in Jamaica and Miami, but never in New York. Recently, I went to L.A., OK, babe, trying to do that bicoastal career thing. Like most Easterners of my age, my impression of Los Angeles was formed early on in "Beverly Hillbillies" reruns. I, of course, want my own cement pond one day, my own Mr. Drysdale, and the desire to live like a movie star goes without saying.

So I get to L.A., sublet a cool little stucco bungalow in the hills, rent a car, get my road maps, and I'm set. Life in L.A., at the outset, is very pleasant—once I got used to its antipulse. There are no changes in weather to keep you alert to the passing of the days; in fact, it's hard to distinguish one from another. It's a very solitary sort of living in that there is no street life. In New York, by the time I get to my corner in the morning to hail a taxi I've had at least fifteen experiences. In L.A., I have to drive a good half-hour to encounter other people. The problem with L.A., as a Gertrude Stein once said, "is that there's no there there." I've accepted the fact that L.A. is a mobile anthropology museum—if you want to observe other people you have to get in your car and watch them in their car. Your car in L.A. is your own special world and you better like it as much as your apartment because you'll spend the same amount of time in the damn thing. It's not entirely dismal though, the car thing, because it gives me three times as much time to listen to music, and cash lasts a lot longer because when your feet don't touch the street, you don't see things you want to spend money on. Not to mention that the absence of walking facilitates the donning of that taboo Manhattan footwear—skimpy high heels—which makes you feel alive and smutty inside. There is one advantage to the lack of street life, however. It cuts out the phenomenally irritating morning ritual of dressing for urban combat—you know where you're going and what you'll encounter upon arrival. The sound of disgusting wet kiss noises from lecherous pedestrians is almost totally missing from the L.A. soundscape. Still, it's not a good enough trade-off to kiss Manhattan good-bye forever.

In my first week in L.A., the transplant was going pretty well. I had precision packed for the three-month sojourn: The wardrobe was coordinated like a Rubik's Cube. My computer with all its master discs in tow for those long L.A. days and nights in isolation, reorganization, and reflection. All my favorite tapes and CDs; my lifetime collection of jewelry. In short, everything that allows me to get out in the street and hustle for what I want. I'm focused. I know what I'm doing. I'm going to find my fortune and bring the loot home. Well, it almost worked. Four days after I had installed myself, I went to open a bank account. Forty minutes later, I turned the key in my front door, saw my TV turned around, heard a couple of guys scuffing around in the back and realized that I was being robbed! "Excuse me," I said and ran down the street in search of a phone. Six minutes later, six shiny L.A.P.D. cruisers showed up filled with twelve fresh-pressed clean-cut officers looking more like the storm troopers than beat cops. They searched the house. The culprits had escaped with all the above-mentioned items. I was scared stiff when the cops told me that the guys had to have been staking me out for at least a couple of days and to be extra careful. I changed the locks, cried my cry for what once was, and went to bed as best I could.

I woke up the next morning determined not to become more of a victim and joined the Beverly Hills Gun Club.

—Los Angeles, October 1991

SHOOT 'EM UP

Learning to Live with the Gun Culture

I grew up in a gun culture. In Detroit, damn near everybody had a gun—in damn near every darn room of the house. Citizens of the chocolate city took to serious armaments during the riots in the cathartic summer of '68. I come from a middle-class family; my father defended his piece of the pie from the roof of our house with a shotgun. My mother maintained the fort from the parlor window with a revolver. The riots destroyed much of the inner city where my family lives. The advent of the Japanese car knocked Fisher Body on its ass, leaving the sons and daughters of sharecroppers who came North in the boom years to find work in the hole. Detroit started to look like Dodge City, and it didn't take long for it to start acting like it. By the mid-seventies, crime of every description soared. Motor City picked up the hideous moniker of Murder City, with the highest per-capita homicide rate of any place in the world. The heartland degenerated into cities of scared people trapped in their homes watching TV. A weapons arsenal was as much a part of daily life as the appliances in the kitchen or beauty products in the bathroom.

It wasn't until I had been robbed three times, on each occasion confronting the culprit, that I began to think about joining the gun culture. The third robbery had taken the heaviest toll psychologically. As I began to digest the experience, I couldn't deny the paralyzing feeling of being a target destined to be victimized over and over again. That's when I made the decision to learn to use a handgun.

It started in one mad moment with a call to the Beverly Hills Gun Club. I was told to come in for the two-hour class Sunday morning, after which time I would be given a certificate of completion and a complimentary session on the shooting range. I entered the ivy-covered, one-story structure and was ushered into a classroom, some twenty-five feet away from the shooting range. The echo of bullets rattled the building.

My classmates for the most part were young women, a few elderly women, and one older gentleman. The instructor, an ex–L.A.P.D. officer, wore sunglasses on his elephant-skin face. The first half hour was dedicated to explaining the legalities of use and ownership. Among other things, the gun had to be carried in a locked box when outside of the home, either in a combination briefcase or a pencil box with a padlock. That tidbit of protocol seemed more appropriate for a duel than an urban emergency. Service-worn .45s and .38s were passed back through the classroom like test papers. The revolvers were filthy to the touch.

"It only takes five minutes to learn to use a gun correctly and safely." He sighed and wiped his face with a gnarled hand, as if to clear out the memories that clouded his thoughts. "I cannot teach you the morality of using a gun." How long does that take? I wondered. "Only you know why you would use a gun. Once your gun harms someone, you will think about it for the rest of your life. I've been shot myself. I've shot people. I've killed people. All in the line of duty and all justifiably, but the questions still wake me up at night. Anytime you shoot someone, even if that person is in your house threatening to kill you, I guarantee you the survivors will sue you. Anything is preferable to a violent confrontation—especially one with a gun."

The rest of the lecture was devoted mostly to "the lady and her gun." We were advised to purchase a gun with "maximum knock-down power." A .38 or a .22 wouldn't do, because of the nature of the bullet. In those small-caliber guns, the bullet ricochets in the body, thoroughly destructive but only after twenty or so minutes. Women were advised to go after a higher caliber where the bullet enters the body and stays in one place dispersing all its energy. It was time for the practical application of the lecture.

A shooting range is set up just like a bowling alley. Instead of requesting your shoe size at the desk, you ask for your caliber of gun, a bag of ammunition, safety glasses, and protective ear muffs. My .38 in hand, I entered the range. At first, I flinched and winced at the sound of gunfire; my nose wrinkled in response to the smell of gun smoke. Nothing separated the lanes, and as far as I knew, no one on the range had been subject to a psychological evaluation. This is America, land of the lunchtime massacre; it made me a little nervous. I figured that if someone were to go loco, it would just be total war. We all had guns, right?

The .38 fired nice and easy with a minimal kick. Next I moved on to the .45, a little bigger and a little heavier. The last gun I tried was a Glock, a semiautomatic from Austria. The body is half-plastic, and it fires seventeen rounds per clip. I squeezed the trigger and the bullet tore loose with a sonic belch. A hot shell flew out of the top of the clip and bounced off my forehead, and the bullets kept coming, smoking and penetrating the target with merciless accuracy. The recoil made my skeleton feel like swirling snowflakes. The pistol had personality, one of destructive rage.

I drove home that day, blurry-eyed and bewildered. I didn't know why. I called my friend Nancy, a woman of extraordinary analytical powers, and recounted the experience. "Well, maybe you didn't realize that you were consciously seeking the capability to kill someone. Now you have it, and there is part of yourself that's a mystery."

—Beverly Hills, November 1991

SATURDAY NIGHT INTO SUNDAY MORNING

I must admit I have a lust for both scandal and spectacle. When I received the heavily embossed invitation for Mike Tyson's thirtieth birthday party at his Connecticut estate last Saturday it seemed to hold the promise of both these elements, which filled me with a kind of stupid glee. I was one of 2,000 on the list for the evening. The invitation was the same format as an official invite from the White House, with a full color picture of the estate enclosed. The R.S.V.P. protocol was the same too, I was obliged to give the full names of myself and my guest and present picture ID on arrival.

The local police, hired as outside security, started rigorous car and passenger checks a quarter mile from the front door. We passed inspection only to stop dead in our tracks at the top of the driveway. The Champ's digs took my breath away. It looked like a kind of Valhalla for Spartacus, a gleaming white structure as long as a New York City block. The partygoers were a stunning mix of black folks—as comically slick as a James Bond casino scene.

You think Tony Montana was living large in *Scarface*? Think again kid, because Mike's place is a high roller's suite extraordinaire. From the suede and marble monotone living room, we popped into the octagonal elevator to the main floor. The doors opened on a raised marble dance floor circled by brass railings. The walls were covered with closed circuit TV's and a permanent neon sign spelling out CLUB T.K.O. Funk Master Flex of New York Hot 97 and BBC Radio One fame was spinning tunes on a riser adjoining the indoor basketball court. If that wasn't enough, it let onto a swimming pool filled with burning candles and pink rose petals. The TEAM TYSON logo painted on the wall of the court and the bottom of the pool personalized the playtoys. Once I walked outside and saw the rest of the grounds, complete with a manmade lake crowned with a spewing geyser and a remote control two-story waterfall, my usual aloof demeanor melted into that of a real rubbernecking tourist. All I wanted to know was, "Where's the white tiger?" Where's Don King? I wanted my picture with both of them. Out of nowhere, the reigning heavyweight champ appeared, passing stealthily, dressed in jeans so tight they looked like they'd been spray painted on his body and a zebra print silk shirt, shaking hands, speaking quickly and unemotionally with anyone who approached him. We followed Mike's trail into the party tent, which had about six hundred people dancing to a special performance of Frankie Beverly and Maze.

All the party elements seemed to be in place and then we went to the bar—juice, water, and Taittinger champagne, and absolutely no other liquor was being served. The champagne was being doled out on a schedule, forty-five minutes of the bubbly followed by a thirty-minute interruption. I couldn't understand what these intervals of prohibition were about, I mean it's not exactly the way to get a solid groove on, is it? Spotting Don King on the other side of the room, my spirits lifted by the sight of his fabled hairstyle and the spoils of an empire dripping from his neck and fingers, I asked, politely, if he could be troubled to take a picture with me. Mustering a wan smile he said, "Yeah. Go ahead." He posed patiently. I thanked him, walked ten paces, and was remanded to a corner by plain-clothes security. "Who are you with?" the hulking gruff figure demanded. Dreading what I might have gotten myself into I demurred, "I'm just a guest." There was a tense silence as he looked me over. He sighed heavily, shifting uncomfortably like he wasn't happy about being put in the position of being an ass-hole, and said, "Give me the film." I sighed heavily and shifted uncomfortably, not happy about being put in the same position, and handed over the film. I was told by yet another watchful security guard that I'd be asked to leave if they saw my camera again. Feeling self-conscious and dejected like a servant girl overstepping the mark, I reasoned that if you're Mike Tyson or Don King pictures can be used in strange ways. Returning to my crew still anxiously lined up at the dry bar, they countered my tale of the photo with one better. They'd witnessed a prominent entertainer being thrown out for smoking a joint.

My motto is "Please make some rules so I can break them." "That's it!" I announced to my crew. "If we're going to be treated like a menace to sobriety, then we're damn well going to act like one!" We organized ourselves in our fight for our right to party, locating where the champagne was stored. Grabbing a case of bubbly, spiriting it past security we hid our-selves far away from the action under a swing set out on the grounds. Everyone admitted to being baffled, perplexed, or dis-appointed by the restrained atmosphere. We gave Mike his props for coming out of jail and doing so well with how he was living and all, marveling that this level of luxury was all from knocking people out.

Then we heard Funk Master Flex from the dee-jay booth plaintively exclaim—"HELP ME! This party's on fire." At which point we burst out laughing—because we had yet to hear a current rap record. Guzzling the contraband booze and bemoaning the pesky security, a quiet came over us. We really felt sorry for Mike that this was his thirtieth birthday party. Just as we were voicing strains of sympathy, Sugar Dice, a childhood friend of Mike's, joined us, shaking his head that Mike was in the room alone watching the TV with the air conditioning.

How could this be? What's going on here I wondered—and then I thought of the transformative powers of what I gather to be the major influences of Tyson's life. Fame. Prison. Islam. Of course, a man who has entered the canon of history has little need for the ogling attention of strangers on his private property. Nor would a recently converted Muslim want to contribute to the rowdy inebriation of his guests. I kicked myself for being insensitive to the fact that he's also a man on parole. Even the slightest transgression could result in the loss of what little freedom a person in his position can enjoy.

—London, July 1996

THE RAPE OF MIKE TYSON

Ringside! Ding! Streaming slobber falling in Pavlovian response like droplets of rain from my unconsciously outstretched tongue. The hottest ticket in America: March 18, 1991. Mike Tyson vs. Razor Ruddock! I roar at the top of my lungs with a zealotry unchecked by morality or propriety: "Kill him, Mike! Hit him, Mike! Take him out, Mike!" All the crowd wants is for Mighty Mike to do the Hammer dance on Ruddock's face, to feel his power by proxy. *Tous les bourgeois* in Afrocentric regalia, wearing Armani and Chanel suits, sitting in $1,500 seats, watching the spectacle of human violence. Spike Lee at my right side, pious patricians Jesse Jackson and the Reverend Al Sharpton behind us, all of us catching the frenzy, waiting for the blood, anticipating Mighty Mike cutting off the flow of oxygen to Razor Ruddock's brain with primal loin-tingling relish. Boom! Mighty Mike connects to Razor Ruddock's ribs. The crowd grunts, screams, recoils in sympathetic reaction. Before I can recover, much to my terrified delight, blows are landed again. Kerpow! A jaw-crushing blow. Ding! The round ends. The fighters separate. The crowd momentarily comes to its senses. Spent and sheepish spectators straighten themselves, adjust hot collars, roll down pushed-up sleeves, wipe sweaty brows. Excuse me, it's like coitus interruptus here. Mike hasn't knocked the guy out yet and we haven't got off.

The fighting continues. It's round seven and Ruddock goes down with a dull thud. The ref counts him out standing above the prone, prostrate figure of Ruddock, recepient of a beat down. All eyes fasten on Mike's gloves, tomato-shaped fists, sailing effortlessly into the air like red balloons—the beacons of victory.

But clutch the pearls! Fighting breaks out in the ring, a little chaos, mild moral confusion, one training camp brawling with the other, a body locking a body in a choke hold spills over the ropes into the well-heeled crowd. Always on the dime, level-headed, soft-shouldered promoters jump in to protect their investments, and remove the fighters from the ring.

The violence up to this point is organized and paid for, one $1,500 folding chair at a time. The distance dissolves, I am no longer the kind, condescending, bloodthirsty bourgeois spectator. Suddenly I find this manifestation of violence abhorrent— as if it wasn't what I came here for in the first place. Leaving the arena, I found myself in an ethical quandary about the relationship of the spectator to violence.

I was hoping the champ could restore himself after Buster Douglas took him to the mat in February of '90, toppling the man once thought invincible. "Iron" Mike Tyson couldn't come clean, he couldn't shake off whatever was polluting the wake of the heavyweight.

In the early days, Tyson had a calm, almost Zen-like demeanor and understanding of his sport. The quintessential underdog became the top dog and had the world by the tail. And then . . .

The glitches in Tyson's career and psychological profile have been ticking like a time bomb since 1988; the incidents, silly rude-boy antics. Swiping a kiss from a parking lot attendant in Los Angeles, back-handing the supervisor who came to her defense, then denying the charges brought aginst him, eventually settling out of court for $105,000. *Tick.* Giving his costly Bentley convertible to Port Authority cops after sideswiping another vehicle. *Tick.* Breaking his right hand street fighting with Mitch "Blood" Green. Mike Tyson is no southpaw. *Tick.* More reflective of boredom, excess, and perpetuated adolescence than a criminal mind, the fans worried. Tyson was relieved of some four million dollars, by his then-wife and mother-in-law, while he was out of the country. *Tick.* Meanwhile "Iron" Mike kept kocking 'em out, and ringing the till, at spectacular speed— ninety-one seconds and $20 million in the Spinks match. Mike moves to promoter Don King, who is said to have wooed the boxer during funeral services for his longtime co-manager and Jim Jacobs. *Tick.* Tyson crashes his BMW into a tree outside of his adoptive mother's home. Speculation about the event ranges from accident to suicide attempt. Tyson tells the press it's the result of a chemical imbalance. *Tick.* Two weeks later the infamous Barbara Walters interview occurs, where Robin Givens characterizes her marriage as "a living hell." We all rooted for our wounded warrior during his divorce, finalized on Valentine's Day. November 1989 brings lawsuits against Tyson on charges of lewd sexual behavior, a faint foreshadowing of what will become known as "serial buttocks fondling." *Tick.* 1989 brought two more knockouts, but Tyson's less focused, not showing the stuff he once had. *Tick.* Punishing the champ for an unheard of ten rounds in Tokyo, Buster Douglas took the belt from Tyson in February of 1990. *Tick.* Tyson continues to grab headlines, a jury finds him guilty of sexual harassment and fines him $100,000. *Tick.*

Hell's bells! Demoralized is the fitting description of my feelings following the announcement indicting Mike Tyson on charges of rape. In the configuration of my politics, I'm a woman foremost and forever. My inclination from this perspective to believe any woman willing to go through the humiliation of prosecuting the crime of rape, especially in so media-friendly a case. (Think of Patricia Bowman's semen-saturated panties paraded Home Shopping Club style on CNN as evidence in the William Kennedy Smith trial.) It's not easy to live through it. Questioning the accuser, and finding myself relegating the charges to the ghetto file "niggers want sex, bitches want money." Backward and ridiculous, trying anything to vindicate the champ, wanting more than anything Tyson's innocence. My empathy is so profound as to engage me in the type of thinking traditionally victimizing women in this predicament. The kind of thinking that allows Clarence Thomas and William Kennedy Smith to walk free, making a mockery of a woman's sovereignty over her sexual being. The nation is rife with sex scandals usually going unpunished, serving as affirmation of the institutional prerogative to harass and assault femininity. Clarence Thomas retreated to race baiting, blaming the debacle on sexual stereotypes. William Kennedy Smith dredged up the scenario of a woman scorned. Both of these men were hideously dishonest in representing their characters. Thomas's and Smith's transgressions were treated as white-collar crime—abstract excusable deviations. Impressive credentials reaching all the way to the Oval Office did not match up to the assumed profile of sex offenders.

But somewhere, somehow, someone had to be brought to justice. Iron Mike fit the bill. Tyson came along just in time to play the fall guy for judicial injustices, in the cases of Smith and Thomas who were forgiven their sexual transgressions. Like most great boxers Tyson comes from a background of delinquency and deviant behavior. Unlike Thomas and Smith, Tyson's sexual prowess is not questionable. Perhaps the greatest mistake was made in his counsel's portrait of the defendant as an "animal with a reputation." The sacrifice was tailor-made; the very things we love Tyson for put him away.

The confusing feelings plaguing my conscience are sorted out by remembering that, above all, rape is a crime of violence, having little or nothing to with sexuality. Why am I shocked that Mike Tyson would be predisposed to violence? What has he been lauded for? What brings the million-dollar purses, the rewards of celebrity? Recalling myself at the fight yelling like an ancient pagan, deriving pleasure from Mike Tyson inflicting pain; then feeling stupid for admonishing Tyson for what I've encouraged and not being willing to deal with the ambiguous emotions surrounding my participation. Boxers are not celluloid heroes like Dirty Harry living in a world of make-believe. Inside the ring, it's skin on skin, requiring a certain pathology to carry out the mission of destruction. Intellectually I believe it's possible—probable even—that a rape did occur that night in Indianapolis. I will never believe emotionally Tyson is guilty—never. Which speaks of the power celebrity holds over human imagination. The blame rests with all of us. I see Mike Tyson as a victim, also eaten alive, one mega-million-dollar bite at a time.

Reading an early Tyson quote on his self-professed "obsession" brings the nature of my ambiguity into focus: "When I fight someone, I want to break his will. I want to take his manhood. I want to rip out his heart and show it to him. My manager tells me not to say these things, but this is the way I feel. People say that's primitive, that I'm an animal. But then they pay $500 to see it. There's so much hypocrisy in the world."

—New York, 1992

FAMILY

My mother,
Marion Webb.

HOUSE MUSIC

These Are the Good Old Days

I t's been twenty years if it's been a day since the last Webb
family vacation. Back in the day, we got up at five in the
morning. The horizon was just shrugging off the pink of dawn.
Outside the screen door lay a dewy world, scented heavy with
the perfumes of urban summers: flowers, gasoline, garbage,
bagged and combustible in galvanized metal trash cans, fusty
little plots of backyard lawns brown and green from August
heat, the comforting dampness of gravel covering the alley
behind our house, palpable as the river's edge. Our neighbors'
houses were still dark and quiet at that hour as they slept the
fitful sleep of factory workers between shifts. I remember tod-
dling along sleepy-eyed, lumbering behind my two older sisters
out to the garage into the family wagon with my parents for the
long drive south from Detroit to Ohio. The thrill it gave me
nestled there in that solid-steel beast, a huge Chrysler Plym-
outh that made Motown so proud. When that royal vessel con-
taining my family and its belongings slid backward out the

garage, the crunch of gravel beneath steel-belted UniRoyal tires gently signified the beginning of adventure.

To my developing mind, the Howard Johnsons and Stucky's restaurants peppering the lip of the interstate were like the Seven Wonders of the World, each one more marvelous than the next. My little eyes transforming them into the Taj Mahals of the American heartland. Innocence. At long last I'd collect my dolls and peel my face off the backseat window as we arrived in the Buckeye state in a little place off Exit 12 called Macedonia, where my mother was raised. It was a different world from Detroit. All the controls of city living fell away there, on my Uncle Carl's property with the cornfield out back. No neighbors, no street lights, no dangers. Family living as it should be. It seemed to me those days and that world would last and last forever . . .

But my sisters grew up and went away to college long before I did. I grew up too, took off for New York, and the family unit of childhood fractured for a decade. Suddenly the days were really twenty-four hours long, and that world dissolved in seconds.

Out on my own, in my tender teenage years, I adopted the world as my family. My sisters graduated from college, had long-term relationships, got married, had children—you know, all the good stuff. I sacrificed that path for another and was too busy or too far away to learn from the example of their lives. I experienced most of these major moments of my family's life through AT&T or Kodak, the technologies of intimacy. This summer, Polaroids and postcards, reaching out and touching, or just calling to say I love you, was not going to cut the mustard. I wanted a family vacation.

If you build it, they will come . . . If you rent it, they will show up. Traveling by air, a 35,000-feet cruising altitude high above the interstates, the Webb family flew from Michigan to the Hamptons for their first visit to New York. Like magic, they materialized in my universe. It was almost hallucinatory to see my father gingerly negotiating his way on my turf as I had so respectfully done for many years on his. I enjoyed the pleasure of watching my mother wander into the cornfield behind the house teaching my niece and two little nephews how to take the vegetables off the stalks, as she had done with us so many years before. My sisters and I followed after, talking about the changes and triumphs of our adult lives, then falling silent. Barefoot in the solid, sloping green earth, shadows falling like the lead joinings of stained-glass windows, the quiet became eerie for a moment. Looking at my sisters, I could not tell if we were adults or children. It didn't matter which we were anymore.

Time decompressed in those seven little days we were together. In the faces and gestures of my nephews, I saw those of my father renewed and innocent. My niece, like a glittering little shadow of my former self, playing the same games with me and asking the same questions I remember posing to my two big sisters as a child. *Plus ça change*, as the French say.

In the odd moment, on the last night of their sojourn, the roles went topsy-turvy as I tucked my parents in bed. My father, who had quietly observed the world I've acquired for myself without much reaction, voiced his conclusion. "I can finally put you down, girl," he said, as I knelt by their bedside as they used to beside mine. "Don't think I ever stopped holding you close to me in my arms like I did when you were a little baby. But I see you can make it now. I can finally put you down and let you walk." The power of that sentiment made me quiver as I pulled the thick blankets over the resting bodies of my parents and turned out the lights.

Morning came and with it the limousine to the airport. The family clambered inside the car. "Ka-tunk," the heavy door swung shut, carrying the sound and weight of a large stone dropping into a river. Waving good-bye through the rain and tears that day, I shuddered as I heard the sound of the tires crunching across the gravel in my driveway. I exhaled and walked back into the house, thinking about the comfort and continuum of the family. It made me feel like life lasts forever.

WEDDING DAZE

Thoughts from the Heartland

"You must be meant to do more in this life than earn a living, find a man, and have kids," my girlfriend Stephanie spouted out over a bowl of cherries. Humph, I said to myself, when you put it like that, it's profane. The words bounced around inside of my skull as I sat on yet aother DC-9 flight to the heartland. Cleveland, Ohio, to be exact, to see my cousin Jeffery get married. I never thought of myself as a married woman; a mother and a grandmother, yes, but never as a bride or a wife. But I didn't see myself as unmarried either. I wondered why. I grew up in the seventies, the era of women's lib. The majority of the information about liberating my coming womanhood came through racy women's magazines like *Cosmopolitan*, stuff my sisters read, or junk I saw on national TV. By the time I was nine years old, I was perched to pitch my bra on a burning pyre of liberation when I got one.

On the flight in the frigid dry air of cruising altitude, I became curious about where this ambiguity sprung from, from whence my twilight-zone vision of adult sexual interplay came. Obviously, my formative years were not so strongly guided by those idle hour forays with Helen Gurley Brown that they would influence my life choices. As the plane glided through the viscous sea of humid air that hung as thick as peanut butter along the length of the runway, I put all these thoughts aside and wanted simply to enjoy my nieces and nephews.

My sister Teresa came to pick me up in a teal blue Chrysler. She and my five-year-old niece had just been to Sea World, and now my sister and I were duty bound to take her to the Dairy Queen for ice cream with sprinkles, out to dinner, and then put her to bed. My sister Teresa's not married, so I am, in effect, "Auntie Daddy" on the occasions of my visits. Late that evening my eldest sister Jennifer and her husband arrived from Detroit by car with their two sleeping infants. With three sisters working on it and my brother-in-law helping to diaper, set up cribs, give medicine, calm and coddle, it took forty-five minutes to get the kids comfortably into bed. Granted, it was a bigger production than on a normal evening, the kids were boiling hot and hopping mad to find themselves awake in the middle of Ohio at the midnight hour. Negotiating my way through the unfamiliar territory of parenting, I was captured by the silent relay system between the two young parents. They responded to one another's needs and wishes, articulated and unarticulated. In many ways, the very thoughts in their heads seemed to be identical. But it is essential to find that level of communication and cooperation if you're going to enter into such a serious commitment with someone. They seemed to have come to a truce of egos. In short, they are not struggling with the dumb shit.

My cousin's wedding came and went on a Saturday afternoon, as they always do, like air oozing out a bicycle tire. As we drove the Chrysler to the reception over dusty gravel trails through the backwoods country of my recent ancestry, my sister Teresa and I got to talking. Why didn't she get married, I wanted to know. "Momma never taught us to get married." I was startled by her reply. I took a minute to think about it, but I couldn't remember any sexual or social instruction from my mother, as far as men were concerned, except "Don't get pregnant." "What do you mean?" I asked my sister. "Momma never taught us to get married," she repeated, as she took a drag of her Newport and flicked it out the window as we streaked past a cornfield. "Think about it, Ma never said that when you go to college you should look for a man, or that you should be married by a certain age, did she?" I got that secret deep involuntary tingly feeling I get between my legs when I'm thinking deep in my memory. I couldn't remember my mother describing any situation where I should factor in a man.

I took a puff of my sister's Newport. I felt confused. But, our parents have been married for better or for worse, for the last thirty-seven years. When I was a child they were some of the few married parents. I knew this at least to be true. "Why?" I asked my sister. She seemed to know something that I didn't, perhaps she had lived through a revelation in my parents' marriage in the years before I was born or had command of the language. "Because marriage is not easy. Most of the time the reward comes through your children. Sometimes you can pay too high a price for your children to have a father. You can pay with your peace of mind." A fresh bottle of perfume came out of my sister's purse. She squirted a little on her neck and wrists, inhaled, and sat back. The new smell, erasing old memories, clearing the air, and defining the here and now with sweet hope. Humph, I said to myself a little later, as my nieces and nephews went buck wild on the dance floor at the reception.

—Macedonia, Ohio, June 1991

DEAR MOMMA

To Mother with Love

Happy Mother's Day. I've said that to you every
year since you taught me how to speak. This
Mother's Day is the first time I think I'm mature
enough to know what's behind those words. That
might sound funny, as though I've been giving you
my wishes on schedule and by rote, but that's not the
case. I have so many feelings for you. Forever you
have been my provider, my comfort, my guide and
the law. It's overwhelming to need someone so much.
All these years you've been like a liferaft for me. No
matter how rough the situation, I knew that if I
stayed close to you in body or in spirit, I would make
it to the other side of trouble. Sometimes during my
adolescence I rejected or rebelled against you, but no
matter how ridiculous my young ego ravings, you
stayed steady.

I saw you as all-powerful as God when I was a little girl. The kitchen was where you did some master-
ful work. A farm girl from Ohio turned working

mom in inner-city Detroit, you could make everything. Baking biscuits or using rendered bacon grease and lye to make soap, I'd watch with fascination and pride when you turned around and cut me a fancy red, down-filled snowsuit the night before the first snowflake fell. You came from the old school—knitting, gardening—you could generate from your own hand just about anything your family needed to survive.

You had a strong identity outside of our family. I loved the way your nurse's uniform reinforced your presence as a professional and a power in the workforce. People today don't wear the uniform like you used to. Since you retired, the profession has opened up to men, and I haven't seen a nurse of either sex wearing military bars signifying rank like yours: Colonel Marion Stewart of the U.S. Army. You made the best of the choices you had, being a black woman in your time. You weren't even a black woman yet but a "colored girl" who shipped out to Hawaii at the beginning of World War II. The other choice you were given was to be a teacher. One of the most impressive things you ever said to me, when I asked you why you chose to be a nurse over a teacher, was that you "wanted to travel farther than the school trip."

I loved how you made me feel so responsible and involved when you came home from work telling tales of gore, heroism, and tragedy about the patients on the wards or the "randoms" in the emergency room. I loved medical terms like some kids are fascinated by dinosaurs. I felt so glamorous being in the bathroom with you and scrubbing the rim of your nurse's cap, being careful not to touch the black velvet band with the nailbrush and washing your stockings with seams up the back that were so provocative I couldn't believe I didn't have to be eighteen to handle them. I appreciated polishing your white shoes and buffing your name tag with alcohol. Helping you allowed me to enjoy your help with my schoolwork because we had a shared goal: being a part of each other's success.

Since I've been working for a decade now, I can relate to the pressure you must have felt in your mid-fifties, with two daughters in college—Jennifer in med school, Teresa in graduate school—and me in private school studying for the SATs. I genuflected to your stamina and bravery for going to graduate school in the evenings at the state university. You saw a master's degree as a way of making more money for your girls' education. To you, our education was our freedom. You never congratulated yourself or bragged about how much you were doing. You didn't have the time—not because you were too busy taking care of business, but because you were too busy taking care of everyone else.

You were never the official head of the household. Being from the old school also meant that we lived according to Victorian values in a nuclear family structure. Daddy definitely had the belt, the crown, the well-placed E-Z chair in front of the color TV— every symbol of ruling the roost. You, however, had everybody cornered when it came to patience and intellect. Never once did you hit me. Never once did you raise your voice. Direct orders weren't your style either. Instead you taught by example, and the idea of disappointing you was enough to keep all of us on point.

Living out here in the world and hearing a lot of stories about people's families, I have to say: Thank you for letting me be free. We never discussed my choice of profession. We never discussed marriage. We only talked about education, and from there you said I could go wherever I wanted. Never did you use my life to fulfill your own agenda, nor did you inflict the emotional violence of your childhood on me—a luxury your parents did not afford you. Every time I asked you about major choices, you would just say, "Make sure you're happy." When I asked, "How do I make sure?" you said, "You have to be doing what you're doing to satisfy you and you alone."

I can't believe how long it's taken me to see you for who you really are. Maybe it's because I'm a woman now, and independent enough to just stand back and appreciate you. Or maybe it's because of the turn of events in life that make it the daughter's turn to take care of her mother. Part of what makes you so precious is that it seems like there is no way that you can ever be broken. And I ask myself: in taking care of you, will I be half the woman you were to me?

Much respect. All my love,

Your daughter

In Loving Memory

R.I.P

My father died. When I hear someone say this phrase it resonates with a crushing inevitability, forcing my mind to cloak itself from comprehension. Swiftly, my soul shivers in silent prayer. Looking away from the living, I offer my respects to the dead. Primal and selfish prayers follow, savage, insistent pleas to be spared of having to ever say those words of my own father. Irrational thoughts become the rational as I convince myself this is something that only happens to other people. But God has a plan in which every dog has its day and nature is His exquisite, ruthless servant in acting it out.

Last Christmas, I felt a precognition of death crawling around the house where I was born. "Did you see the Grim Reaper?" a friend asked when I told him the story. "No," I said, "it was Christmas, he must have been on holiday." Rather, it was a sentiment palpable and ephemeral like a low-lying, humid fog licking at my ankles. "Ask not," as it has been said, "for whom the bell tolls." I thought it was my own death I sensed. And I fled the scene.

It is much easier for me to indulge in the morbid narcissism of imagining my own demise than that of someone I love. Easier to make sense of that than my world spinning on an axis absent of such an important figure as a father. Choosing to ignore the question, I soothed myself by taking my father's existence as much for granted as I take my own young life.

When I discovered it was not my own death coming to call, I started the difficult work of understanding my relationship with my father. Who was he as a parent, as my mother's husband, and as another individual stripped of all the dividends of a child's acceptance? Ours was a complex relationship. I loved and hated Daddy with equal intensity at every moment.

My father was an elegant man in both dress and speech. Every morning during the ten years after he retired from his job as an electrician, he shaved and dressed in freshly pressed clothing and hard-soled shoes by the time he arrived at the breakfast table. The rest of his day was spent reading every article printed in both Detroit newspapers. My father was informed and held us all to fastidious standards of correctness. "Don't get caught out there," he used to say. Besides cashew nuts, fried shrimp, and the good grace that we might all live another day, it was clear that education was the one luxury to which his children were entitled. If we couldn't provide ourselves with the rest of life's luxuries by way of our ingenuity, his only response was, "I can't help you." My father lived a long time and was not easily impressed. He was stoic, if not stingy, in doling out compliments. "Just make sure you know what you're doing," would be his praise at the news of one of his children's major achievements. I found that motivating. Daddy also had a flamboyant temper that was easily aroused; that aspect of him was wounding.

I think the unconscious mind does great things to comfort

the small conscious portion that guides us through the mundane duties of living. I laid no claim to the fact that reviewing our time together meant preparing to say good-bye.

On a beautiful day near the end of June my sister called. I was standing alone in my kitchen. "It's about Daddy," she said, and then repeated the doctor's prognosis of acute bone marrow leukemia into my ear. "Irreversible, untreatable, and terminal" were the words that followed.

Three weeks later, the dining room of our house had been converted into hospital quarters. Three generations of the family formed a ring around the bed where my father lay unconscious. On this night, the adults were aware they were holding the final vigil. I sat next to my father, holding his hand. He may have been conscious of me being there. Probably not. It's funny how often my father had said to me in the fits of frustration parents have in controlling children, "I brought you into this world and I can take you out." He did indeed bring me into this world and now it was his children who were ushering him out. His soul was in the gentle process of decanting itself from his body into whatever place it is that souls go. I watched his eyebrows knit together. And then his face assumed the final flaccid expression of sleep. His hand stayed in mine until I felt the flow of all life pass from it. In that moment any fear of a natural death passed from me. I know of no experience more intimate.

Seven days later I was putting the house in order for the life my mother would continue to live there without her husband. I was jarred by how quickly the articles of my father's world became static and meaningless. Daddy had built a small empire of pajamas and printed material. We could have opened a department store and a newsstand with what he left behind. I felt like I was going through a wallet tightly packed with discontinued currency, serving only to remind me of times gone by and what I can't have again. I tried to conjure my father's presence by looking at photographs of him. But the pictures were like slips of paper, no more than leaflets from a party I never attended. I had to accept that Daddy had left the physical world. And the only way to summon him is through memory.

—Malibu, July 1993

LOVE

Peggy Sirota

THE JOYS OF MASOCHISM

*Doin' What I Don't Like to Do
and Lovin' It*

Life is an exercise in masochism. Sitting here chained to my desk of pain I don't think the statement is necessarily negative, it's my experienced opinion. On the most basic level, how many things do you do every day, that a) don't feel good, b) don't look good, c) only serve the needs of polite society? If you take a minute to think about it, there's plenty. In my adult life it's no surprise I've become a glutton for punishment on an epicurean scale. I can trace it back to my childhood. "Drink your milk," my father ordered as I downed yet another wretched glass of pasturized cow snot, "it will make strong bones." We can all relate to the super masochistic hyper-duty knocking ourselves out four months of the year just to pay taxes, even before we get to make any spending money. (If you mark July 1 on your calendar, November 1 will be the next day you work for yourself.) This debilitating fact of life has never deterred the workaholic in me; if I wasn't a masochist I would never have chosen to work over a blinding computer screen, stuff my feet in oppressively high heels, or hock my emotions for the amusement of the general public. But, don't get upset, just try to bring the suffering into sharper focus. After all, you should learn to love your misery. Misery is your most reliable companion.

The next most universally accepted masochistic practice is, of course, relationships. I advise you to reach for that box of bon bons, that pack of cigarettes, or whatever self-destructive vice suits you. Throughout my romantic life, I've never been with a fella who wasn't a fool for the gridiron. Although I'm a boxing fan, I hate football. I probably hate the game because the players engaging in this ying-yang balance of sadomasochistic pleasure seem so complete. I'm jealous because they like taking a hit as much as they like giving one. I should be so lucky. I've never been able to give back as much pain as I can take. But, I'm working on it. How many times have you begged your man to share in shopping trips, cooking, or hanging out with *your* friends? The agony of these forays can never rival the agony of Super Sunday. And what would you get anyway—a disgruntled sidekick who spoils all the fun. Why not squash him like a roach at the first sign of trouble? What's stopping you from lowering yourself to plead for his socially irritating company? Simple, the masochist in you.

And then there's the daily reality of the jimmy to the jane. Now, ladies, how often, in that awful rowing toward the big "O," do you end up sore and unrewarded? He's snoring and you're dashing down the avenue in the heat of night on the way to Carvel's ice cream store in search of Fudgie the Whale. But, don't you hit the mats again the next day, your body and mind begging for more?

And let's take time to deal with the ravages of Fudgie the Whale. I'm a freak for cholesterol, saturated fats, and other poisonous foods. It fits the m.o. As I gnaw my way through candy bars, ice cream, and fried chicken I know that I'll be seeing my trainer's face. Fully aware that I can take any amount of punishment, he works me to a point where I wail for mercy, knowing that he's incapable of pity. For a masochist, this is the perfect relationship. Because, when all is said and done, I'm paying hard currency for the pain.

It is said that those who hurt you help you. How reassuring if you're a masochist! It's good for you it's got to feel bad. Consider everyone you've ever been in love with: Think about how many times they've hurt you. And, on the immediate level, it sucks. But, on the grand scheme of things aren't you a little smarter and a lot tougher for it? I'm a mercenary soldier in the pursuit of true love. Love is war. Where there is warfare the mighty runt of diplomacy is never far behind. Men tend to serve as the berserk, unreasonable island nation demanding the world bow down to its demands. I've heard it can be the other way around—but I don't believe it. That is, until I see a woman's face on a dollar bill. Love is necessary and good for you. It takes a lot of work and it's painful. Oftentimes love is accompanied by a long drone of upsets and compromises that are swift enough to make the brain bleed.

But in those moments of pleasure, when the brain releases a storm of endorphins, it's all worth it. After all, how could I enjoy being a masochist without a sadist to share it with?

—New York, 1990

LOVE'S THEME

The Expensive Lessons of Romance

I am struggling to the death with the idea of romantic love and its practical application in relationships. The cursed questions more often than not bring pain to the surface, spilling tears from my eyes. I believe the only way to really arrive at the doorstep of the divine state is by possessing the robust spirit of an adventurer and the appalling faith of a visionary. "A visionary!" a friend of mine winced, spitting the words back at me like rotten mush. "You know what happens to visionaries, don't you? They end up in the desert talking to snakes."

That may be so, but I am willing to step through the portals of suffering that go along with following my vision. I believe that most of us start as visionaries with unjaded loins and unscathed hearts. Once the adventurer in me leapt out, beginning to explore other people, I realized that love is not "free," like the song says. Love teaches some very expensive lessons. I have paid some high prices. If you've been in love, you've been there. My self-confidence has capsized in the wake of failing relationships, my self-image has been hobbled more than once, my spirit has shuddered, crawling stiffly in arthritic procession to death's door. When I knocked, the Reaper was not answering. I have been forced to face things about myself that I do not like—chiefly among them: once my faith has been betrayed, I do not forgive. Love affairs have a way of preying on my freedom to trust, and there have been eerie moments of horror when the dynamics of a particular relationship have shattered my belief that a real love does exist for me. Love has left me wounded and running for my life. I know that I am never a victim in a relationship, but a participant. Nietzsche said it all in this phrase: "That which does not kill me makes me stronger."

Controlling a relationship is impossible. Things never work the way you might want them to; things work the way they work. Nature decrees it. Science proves it. So, face it. My joys, my discoveries, and my mistakes have culminated in the creation of a stalwart warrior able to weather the battle of reality versus perception. Barry White once said to me, "No one can break your heart, the heart is a muscle. What happens is, they confuse your mind—you thought one way and they did another." For me, this is as simple and profound as the fact that the sun does not rise and set each day; the earth rotates. Thinking that I was in love, and someone telling me they loved me, have not always jibed with reality. Finding myself in the pattern of loving people who could not love me back; choosing mates incapacitated by constitution, ego, or fear of returning love is one of life's most polluting experiences.

The polluting element in relationships, I'm finding, is what I call "the silent partner." "Silent partners" are the sneaky little demons nesting in the psyche; those issues that harken from past events and exist independently of any experience you've had with the person you are involved with. I've been burned, we've all been burned. Anyone emerging from the flames without injury is either phenomenally repressed or deserving of a

Purple Heart. Rarely does life offer the swift, immediate retribution to the offender of the senses. So the senses carry this mark in a passionate, childish way; oftentimes the dialogue with the offender continues for years after the person is gone. Let me ask you, have you ever been alone and the thought of an old lover materializes, spontaneously thrusting you into a full-blown argument with yourself? A memory becomes a "silent partner" in a new relationship, manifesting itself, infecting the here and now. The task is separating out one set of experiences from another.

Knowing it is hardest to first realize; doing it, I perceived my battle won. Wrong. In reality, it is hardest revealing myself. Revealing my intellect and heart is the initial step of the adventure. It can be empowering in combination with the right person. I know that it is the wrong man if he tries to seize power. There are other definite clues to understanding I am not on the trail of a new adventure, but the familiar road to nowhere; being shamed, fearing judgment, feeling that I need to make a series of compromises that will ultimately lead to a network of internal lies. Loving someone in earnest requires the strength to ask yourself the question, "Is what's going on here mutual?" If the answer is no, it's over.

I am well-versed now with what love is not. Taking the experiences I had as an intrepid fool and debutante, I am beginning to formulate a revelation. Vision is not what my eyes see but what my spirit is relentlessly desiring, seeking ruthlessly. Loving someone is to share kindness. Without that I can only endure, but I cannot thrive. If my generosity is abused, I become faint of spirit. Love's highest function is to be free from fear—too much of the world serves a loveless and fearful agenda. In the private quite hours of my life, I want to experience sanctuary. That is love.

—Paris, 1992

THE TEST OF LOVE

*Show Your Love by Taking
an AIDS Test*

T he best present you can give someone this Valentine's Day—if it's someone you love and are sexually active with—is an AIDS test. It took me three years to summon up the courage to be tested for the virus. More than just finding the courage to face your fate—should the test turn out positive—is accepting that no matter who you are, or who you think you are, AIDS is real. For the longest time, I thought that by simply defending the fact that AIDS was not the product of depravity, or a wrathful act of God, I was helping to create a climate of empathy and understanding. It took a lot of thought and a lot of searching to realize that coping realistically with my social responsibility means, first of all, getting tested. I think all of us who are healthy brandish the psychological shield emblazoned with a gleaming crest of invincibility. I believed that I was untouchable.

For years, the HIV statistics didn't include me. I'm a heterosexual woman, black, and in my twenties. I have never had sexual relations with a bisexual partner, to the best of my instinct and knowledge; I have never been an IV drug user. But between lovers, there is no accounting for gaps in information. There are some things that people like to keep personal; you don't know anything when you're in the early, euphoric, psychotic states of that thing called love.

The message that pushed me to action was delivered during the morning news on KISS-FM. While eating my daily bowl of cereal, the dee-jay shocked the stuffing out of me when he said: "The leading cause of death among black women ages fifteen to twenty-five in the tri-county area"—with appropriate journalistic detachment, I held my breath while he went on—"is the HIV virus or AIDS." My face hit the bowl. I didn't have to look in the mirror to know who he was talking about. I wondered how long it took the government and the medical community to figure this out? How long had I been at risk? What was I supposed to do next? As in a fire, remain calm.

On the heels of that bad news came some good news—this time the messenger was Cupid.

I had to be really in love before I could meet my responsibility. It took three weeks of serious conversations with myself. What if the test is positive? Who will I tell first? Where will I go to die? How long will it take? What will this do to my family? Will they accept me? My medical insurance has expired! I grappled with my fears to the best of my ability, and decided simply to dance to the music should I hear the tune. It was useless for me to whistle away in the dark.

I went off to my annual checkup with a very serious objective, which I planned to casually slip in between the blood pressure cuff and the tongue depressor. I sat down in the doctor's office, and we had the usual chit-chat. Blah, blah, blah. I couldn't stand it! Let me know if I'm going to live or die! Of course, it's all going to be all right, calm down, and tell the doctor what you want, interjected the quiet guide of reason in my head. So, I asked. He told me quite plainly that I wasn't really at risk, not to bother. I quoted what I thought was a profound and correct statistic from that radio broadcast. It was unqualified, he told me, it applies to IV drug users. I don't have any needles in my life, but I just don't think that doctors are fully aware of every cause of the ailment. I was infuriated and insulted; I felt that someone somewhere was making a mockery of my intelligence. Why would my trusted physician—a medical professional—tell me not to protect myself and my significant other?

"Why do you want to be tested?" he asked. "Because I found someone I really love. I don't want to harm or do something potentially lethal to him. I want to know if I'm planning a future that's a pipe dream. How can I think about marriage, children, tomorrow—anything—until I know?"

My doctor put me through the motions. He told me to make sure that I was serious, that I had thought through the consequences, and that I was in at least some state of readiness should bad news come my way. He told me that he used to give the test automatically, as it's a free service of the Department of Health and Welfare in New York State. My doctor stopped routine testing when a patient who tested positive committed suicide. I told him that I was as ready as I could be, and felt that I just could not go on until I knew for certain that I wasn't infected.

The procedure is simple. The physician submits two cc's of blood to a government lab. A number is affixed to the lab order to safeguard the individual's privacy, a signature is required for the doctor's files, and that's it. I went home to wait for three weeks and realized there was absolutely no turning back. Period.

My test came back. It was negative. I am relieved, for now. But this is a mysterious killer. Some say it incubates for up to seven years. Which means that I must repeat this process again in six months. I believe we are all at risk. Acquired Immune Deficiency Syndrome has no respect for people, for hopes, dreams, or accomplishments, for you, or the future of anyone you care about. Test yourself. It is an act of love.

—New York, 1990

HIDDEN VALENTINES

Love Is All Around You

I f you care enough about tradition and sentimental things, Valentine's Day can be one of those devastating holidays. Not because you need someone else to fulfill your wishes, but because the urge to want more or newer love—or even some other love than the love you have—is overwhelming.

I've been truly miserable on enough Valentine's Days to feel uncomfortable admitting it. But the reason for my suffering was not obvious to me until yesterday: I realized that the pain I have felt on so many occasions was self-inflicted and that I rarely find myself taking stock of and appreciating the love I already have. Valentine's Day, I think, would be a lot more successful if I treated it more like New Year's Eve—a time to reflect upon how much I've grown over the past year in my ability to be loving in every type of relationship I'm fortunate to have in my life.

Valentine's Day should be like a Thanksgiving for love. Cause for celebration shouldn't be reserved only for those who are romantically engaged, leaving anyone without flowers and a box of chocolates feeling like they're on the outside looking in, aching and desperate. Love is the thing that sustains and nourishes us—I know if ever a moment came when I truly believed that there was no love in this universe for me, my lights would go out and I'd fall over dead. I could never imagine myself starving, so how could I imagine or indulge in thinking that I'm not getting enough love? Looking for some "perfect" love, that's how. Thinking that other people are enjoying the fairy-tale scenario of a flawless love that has rescued them from loneliness. When I'm overtaken by such thoughts, I feel inadequate because I haven't achieved such a love in my own life. And, without fail, any other love I have pales in comparison to this fantasy.

It's hard to evaluate the love that parents and family give to us. It's not snazzy, and it is binding in a way that I suspect is deeper than taking a vow for better or for worse. I get uncontrollably embarrassed and emotional when I think of how completely and selflessly my mother has loved me all my life. When I think about our relationship, I get a feeling that surprises me like an apparition. Accompanying my recollections of childhood is the release of a feeling that is both sweet and painful. I don't have a name for the feeling; its effect is bizarre—it makes me sob with gratitude and shake with terror. The terror I experience probably comes from the knowledge that I can never go back to that time. What haunts me once I'm calm again is the thought that my mother's love is so profound that I'm powerless to think of what an adequate reciprocation could be. What she gave me was perfect and unconditional love, a love so steady and strong that, through the years and across the miles stretching between our homes, I know that she is always there, like a force field. Even when I was difficult, my mother let me know I was a delight to her. When I did wrong, she scolded me, but she still loved me without compromise. There is no greater gift for starting out in life than knowing that I was loved that way—and that her love can transcend everything. I have always known that, whatever my problems, my mother's love is protecting me like a force field. She is my valentine.

I have a great longing to want my mate to love me as much as my parents do. But it is unfair to expect unconditional, maternal kind of love from the people I have chosen in my adult life. I believe that realizations like this will help me grow in love. If I want to recapture the love and devotion I experienced as a child—and I think it is achievable—I must choose someone who will meet me halfway, and I must develop the patience to make do with what I have.

And there is friendship. In a way, the bond between friends is the most selfless of love relationships. Friendships are highly mysterious and complex because they are not based on any primal drives. There is no sex to express and expand the measure of your fascination with one another. Friendships, because they are devoid of sex, don't contain the impurities of romantic love. The value of friendship is that friends bear with you, and its basis is admiration, which then grows into fondness. There is no malice in real friendship, whereas in love you constantly live on the edge of malice.

Friendship is the place where you find acceptance and room to grow. Think about how gleefully you report new discoveries to your friends, and how eager a friend can be to respond to them. Friends reinforce your successes and triumphs and put out the doormat to welcome you even when you've failed. I admit I'm guilty of not appreciating my friends and family as much as they deserve. I can get sidetracked by my romantic relationships and let friends fall by the wayside—or get so lost in some new career pursuit that months can pass without returning a phone call. My friends let me know in the strongest possible terms that I have to do better because they care about me. And I don't feel under pressure when I get called out by them. That's real friendship—people don't want to lose you. So, on this Valentine's Day, besides that "someone special" that Hallmark card is for, I'm giving love to family and friends.

—New York, 1994

STUPID CUPID

The Valentine's Day
That Never Comes

This is New York City. For many of us, anticipating Valentine's Day is like a child in war-torn Bosnia looking forward to Christmas. Expectation is high. Prospects are bleak. Every year I wait for Cupid to come with the same unwavering shiny-eyed belief that I had in Santa as a child. During the long interval before Cupid makes his regular visit to lovable boys and girls the world over, I try to be caring and sincere—because Cupid, like Santa, makes a list and checks it twice. Each and every day people in search of love, as well as those who are in love, compose lists of a lover's qualities that they hope Cupid will be kind enough to deliver. And while I prepare for the promise of the holiday, there's a little verse I like to recite.

'Twas the night before Valentine's
And all through the house
Not a creature was stirring—
Not even a mouse.
All the young singles lay snug in their beds,
Whilst visions of commitment and erotica
Danced in their heads.

To the rest of the world, I like to pretend that my heart has turned to a cinder on Valentine's Day. All the decorations are so persuasive. The heart-shaped boxes and the red crepe paper Cupids flying through the air in all the shop windows—how romantic. And the cards for every degree of love: "Special Friend," "Teen Girlfriend," "Lifelong Love," "Passionate Love." And the most intriguing category, "Blank Inside"—maybe that's the Zen state of love. Just when I thought I was out, the card rack pulls me back in.

Valentine's and New Year's have a lot in common. Deep down, who doesn't want this year's holiday to be the perfect cocktail of cunning and serendipity? Complete with an unforgettable kiss at midnight and the proverbial big bang just before dawn. I can't just ignore Valentine's like I can New Year's, preferring simply to be woken when it's over. I wish Hallmark, who invented the holiday, had taken Joni Mitchell's polite advice: "Don't wake me unless you love me. Otherwise, it's too hard to get back to sleep." Everyone says that what you do on New Year's is a good indication of what you'll be doing the rest of the year. Valentine's is a sentimental New Year's Eve—its indication is much graver than "Auld Lang Syne." I always think it's a predictor of how I'm going to feel for the rest of my life. That's the trouble with holidays—prescribed feelings are not always the best medicine.

I had to let go of my faith in the Easter Bunny and my faith in Santa. When I found out there was no Santa, I wasn't so devastated that my parents had lied to me, but that all the times I didn't get what I wanted it was because they wouldn't buy it for me. My mother was right there by my side telling me to look on the bright side—at least I wasn't unrewarded due to lack of character. It was an omen. I knew the Easter Bunny was next. When they told me, I covered my ears and screamed aloud in gibberish in order to block out the terrible message. Then I thought about it. How much did I really care about boiled eggs and chocolate candies? And then—no Tooth Fairy! I miss her. She always brought cash. But something is wrong here. I'm almost thirty years old and I still believe in Cupid. There has been no rite of passage to help me accept the nonexistence of the last mythical "giver."

Most of my adult friends believe in Cupid. Some are agnostic about it, but it is the rare dove who wholeheartedly denies his existence. One of my friends says he gives Cupid credence because he just knows he's going to fall in love every time he walks out of the house. Another friend says the little cherub is real due to the "theory of angels." "My sister died a few years ago," he told me. "She wanted to be the angel in charge of snow. When she passed on, it snowed all day long. There's an angel responsible for everything." One of my closest girlfriends won't even hear of it: "I found out about Santa very early on, so all the rest of that stuff is just bullshit to me. I can't believe there are people out there waiting for somebody to shoot them. With a gun, maybe, an arrow, no."

Even if Eros is a shell corporation and Cupid no longer delivers in favor of doing endorsements—why do some of us hold out in hopes of there being a Cupid? It's an important visualization of there being somebody out there who's wishing for you. And of somebody up there who believes you should get what you wish for just because you deserve it. And both heaven and earth are on patrol to make sure it happens. The idea of the little guy in diapers with the quiver of arrows aimed at your heart helps stave off the bitterness that comes with the daily realization that the world is not a fair place. As sickening as it is, I just can't give up on the myth of Valentine magic. After all, if there is no Cupid, silly rabbit, then what's left for us grown-ups? Happy Valentine's Day.

—New York, February 1993

JUST CALL ME

Get Over Your Hang-ups

[Ring] Where's the phone? Panic. Excitement. I'm running across the wood floors of my apartment, sliding recklessly in my stocking feet, because I have to get my hands on the cordless phone before the answering machine picks up. Finding the phone is like a game show. Running like an idiot from the linen closet to the bathroom. Trying to reach my goal before the time's up. Ring. Okay, okay, the phone must be down in between the bed pillows! Voila! "Hello?" Oh, no! It's only Mr. Dial Tone. I'm too late. The caller hangs up.

No matter how annoyed I get with the intrusion of the phone, or the search for said intruder, a ringing phone is still a signal of welcome serendipity to me. I hardly, if ever, know who's calling or what information might come across the wire. And the added attraction with the cordless phone is that neither party knows what the other is up to on the other end of the line.

Today, I'm taking an informal poll of the people I talk to

most about which chores or pleasures they perform during cordless phone communiqués. My longtime girlfriend in California confesses with embarrassed laughter to having a "Pavlovian response" to the ringing phone. "It makes me have to pee," she admits. Another one of my phone buddies in the music business says that when he has to deal with people he doesn't like, he pretends to be seated in an easy chair. Hmmm, sounds innocuous enough, like some kind of executive visualization technique to make you more effective. I asked him if what I was seeing in my mind's eye was indeed the case. Not at all, he told me, "You know those sounds that people make when they're trying to get comfortable in an easy chair? You can pass off the same grunts and pauses when you're on the bowl passing your morning constitution." Think about that. Years ago a phone in the bathroom was the height of luxury. You had to be a millionaire to exact that kind of petty revenge. Before we can really get into praising the invention of the cordless, my call-waiting goes "boop."

Press flash. Click. Click. "Hello?" I hear more bathroom sounds in the background of this call. Maybe it's a pool party. Nothing so exotic on this cold winter day. It's just one of my girlfriends dialing from the shower. She's desperate about getting ready to go out for the evening. She needs me. "You know, I was just saying on the other line how handy the cordless is . . ." then "Boop."—"Hold on, okay?" I don't usually bother to wait for an answer to this question, unless I'm romantically involved with, or really kissing the ass of, the other person. "Hold" is both the great convenience and the distraction of modern communication. "Hello?" "Veronica, hi!" shouts a familiar but very distorted voice. Oooh! It's a romantic call from an airplane—I love those. I have to make one of those split-second etiquette decisions. Do I go back to my desperate friend in the shower or hang out at cruising altitude with my loved one? I decide to leave my girlfriend in the shower, rotting on hold.

Ground-to-air communiqués are always a ripe moment for passion. "I love you" is the best thing I can say to someone on a 747. It's probably the extreme crackling of his AirPhone going to my head. "I can't hear you," my dearest one shouts down the phone toward Earth. Willing to work with the constraints of technology, I repeat myself. Click. Across town, "Desperate" in the shower gives up. A second click interrupts transmission of my love message. "What," he shouts again. "Forget this. I can't hear you. I'll call back." Click. He's gone. Dialing his destination to leave a message—"Boop," foiled again. Glaring at the phone in the palm of my hand with much contempt, huffing with indignation, I press the flash feature.

"Hello?" Male. Heavy breathing. I'd hang up if I wasn't used to it. It's the m.o. of one of my old boyfriends. It sounds like he's doing something I wouldn't consent to if I was there, but I know him to be a fitness freak. "Oh, hi. What are you doing?" I know the answer won't be scintillating. "StairMaster," he says, bellowing between strong exhales, inhaling a drag from a cigarette, deciding not to be so lazy, I go to do something physical. Taking the tweezers out of the bathroom cabinet, I start plucking my eyebrows. The smug satisfaction of improving myself overwhelms me. Midway through the old beauty and the beast routine we've always shared—"Boop." Saved by the bell.

Press flash. Click. Click. "Hello?" Genius! A call from a pay phone, the lowly donkey of the phone system. I won't hold this gap in chic against my Rollerblading partner. It takes about two minutes for him to coax me out on my skates. I love skating for reasons other than touring Manhattan. It's the perfect opportunity for me to utilize the Zeus of the communications pantheon, the mobile phone. Sliding through the frigid night air, I dial my loved one at his faraway destination to once again profess my love over a clear line. I get the hotel. In the middle of dictating my message, call-waiting chimes in on the mobile. It's him! Calling from the plane. "Honey," he says, the pride in his voice squelching the crackle of the airphone, "I got you call-waiting on the mobile as a surprise." I think it's time to say "good-bye."

—Los Angeles, 1992

CUT TO THE CHASE

Playing Tag with Love

Sighting a person who pleases one's senses sets physiological responses zinging like pinballs through the human Bermuda triangle—heart, head, and loins. The same childish tingle of danger and delight rise as the senses cry out upon encountering the new person—"You're it!" The best game on the playground of adulthood begins with meeting someone whose wit, body, and charm sets you racing. It's like playing tag.

The chase is on. Being pursued, we are conditioned to run like hell, screaming and giggling with each stride, all the while holding a fantasy deep inside of being taken prisoner. Finally, the pursuer gets close enough to touch the pursued. If that touch is delicious and intriguing, the dynamic of the game reverses—and goes to a whole other level.

Fantasy fizzles. It was only a tease. No one takes anyone prisoner, willing captive or not, with great ease. Once we conquer, nature tells us to flee. It hurts so bad, as the person who once pursued us with a passionate determination turns on their heels. Children love to be chased, it's a primal ego trip. (And just because you're over twenty-one doesn't mean you stop liking it.)

Having been tagged, caught, and then rejected is spellbinding. For those of us who are more predatory, being tagged is also to taste blood. Nostrils snort "I'll get you back!" The predatory animal within sees red.

It's a fine line between the feeling of wanton abandon and the abasement of being abandoned. In games of childhood we mindlessly perpetuate pursuit. In the arena of adulthood, the mind pumps furiously through its subconscious labyrinth in pursuit of the fleeing body.

On and on it goes. Players tire and part ways, or go into less passionate games, like working and playing house.

Welcome to the mating game of adulthood. Its twists and turns are really no different than in the school yard—only the stakes are higher. Every relationship, no matter if it is a milestone or a discard, engraves its face on the totem of the senses. It's called playing for keeps.

The rules are far more complex. Codes of conduct on this level of the game are unpublished. The rules are particular to the individual, encoded by personal experience. How well people play depends on how fair they wish life to be, or how fair other players have been to them.

We all know when it's time to get into the game. These are instances when a timid little "no" or two is whispering in the back of our minds. But, one eager "yes!" quickly deafens a person to the resistance of every whispered "no." Subject to the same disregard for plight as a calloused New Yorker can have toward a tattered tramp on the street corner tinkling coins in a cup, "no" struggles behind. "Yes!" jingles the triangle.

Chemistry on contact. Love at first sight. Acting upon either impetus is at once fantastic and terrible. In romantic relationships, allowing the touch of the other to play on our physical, emotional, and logical responses is nothing other than submission. Romantic submission is the softening of any rigidity that would otherwise shut out interaction.

Acting with wanton abandon oftentimes leads to abandonment. There is an innocence in all lower drives. The emotions of wanton motivation are real—and raw in the extreme. Some people like to play on this level. Others do not. From the christening to the last rites of any relationship, emotions are always in a wash of near infantile vulnerability after sex.

There are only two postcoital revelations: I am happy, satisfied, and do not want to part from this person—ever. I am unhappy, unsatisfied, and want to escape from this person—immediately. Equal in intensity and urgency, either response can evoke comfort or terror. The thoughts and emotions in this state are never vague. Do I flee, do I chase, is this a truce? There is nothing to pad feelings over; no distance, no distraction.

Conquest and contempt are closely related. Sex can bring us closer only if it feels mutual. If not, sex can drive a bitter wedge into the heart of a relationship. One person can feel taken, and the other becomes the villain, the taker. No question, sex is where the truth comes out. It has been said, "Truth is a bludgeon disguised as a gift."

Who we are playing with, and what we are playing for, is revealed in the daily quest of understanding someone intimately—lying down to commit the act of opening loins, followed by the mundane getting up and going on together to the next thing. Seeking insight into a new playmate through a walk in the park or observing their table manners—this is the narrow path allotted to find out if one has met one's match.

Are both players proceeding with the same level of sportsmanship, are both players playing as aggressively, as consistently toward the same goal? A relationship is in effect once those questions and feelings have been addressed. It's official.

Asking someone to verbalize the answer resembles the dialogue between Alice and the Cheshire Cat. "Who are you? Explain yourself," the Cheshire Cat demands of a bewildered Alice. Alice says, "I can't. I don't understand myself under these circumstances."

The confounding element in relationships, no matter at what phase, is the frequency with which we bump up against our own expectations and shortcomings. Even when unwittingly provoked, either will cause players to chase each other. Each player is trying to tag the partner accused of being overzealous, or the partner accused of under-delivering. The crux of loving someone is caring enough to make their problems your problems. It's not possible to measure one's true character without the experiences of constant, intimate contact.

—New York, 1993

POP CULTURE

Darren Keith

JUNGLE DIARIES

I don't believe there is one person in this world old enough to have been exposed to cinema who hasn't dreamed, at least once, of being a movie star, or at least in a film. Anyone who would tell me otherwise, I'd be inclined to call a liar. As a kid growing up in Detroit I watched endless hours of afternoon movies on television. When I was old enough to take the bus, I cut half of high school in favor of the foreign film series at the Detroit Institute of Arts, dreaming all the while of all the worlds, and all the women I could be beyond the Motor City.

Jungle Fever, directed by Spike Lee, is my first film. As I sit here writing this article I have no idea if all the scenes I shot are still in the movie, or what my performance will be like in the overall context of the film. My director has yet to give me more feedback than "Don't WORRY." I won't know what will happen until the premiere in New York next month. This is just a description of my experience of making a movie for the very first time. I can only liken it to Lewis Carroll's *Alice Through the Looking Glass*. I have yet to come out the other side, into the mythical world of celluloid.

June 16, 1990: "This is Spike Lee," a gruff voice crackled out across the Atlantic from my answering machine. I had to rewind. I had to listen twice. He said what I thought he said. "I want to audition you for my new movie." I called my agent. "David, David what the hell is this? Spike Lee called my house about some movie." The excitement made me almost hostile. "You're going to audition. I think that you can get this part. Where are you?" "I'm in Paris working for *Elle*." David Schiff, in the brass-tacks wisdom that Hollywood agents sometimes have, told me, "Get on the plane and come home."

June 17: The auditioning process began. I went to pick up what are called "sides," a short scene usually of about two pages in length from the existing script for the film. These few lines are the actor's material for the audition. From this limited amount of dialogue, actors are expected to create an emotional connection to the circumstance, and surmise what the character might be. Figure out the acting, come in one or two days later, and live it out truthfully, as though it were happening for the first time. It can take me up to twenty hours to conquer one page of text. In short it is an exercise in alchemy.

I was instructed to pick up the sides for "Vera." The receptionist at the desk told me that there were only sides for "Vivian," as far as she knew no character named "Vera" existed. I spent two days obsessed with the material.

June 19: It's hot as a firecracker outside. Nelson Mandela arrives in New York. At four o'clock he will speak at City Hall. Today is the proverbial "big day." I was scheduled to read for Robbi Reed, the casting director, at the same hour. I consoled myself with the fact that Mandela would be in town all week and I would have other chances to see the great African leader in the flesh. I would not get the chance to see Mandela, this was the first indication of how film takes over a person's life.

I rode my bike to the casting office. Signed in, sat down, and waited my turn. I found out after my reading that I had picked up the wrong material. Can you imagine yourself in a twenty-alarm fire trapped on the top floor of the World Trade Center? Knowing that if you don't jump you might burn up. I was given the correct text, and Robbi gave me the option of coming in another time or working it out in a few minutes and giving it another try. I didn't trust that if I went away with the material for two days the exact, right, perfect person for the part wouldn't walk in behind me. My mind said now or never. The scene happened to be about racial prejudice between dark- and light-skinned blacks, something that traumatized me often as a child and still comes up in my adult life. By the grace of God, in an instant I found a connection to the words. The scene was meant to be funny, my interpretation recorded on videotape was the contrary. Robbi asked me if I was all right when the reading was over. I said yes and thank you, and left. I had no idea how my work was received, actors rarely do. I felt small and spent. All I could do was wait.

"Yeah. This is Spike Lee," this time the voice on the phone was live and direct from Brooklyn, and just as gruff as the first time I had heard it. "I saw your tape. I liked it. Why did you break down like that?" I really couldn't answer what prompted my response in the scene. It was a lifetime of experience with the issue. I was leery of going into with a stranger on the telephone, director or no director. "I can't explain," I mumbled. "I'm sorry." Thankfully Spike was accepting of my answer. "I want you to come in and read again. You should have a script and we should meet." I couldn't believe I had gotten this far.

June 22: A second reading was scheduled for six o'clock this evening. Nelson Mandela is speaking at the Tribeca Grill tonight at six-thirty. I had to miss it. I left a shooting early to get ready for the audition. I waited at the casting office with the casting director until it became apparent that Spike was not showing up. He had gone to the Mandela event.

June 24: I took the R train to Brooklyn at the invitation of the director for lunch and a script. In all the years I have lived in New York, of all the people I know who have worked with Spike, throughout all my travels our paths had never crossed. Spike is someone I've always greatly admired as an artist and a force in American culture, but chiefly my admiration of the man stems from the fact that he has had such a profound and positive effect on the lives of so many young black people. I tried to keep my mind on James Baldwin to combat my nervousness and apprehension. When I arrived at the four-story firehouse headquarters of Forty Acres and a Mule Filmworks, I was told Spike was running forty-five minutes behind. Maybe it was nervousness, or because I was hungry but I fell asleep on the couch in the waiting room. I heard the door open and saw a slight figure approaching. Mars! Mookie! Spike! the genuine incarnation. I got my wits together. He gave me an odd look, I thought it was because he caught me dozing. I came to find out in the following weeks it was because I was so "regular." He had expected me to look more like a model, whatever that means, my profession of trade. We walked into the city for lunch across the Brooklyn Bridge. Spike was usually a few paces ahead of me and when he wasn't, he was interrogating me with some very provocative questions about my personal experiences. End result, I was told to read the script in preparation for a final audition.

June 26: Spike called to ask me if I was the person who had written the cover story for *Interview* magazine on Denzel Washington. He said he liked the piece and would I interview his sister, actress Joie Lee, for an issue of *Spin* that he was editing. I really didn't feel entirely comfortable with the idea, because it put me in a precarious position in several ways. I was trying to get a job from him, so I decided to treat the article as part of the audition. Spike is not a person that takes no for an answer.

July 2: I had to go to Florence, Italy, over the weekend to do some modeling work. I missed my plane to New York and arrived late last night to my flooded basement apartment and an eight A.M. call for work. To top it all off the most important audition of my life was at the end of the day. I felt harried after the weekend of trans-Atlantic travel, jet lag, and work during the day and nights dedicated to completing the article for Spin.

The appointed hour came. The final audition lasted some two hours. Most of which was improvised from scenarios that Spike set up based on the relationship of Vera and Cyrus. There wasn't so much a romantic type of chemistry between us as an interesting friction of two personalities. Everything was taped. When the audition was over I knew I had done everything I knew how to do to the best of my ability. I said thank you and good-bye to everyone. I was happy just to have had the chance to act and to have gotten a taste of what it would be like to work with Spike. I handed him the article on his sister and turned around to walk to the elevator. I heard Spike say, "You got the part." I was puzzled. I had the sensation of being in a car accident, when time folds back in on itself when the sounds and details of each moment take on a clarity that makes the familiar become surreal. "Excuse me?" I said. "You got the part," he repeated. "In what?" I managed to eke out. "You got the part!" "Well, what do I have to do now?" I think my despondency exasperated Spike. He called for Robbi Reed, the casting director. It took the two of them several minutes to penetrate my disbelief. A quiet thank you spilled from my lips, and I left.

When I got to the street that's when it really hit me. I sprinted through the streets back to my apartment rehearsing the whole way how I would tell my parents back in Detroit. "Hello." My mother's little voice materialized on the phone. "Momma! I got a part in a movie! A Spike Lee movie!" "You did? Who is that?" my mother asked in all earnestness. "Spike Lee! He's a great director. I'm opposite him in the movie! I'll play his wife." "Is he black or white?" my mother wanted to know. "He's black, Momma." "Okay, when does that mean you're coming home again?" "Soon Momma. Let me talk to Daddy." "Hi Daddy! I got a part in a movie with Spike Lee! I'm going to be opposite him, we're playing husband and wife." "Well, it could be worse," my father said, "it could be a porno movie. Do what you gotta do, girl, and come on home." They were happy for me.

July 3: I woke up numb. It's one thing to compete for a role, it's a whole other thing to be awarded the honor and responsibility of performance. I picked up the script and began to work out my performance, in the same way a musician works out a piece of music, one note at a time. I soon came to realize that Vera had no profession. I'd have to think of one for the role. For all the strong views my character has about race relations and racial identity, there is nothing in the text to ground her point of view. I would have to invent a philosophy. Spike is not a director that is precious with text. His writing is based more on ideas than language. He explained to me as I came to him with ideas and questions concerning my role, what makes his films live and breathe the way they do is the freedom he gives the cast to discover and inhabit the characters.

Spike had some input of his own on what Mrs. Vera Flood would look like. He thought Vera should have a tattoo. Tattoos can be painted on temporarily, so I had no objection to that. I chose a heart with Cupid's arrow piercing the middle and the words *Daddy's Girl* to be located on my left shoulder. Spike and I both agreed that I should have a haircut. He told me to watch Jean-Luc Godard's *Breathless*. He thought Jean Seberg's hairstyle in the film would suit both myself and the character. He was right. What I did find objectionable was when Spike told me he loved "fire truck red" lipstick. It's his favorite because his grandmother wears it. Red lipstick! I thought I would look like Bozo the Clown! I hated red lipstick at the time. Spike insisted on it. So I began to wear it in my everyday life in order to get used to it.

July 11: I decided that Spike should come with me to pick out wedding rings for our characters. I convinced him to go to 57th Street with me and buy some costume jewelry. It took about an hour before I found the perfect ring for Vera's fingers. When I did I asked him to propose to me, as much for a goof as I thought it would be necessary. He didn't like the idea too much. He thought that it was going too far. I insisted; it didn't take him too long to realize that he has found himself a nutty person to work with and got with the program. The next day he sent me a dozen dead roses and a butter rum cake with the words TO MY WIFE VERA written in red icing. I wore my ring until the final instant of filming.

July 12: I met with Lonette McKee for lunch. She was a million times more wonderful than I expected her to be. There is not enough space in this article to explain how giving, helpful, and essential she was to my survival during filming. We made a pact to be 100 percent available to one another for any reason on the project and we spent many hours doing our actors' homework together. I introduced Lonette to members of the fashion industry for her research, and she shared her years of expertise in the film industry with me.

July 23: *Mo'Better Blues* had its world premiere in New York City. The turbulent reception the film received from the critics didn't dampen the Afro-American spirit of achievement and celebration that night. It was a premiere unlike any other I had ever been to. Everyone turned out, black literati and glitterati, members of every branch of the press, actors, athletes, and politicians. Mayor David M. Dinkins sat behind me with a bucket of popcorn. Everyone was dressed to the nines. Spike took a moment out to honor Mother Hale with words of praise and big fat checks from Spike, with matching funds from Nike, to help with the continuation of her work with AIDS babies in Harlem. A portion of *Jungle Fever* was to be filmed in Harlem. I was touched by the fact that Spike would think to give back to the community before he even began to take. I felt proud to be part of the Forty Acres team.

August 6: I can only say, when *Jungle Fever* was read through with the full cast for the first time I was petrified. There I was going into my first professional experience paired with some awe-inspiring talents. Ruby Dee, Ossie Davis, Lonette McKee, Anthony Quinn, John Turturro. I ate my breakfast that morning and threw it up before I got out of the door. I didn't know if I could make the grade. I was fearful maybe there would be resentment or prejudice against my coming from the fashion industry. No such thing happened. Working the rag trade can make for a claustrophobic point of view. Most people don't follow fashion, and are familiar only with the most obvious symbols of the trade. It was a welcome insignificance. I gave the reading my all, and even got compliments from some of the other actors afterward. It was a relief to get over that first hurdle.

August 10: Hair and makeup and lighting rehearsals and the choosing of props is a very important part of filmmaking. It was my job to figure out what Vera would look like and what individual props I would need in order to support her world, what would she read, drive, and carry on her person in each scene. This list has to be reported to the prop master. Spike's cinematographer Ernest Dickerson does brilliant work. He's been responsible for the look of Spike's movies from the very beginning with a student film he and Spike made, *Joe's Bed-Stuy Barber Shop: We Cut Heads*. I confided in Ernest that first day. I knew a lot about cameras, but nothing about that huge Panavision camera we would be using. Ernest assured me it would be easy to learn the camera. I was surprised when he told me that he often used fashion magazines as reference material. Later that day all the principal actors were required to take a brief physical for insurance purposes.

August 11: The next two weeks were all rehearsals, publicity stills, and fittings. Most of my rehearsal time with Spike was dedicated to helping him learn his lines. And talking about changes in dialogue that I thought up. Spike slated in extra rehearsal time for me as it was my first film. I'm new to acting, and at times felt unsure of myself, Spike reassured me that he hired me "for my instincts." He warned me not to get too complicated, just to work hard, and not be afraid to act. Rehearsal time is a luxury item with the price of film these days, most of the smaller scenes in the film were rehearsed the night before, but most often the day of filming. The rehearsal period is the time when most of the cast members meet, waiting for costuming was when I had the occasion to meet Anthony Quinn. I was ecstatic when Spike cast Mr. Quinn in the role of Lou, John Turturro's grieving Italian father. I've been fascinated by Mr. Quinn as an artist since I read his autobiography *The Original Sin*. Talking to Mr. Quinn, I was surprised how open and available he was to discuss the acting process. He told me that he was searching for an impediment for Lou, he didn't want to do a stroke, he just acted a couple of characters with that impediment, and he had already done heart disease. I had a million questions and a million more compliments for the great actor, all of which he answered and accepted with wonderful good nature. What makes Mr. Quinn so appealing is that he is very much a student of humanity and his craft.

September 6: What was commonly referred to as the "girl-friend" scene was rehearsed at night for filming in the morning. The rehearsal went well, Lonette, myself, and three other actresses spent three hours alternating between straight text and improvisation in the rehearsal space at Forty Acres. During rehearsal, the actress cast as Nilda started to make comments about white women having a lurid sexual disposition. From Vera's point of view these comments were outrageous and absolutely unacceptable. In the context of the scene those were fighting words for the two characters. Spike and Robbi watched the rehearsal, and then left. The minute Spike was out of earshot, the actress playing Nilda hauled off and personally attacked me, vilifying my performance in a strong warning that did not preclude physical violence. "I will kick your ass! I don't like the way you made me come off in the scene. I want to be the good guy. I want to be liked. Don't you dare do that to me in the scene." I apologized if I had hurt her feelings in some way and assured her that it was nothing personal, but in order for me to be true to my character (Vera's mother is written as white in the script) I had to respond the way I did. "I don't care," she continued, "you heard what I told you." I realized there was no reasoning with this person, and words erupted between the two of us that the other three women in the room were obliged to stop. Cathy Tyson asked me if my mother was white, I said no, both my parents were black, but that was not the issue. My duty here was to serve and protect the line of the part. In retrospect, I realize that the whole exchange was totally unprofessional on the part of the other actress, and equally unprofessional on my part to let myself get involved in it. Any likes or dislikes, or disciplining of an actor comes from the director. Period. I should have called Spike back in the room the moment I realized the game she was playing with me. It was a cruel thing to do to another actor especially one that had never set foot on a film set before. I left rehearsal enraged, but worse than that I doubted myself for an hour or so. I wondered if I had violated some unspoken rule. I realized that I had just experienced one of the pitfalls of the film industry. My first day of filming was eight hours away.

September 7: Call time five-thirty A.M. Going to sleep that night I was like a six-year-old anticipating the first day of first grade. This time the school house was the big bad world of film. I packed my bag the night before full of all the things Lonette told me I would need in my trailer: two towels, incense (she knew from experience that the toilet systems can get a little rank on occasion), a sleep mask for quick catnaps between takes, a bar of soap, vitamins and a box of Kleenex. As a present Lonette gave me a pair of slippers to wear around the set, and a box of ginseng. I waited dutifully by the door for the car to come pick me up, and take me to the set on Strivers Row, the most beautiful block of brownstones in all of Harlem. The minutes passed. The car was late! I panicked. I'll be late and I'll be written up. Why aren't they here? Horrors of horrors, Oh No! I've been replaced! I rushed downstairs and called the production coordinator. "Hello?" a groggy voice answered. "H.H." I wailed into the phone, "they forgot me. The car isn't here." "What time was it supposed to be there?" "Five-fifteen!" "Veronica," he answered patiently, "it's four-fifteen. The car will be there in an hour." Gee, I felt dumb. "Okay." Relief! I hadn't been replaced. I hung up and went over my lines.

Five-thirty A.M. I arrived on the set right on time. My eyes met with an unforgettable sight. Malcolm X Boulevard was lined with silent, exquisitely composed, clean-shaven young men, in black suits, white shirts, and crisp black bow ties. These beautiful young men were the Fruit of Islam, our security force. Municipal police are not the welcome sight to a lot of people of African-American descent as they tend to be hostile, and often a dangerous presence where blacks are concerned. I've experienced unwarranted racist-based police harassment on several occasions in communities all over the world.

I was introduced to my trailer. A little compartment in a Winnebago about the size of a double bed. With a cushioned bench, fluorescent lights, and a toilet separated by a movable screen. Not the prettiest of sights at the crack of dawn. Finally, after I had my hair done and finished my makeup, and the other actresses in the "girlfriend" scene were ready, we were led to the set. From seven A.M. to eleven A.M. we repeated the scene until twenty or so takes later Spike called "Cut! Thanks ladies." I was alive and in one piece. I began to get to know the people on the crew, and to understand the workings of film. As I was leaving the set I was told I'd be reporting for work tomorrow.

September 7: Scene #62 was on the slate today, a relationship scene between Vera and Cyrus. I must have waited about three hours in my fusty little trailer before they called me. Every ten minutes or so a production assistant comes to your trailer to check if you need anything, but mostly to make sure of your whereabouts. In the waiting time the temptation is to wander off. Eventually, I came to dread the crackle of the walkie-talkie, the signal that a production assistant was coming to tell you that nothing was happening yet, but hurry up and get ready.

Film sets are very much like ant hills. There are hundreds of people in motion eighteen hours a day: caterers, costumers, prop people, lighting people, teamsters, moving, moving, moving while you are waiting, waiting, waiting.

September 9: The "dailies" (what most people commonly know as "rushes") of the "girlfriend" scene were shown. Seeing myself for the first time on film was kind of horrifying. My head was about the size of a car engine. I felt like one of those balloons in the Macy's Thanksgiving Day Parade. Everything is so huge. I kept waiting to see my arm float up with a string attached to the palm of my hand. I didn't even look like me. Mostly because I never see the back of my head, what I look like when I'm emotional, or what I look like when I'm walking away. To top it all off I had erased a lot of my own mannerisms. Dailies are an instant educational tool for an actor. What's good and what's bad rewards or slaps you in the face right away. The actors involved in the scene are present, along with crew members and the director. It's the first test of audience reaction, and I liked it.

September 11: Scenes #72 and #73 were the most important scenes I had in the film, in which Vera reveals her views on racial identity. Lonette patiently acted as my sounding board, listening to me, and helping me solve some of the acting questions involved in the scene. The scene starts with Vera giving Cyrus a bath, and then moves into the bedroom. This is when a lot of things that have to do with continuity came up. During the first shot, or master shot, the camera was on both Spike and I. Fine. Then the camera changed to my point of view. Fine. Then it changed to Spike's point of view. I was astonished as the crew removed the bathtub from the wall lickety-split, and the camera was set up on the other side. This was when my inexperience began to show. I was told by the continuity woman to continue the same action of washing Cyrus's chest. I did so. A few seconds later Ernest Dickerson the cinematographer said to me, "You are in my frame." I stopped what I was doing assuming that he meant "get out of frame." When the last take was over the continuity woman was very worried that the film wouldn't match. I explained and apologized if I had ruined anything, but there was no time or film remaining for another take.

We took a break while the crew set up the bedroom for the conclusion of the scene. Scene #73 is a heavy one, the aftermath of a marital argument. I had no lighting stand-in that evening, and had to take my position for the camera and more or less hold it for a few hours. For technical reasons I really couldn't leave the room to be alone with my feelings between takes. The crew was quiet and respectful, but they still had a lot of busy work to do, most of which took place right under my nose. I had to actively struggle to maintain my emotional state for the monologue. Most of the work and preparation I had done in the weeks beforehand was geared toward delivering those words. We did five takes and then it was over. I went home spent from the doing of it, and anxious about the final result. It's not like a play, where the night's work dissolves from existence and tomorrow is another chance to live out and perfect the performance.

The next day at "dailies" all was well. I happened to sit behind the continuity woman and watched her throw her hands up in the air, when the film proved that I had made a mistake during the bathtub scene. I took it as a personal failure instead of a learning experience. I was so ashamed. It was a small mistake, but film lasts forever.

September 14: I thought scene #16, when the audience is first introduced to Vera, would be one of the easiest to shoot. All I had to do was come in from walking the dog after work, say "Hello" to my husband and his best friend, unleash the dog, take off my coat, throw my bag down, and sit on the bed. Those simple actions turned out to be a nightmare. It's one thing to give a person physical directions, another to have a human and a canine actor execute the same set of directions in one fluid motion. The first time the dog got its leash wrapped around my legs and I fell. Another time he licked me smack in the puss, and my makeup had to be redone. Then we had to reblock the scene where most of the lines were delivered crouching against the doorjamb, in order to have greater control over the dog. I had a lot of marks to hit, and I made some of my own mistakes.

Spike and I were tired and we went up on our lines a couple of times, calling each other the wrong names. Twenty-two trying takes later it was finished. It will probably end up being about ninety seconds of audience enjoyment.

The crew had moved to the notorious section of Bensonhurst, Brooklyn, one of the hotbeds of racial tension in the city. It was on national news the summer before when Yusef Hawkins, a young black honor students had been murdered by a gang of baseball-bat-wielding whites. I was concerned for the crew. I have to admit, I was thankful I had no cause to be on the set at the time. Several days after the cast was present the *New York Daily News* printed a sensational front-page headline, "Cops Guard Spike Lee." Spike told me the reports in the paper were exaggerated, and there had been a few minor incidents.

October 17: I had nearly a month off from filming. I was glad to get back into things. This time, the crew had moved into my neighborhood, the East Village. The set was only two blocks away. All the remaining scenes were to be shot at night. I had to change my sleeping habits in order to accommodate the new hours. I arrived on the set at five-thirty P.M., one of the actors necessary for the scene was nowhere to be found. The crew went ahead with some other scenes. I was peeved, I was ready to act! Maybe it's the ham in me, but I wanted to go on! After three hours of waiting for the missing actor, I was put on all night standby. I went back home. Production called me around midnight and said to prepare scene #90, my final scene in the film. Someone would be there to get me at two A.M. The weather had started to turn bad. Cyrus and Vera were on the road that night. I knew it wasn't going to be a picnic to drive the little convertible with its top down on the F.D.R. Drive. It took over two hours to conceal the lighting in the tiny sports car. The car was secured to a flatbed on a specially built truck, capable of holding the big Panavision Camera and the crew. In general, cars are towed in movies, at extremely slow speeds unless a stunt is taking place. There were no stunts planned for the evening.

We started off down the F.D.R. Drive, and drove in what seemed to be endless loops under the Brooklyn Bridge. Ernest acted as director while Spike was doing his scenes. Between takes Ernest called out to me, "Watch the overlap!" I thought overlaps were some structural things under the bridge, I looked up in the night sky to see what was overlapping us. The camera caught the exchange on film. Six-thirty A.M. rolled around, we had just finished the final take when a peal of thunder cracked in the silent Saturday morning city, and a near monsoon kicked up.

In dailies the following day everyone roared with laughter at my eyes searching for the "overlap." "Overlap" is a film term for overlapping dialogue. I was a little embarrassed at my naivete, but it's this kind of stuff that lightens up the serious responsibilities of making film.

October 20: I reported for night shooting. The weather was inclement. Cold and raining. Bad weather makes everybody's job doubly difficult. The rain was freezing cold and punishing the thin plastic rain ponchos the Fruit of Islam security force wore over their suits. We were all obliged to dress on set, as there was no way to protect our clothes from getting drenched on the short walk to the set. We started filming about midnight, a short scene in a sparse loft apartment. The crew was in good spirits, despite the rough weather. Ernest had a funny habit of whistling the theme to the quiz show "Jeopardy" while his technical assistants solved lighting problems.

The final portion of the scene was an awkward moment between myself and Annabella Sciorra, who played the mistress of my best friend's husband. It was really the first time Annabella and I had met. Our scene was left basically unrehearsed, Spike is known to do that in confrontation scenes. A swinging camera motion was used for the scene. The camera operator had to smoothly sweep the heavy shoulder-mounted camera first toward Annabella, then back to myself, as we each delivered our lines. Once or twice the two of us started giggling, because the cameraman took on the appearance of some kind of high-tech Minotaur. Two little boxes were taped off on the floor, our feet were not to stray one inch beyond, that left Annabella and I plastered against the walls in the tiny kitchen. Physically uncomfortable as it was to stay on the marks, it worked very well to heighten the tension. Spike called, "Cut."

I went downstairs to the holding area to change out of my costume, sign out, and recover a little. It was two A.M. and pouring rain. It was my last day on the film. I had done my job. I really didn't know how to feel, except that I didn't want to say good-bye. I tried not to call attention to the fact that my experience with all the people I had spent so much time with had ended. I slipped off the set into the street. I walked through the rain passing my trailer for the last time. I bumped into a few crew hands scurrying along carrying things from the vans to the set. Some of them congratulated me and said good-bye. I really couldn't speak or face anyone. I just didn't want it to end. Walking home in the night I was shaken by the thought that from this point on everything to do with the film was out of my hands. I wondered what the editing process would do to my acting, did I do the right thing? I did my best. There was nothing more I could do to affect the outcome of my performance.

I sat up the rest of the night, shaking my head and blinking my eyes thinking about that one in a million chance. I felt like the apex to a pyramid built on a strong family foundation. I had fulfilled a lifelong dream. I thought about my grandmother, who died in 1911, and the life she lived in the Jim Crow South. I never met her, but I would have given anything that night if she knew what I had been able to do two generations later. I better keep working my butt off. This is only the beginning.

—New York, 1990

MARY J. BLIGE

A t age twenty-four, Mary J. Blige presently holds the title of queen of hip-hop soul. This medal first came to Blige directly from the hip-hop community because, responding to rap, she developed a style of soul singing flowing right on top of the beats on her 1993 debut album, *What's the 411?* (Uptown). Since the release of her second Uptown album, *My Life*, last fall, she has been referred to as the "Aretha Franklin of Generation X." As usual, flattery and fame have their price, and Blige is in the doubly precarious position of being expected to live up to all of this.

I went to meet Blige at a private airplane hangar in Santa Monica, while she was shooting a $300,000 video for the track "You Bring Me Joy," which will be the third video from *My Life*. Three and a half hours after my arrival, during the dinner break, I was allowed my first encounter with Blige. I had been warned that she is not at all political. That she is moody. That she can be attacking. When the director calls for a dinner break, I hear her cousin and traveling companion Marco rename it a "chronic break." True to word, Blige and her sister LaTonya, along with Marco and a few attendants, sit in Blige's Jeep, listening to the rapper Method Man on the car radio, passin' reefer and drinkin' forty-ounce beers. Someone summons me to the car to introduce me to Blige. When it becomes clear to Blige that I intend to interview her that day, she is openly infuriated that she had not been briefed that I'd be doing more than just "hanging out" the first time we met. She's through. Windows start rolling up, the doors on Blige's Cherokee slam shut, and I awkwardly retreat to my car. I'm parked in the space next to hers. She's given me the pop star treatment: They bring you up, and they let you down.

"Keep it real" is the pledge of allegiance at Camp Blige. It isn't long before the "chronic" is in full effect and the parking lot becomes a block party. Taureen Bennett, Blige's soft-spoken, 6-foot 3-inch bodyguard, stands next to the passenger side of her Jeep Cherokee and rocks the vehicle and its occupants to the beat. It looks like a ride at an urban amusement park. When Taureen works up a sweat from rocking the Jeep, he sits down in front of Blige's dressing trailer next to her Jeep and sips a wine cooler. Hours go by, and the party continues. Marco and LaTonya bring back Styrofoam containers of fried chicken and greens. Under the streetlights in the parking lot, Blige teaches her sister and Taureen the steps she dances in the video. It's a ghetto extravaganza.

Blige needs a pack of Newports. Sensing my total frustration, she asks me to take her to the store. The two of us go together in my car, followed by Taureen in his car. My frustration and resentment immediately turn into gratitude. I'll do whatever it takes to get a story.

Sizing me up at the liquor store, Blige tells me, "You need a drink, girl." Politely, I decline in favor of Gatorade. "No! Let's get a bottle of Malibu." It's not an offer—it's an order. I need to know what Malibu is. "You ain't never had no 'bu, girl? Well, you here now." Blige picks up the Malibu and goes over to the cooler and pulls out two cans of pineapple-coconut juice, asking the cashier if they're "all natural, no MSG?" Then she asks for a pack of cigarettes.

Taureen shadows my car back to the set. Blige invites me into her trailer on the condition that I "troop" with her through that bottle of Malibu and a few beers. She shows me many different sides of herself: pop star, spiritual leader, project princess, bitch, and good girlfriend. The overwhelming thing about Mary J. Blige is that she does exactly what she wants to do, regardless, or maybe because of, her point of view—that she is constantly under siege in a world that's hostile to who she is. And because of that I won't forget her. She is someone who will be famous whether her story turns out to be a tragedy or a success.

VW: So, is this everything that you ever wanted?

MJB: This is some bullshit. I'm happy though. But I'd be happy either way. I got to be.

VW: It sounds like that's your goal—to be happy.

MJB: Oh, definitely. To be content. To find my right mind—peace—and do it while I'm here.

VW: But there's a lot of stuff that took you away from that, right?

MJB: Like what?

VW: Well, we all have stuff that takes it away from us.

MJB: Well, you know what takes it away from us? We take it away from us, when we feed into negative bullshit and shit that's going on that we are not supposed to even have anything to do with.

VW: But sometimes it's not even negative bullshit. When I started modeling, I was nineteen years old, and suddenly it was like planes, money, and hotels.

MJB: That's positive when it's showered on you the right way, but it's negative when you can't handle it, when you don't know what to do with it. It's good, it comes, you spend it, but don't act like an asshole. Just stay you, remain the same—humble and kind, a nice person. Do your thing. You demand respect and you'll get it. First of all, you give respect.

VW: So what does it feel like, Mary? Everybody wants to know, what does it feel like?

MJB: What does what feel like?

VW: What does it feel like to have a gift inside of you, and it's just something that you live with, and then suddenly everybody steps up and they recognize it?

MJB: It feels good. There ain't no bust about it.

VW: It must be scary sometimes.

MJB: You just got to look at it as all good. It is scary. Life is scary if you look at it. So you just got to live. You got to be happy without a care in the world. You got to be all right in your heart. Fuck the outside of you, as long as that heart is clean. I mean, I know my heart is not clean, and your heart is not clean, and none of our urban hearts are clean. But you can be washed again.

VW: Mmm-hmm. It's hard.

MJB: It's very hard. So no one should judge you, because it's hard for everybody.

VW: You talk about violence a lot in interviews. Did you grow up with it?

MJB: Yeah. I grew up on it—in it, on it, all of that. It's not the right way of life. But yo, it's the way of life. And it's how you go about it, too.

VW: Do you worry about people judging you? People judge you all the time. They listen to your records. They write critiques. They talk about how you dress, who you go out with, what you eat, what you smoke, what you drink.

MJB: Well, it's like this: Ain't nothing I can do about it. So I got to live for Mary. Fuck thinking about judging.

VW: Was there a point when people first started paying attention to you where you were like, "Damn, why?"

MJB: There ain't nothing you really say. Of course, when you're younger, you're going to ask "Why?" to a lot of things. But when you find out the answer, there's no more question. Do you believe in loving your neighbor?

VW: Oh yeah. That's real basic. What made you think about loving your neighbor?

MJB: 'Cause you have to. It feels good. And it should all feel good.

VW: But why did that come up? Are you living in a way that's different now because you've got a lot of neighbors? Everybody who picks up *Essence* and reads about you becomes your neighbor. Everybody who listens to your record becomes your neighbor.

MJB: No, they don't.

VW: Have you ever felt like maybe it wasn't going to work, maybe you weren't going to be happy?

MJB: I never thought like that. I mean, all my life, I never really thought negative about nothing. Never.

VW: Your last album established you as part of the big boys' club. *My Life* is more of a girl's album than your last album.

MJB: And people, when they hear pain, you think of pain and that's the bottom line. Everybody will be hurting. Listen to a baby crying, and you'll cry, you'll hurt. You know what I'm saying?

VW: I do understand. What makes you think I don't?

MJB: You look like you don't.

VW: I was just thinking it through. Did you write a lot before?

MJB: I didn't write anything on my first album. There were a lot of my emotions in it.

VW: What made you want to write, because it seems like your songs are mostly about hurting?

MJB: Pain. Pain. I couldn't take no more, and I had to sing.

VW: Were you going through relationships?

MJB: Yeah. Many relationships where I learned . . .

VW: What were you trying to achieve in your relationship with your boyfriend, K-Ci, of the band Jodeci?

MJB: As far as men [and relationships go], that's where I think respect should come in. I respect you, and you respect me.

VW: Otherwise, why be in it?

MJB: You know, me and my weaknesses . . . [pulls cap off a Heineken bottle with her teeth] 'cause I'm all right. But I can fuck you up the same way you can fuck me up, too. And it ain't got to be physical.

VW: No. When it's mental, it's worse, because it takes longer to figure it out. And it takes a lot longer to get over it. When somebody who you trust—who you love—starts doing that shit to you, you don't expect that. When I let somebody close to me, especially a man, and then they're critical, negative, and destructive, it used to be I had to get hit three times between my eyes to figure it out.

MJB: You don't got to be hit at all now, do you?

VW: No. Now, I know when to duck.

MJB: No more. Finished. I'm not dealing with this any longer now. I'm going to need nothing but natural resources. [Runs hands from her forehead to her toes.]

VW: But that's the hard way to go.

MJB: It's hard, baby? I'm going to make it easy for you.

VW: Not dealing with shit from men in relationships takes a lot of discipline.

MJB: If I've got to die doing it, I'm out of here. 'Cause I'm not going to make an ass out of myself for the world. I'm just going to love, love, get respect, demand it 'cause I give it. Give it 'cause I demand it, whatever. It's a respect thing. And that's my way of living. That's me, okay?

VW: You know how you watch TV as a kid, and you think that's how relationships are going to be?

MJB: You thought that? Why? You didn't see the real shit happening in your face?

VW: I was trying to block that shit out.

MJB: No, don't block that shit out, block that TV shit out. You'll never block reality. Reality's in your face. Reality is the shit you can't hide from.

VW: But you never did that as a kid?

MJB: The only thing I did [was] movies when I was a kid; as far as TV goes was when the Chinese women [in kung fu movies] used to come on, I used to act like them kung-fu motherfuckers and try to fuck everybody up. But that's it. "The Brady Bunch"? Happy ending? Get all emotional and all that shit? Go back to reality. In the streets all you see is reality. Back to reality. And reality is what we feel here. [She places hand over her heart.]

[Mary's cousin Marco chimes in.]

MARCO: That's why most people can't understand Mary, all Mary sees is reality. When you've been growing up in the streets all your life and this shit hit . . . it's nothing big, really. It might be big because you've got a lot of dough in your pocket at first. But once you settle down, it's just a regular job.

MJB: And you, fuckin' around trying to be Alice in Wonderland?

VW: I'm trying to keep up, Mary. I'm not a drinker or a smoker. But I'm trying to keep up. Do you like this life?

MJB: Do you like being in this life?

VW: Yeah, I do.

MJB: What do you like about it?

VW: In a lot of ways, it's freedom. I like being off the block.

MJB: You think it's freedom? You've got a point.

VW: You know what's not freedom? Standing in the welfare office.

MJB: But you know what? I'm going to tell you this right here. [This life] is freedom, but it's hell.

VW: I'm not so sure if it's really hell.

MJB: It's reality. You can't walk out of that door and think it's going to be Alice in Wonderland.

VW: It sounds like you need to maintain a lot of control— like you'd be regulating—

MJB: I don't regulate. I regulate within me. I got Mary together. I speak to Mary. 'Cause I'm no better than you, you, or you. And I can't get on no throne and preach 'cause I'm not God.

VW: No, it's not about getting on a throne and preaching.

MJB: That's what I'm saying. I can't get on a throne and preach. I can't make the world sit down. And that's the bottom line. Because that's the most powerful source right here, [what] we have [within ourselves].

VW: At the same time, you're a woman. And the business is not set up for women. Usually people wouldn't listen to you when you say, "I want to do this or that."

MJB: You can't restrict your mind on the business. You've got to restrict your mind on the work and how you want to live.

VW: Do you have different survival skills now?

MJB: I have survival skills, period.

VW: Did you add new ones?

MJB: Uh-huh.

VW: What about the etiquette course you enrolled in with Angelo Ellerbee from [the public relations firm] Double Exxposure?

MJB: Angelo Ellerbee is the perfect example of what we need to be. He can't be fucked with.

VW: Why not?

MJB: I'm thinking about it. Do you know why? I would have figured it out if I was you.

VW: Why? Because he's happy in himself? Because he knows where he comes from? Why? What did he do with you for twenty-four weeks?

MJB: I wasn't with him for twenty-four weeks.

VW: Really?

MJB: That was the length of the course . . . [Blige attended it for seventeen weeks.] See, the more you ask me stupid questions, the more I'm going to give you stupid answers.

VW: Why was that a stupid question? That's consistently in your press, Mary.

MJB: It really is consistently in my press. But why do you think I went? Why do you think I went for such a short period of time?

VW: Because you knew a lot of it already, and you learn fast?

MJB: Well, why are you asking me the question? We need to be alone, right? Because we're going to fight, ain't we?

VW: No, it takes a lot to offend me. I might be offending you. [Mary balls up her fist and stares at me.]

MJB:No, I'm not trying to offend you. So we need to fight.

VW: No. Why would we need to fight, Mary? Over what? [laughs] You might need to scold me a little bit, because I've got a feeling that there's something I'm missing. And that's okay.

MJB: You ain't missing nothing. It's all good. I'm trying to tell you. Everything is good. The bad is good.

VW: Yup.

MJB: Take me away. Kill me. Stab me. Shoot me. One day I know I'm gonna have to get up out of this bitch [this life], because my God won't stand for all this unfairness.

VW: Well, you're only going down once, right?

MJB: You're only going down once. You don't come back. You're outta here, and then after that you're searching. So, you want to be happy searching.

VW: Clearly, that's home base for you.

MJB: What?

MJB: Being happy. Everything comes back to that. Tell me about recording "Freedom" with the other female R&B singers for the sound track to the Mario Van Peebles film *Panther.* Was that the first time you've been in a group of girls like that?

MJB: Yeah, that was my first time.

VW: What did that feel like?

MJB: Like nothing. I mean, it felt like everything living in me.

VW: Yeah, but I mean, you've got Patra, she's a Jamaican party girl. Then you've got Me'Shell Ndegeocello . . . it had to be different than watching Method Man work when you two recorded the duet "I'll Be There for You/You're All I Need to Get By."

MJB: Who am I watching? Can you rewind that? Veronica, I don't watch anybody. Listen, sit down. Let me tell you something for your own good.

VW: Okay.

MJB: I don't watch shit. I don't watch nobody.

VW: Right. So in that room with Latifah and Patra and everybody else, you were just listening?

MJB: Ask the question again.

VW: So you were just focused on you?

MJB: I'm focused on the good shit in life. And the good shit in life is man and woman. So you can't watch it. You've got to feel it.

VW: There's a lot of negative stuff that I don't see because I don't want to see it.

MJB: Don't see it, baby. [VW laughs] No. There's your answer to everything . . . and then whatever you're going to express, that's okay. And this tape's for you, baby. Don't worry like that to the world. You're like me, going crazy. People want to see a nigger like me locked down in jail, doing drugs. And that's just the rub of the way of the world. Like what they did to Tupac. They put him under. He didn't do a motherfucking thing. They put Mike Tyson under, he didn't do a motherfucking thing. They tried to say Michael Jordan's father was doing drugs and gambling. But that was his business.

VW: Whatever, he didn't deserve to die like that.

MJB: Don't lock me down like that. Don't chain me up like that. Don't bring me back to slavery days because I'm living my life. You're living your life when you get ready— and can't nobody fuck with how I live my life.

—Chateau Marmont, Hollywood, 1995

You're a Woman Now

Sharing Milestones with Prince

"I was dreaming when I wrote this/Forgive me if it goes astray."—Prince

It wasn't exactly a nightmare rattling my id late the other night, but some message coming up through the dungeons of my unconscious waking me. "You're a woman now," said the whisper inside my skull. What fresh revelation is this? "Prince's greatest hits are out on CD," mocked the little whisper in reply. I wish my psyche could keep more convenient hours. I conceded to the pillow I knew what was messing up my sleep. I was just fifteen, becoming a teenager, when I bought the first Prince record. And it was on vinyl.

So it's official. The generation known as X, or the 13ers, or whatever moniker you want to attach to us twentysomethings, has come of age. *Prince: The Hits* is a generational milestone. If you don't think that's proof enough, think about the first time you heard "Little Red Corvette"—you were probably psychologically and emotionally limber enough to think about getting down in a bucket seat.

Back in the pioneer days, before cash cards, before the big disease with the little name, before commercials on MTV, before black music was on MTV, there was only rock 'n' roll and R & B. The two cultures had yet to marry or remarry in that era. In those days, R & B was either a staid exercise, buttoned up in silk suits and floating on Italian slippers, like Teddy Pendergrass inviting women to "Close the Door," or a flashy disco style extravaganza like Earth, Wind & Fire was singing "Reasons," in metallic platform boots. The relationships in those songs were not very complex, and the personalities plucking the heart strings seemed to be straightforward in their sexual orientation.

In true pioneer spirit, Prince came onto the pop horizon. His Royal Badness was the perfect marriage between Bootsy and Pendergrass. When 1999 still was a long way away, Prince's sexuality seemed even more distant. His sexual persona embodies cock-strong and feminine at the same time. Strange that he can be 100 percent man in full hair and makeup, not to mention the high heels and lingerie. The exploration of sexual ambiguity and alternative sexuality was a major part of the American search for self in the eighties. The exploitation of these themes is now a part of American entertainment in the nineties. Think of Cindy Crawford and k.d. lang in mock lesbian embrace on the pages of *Vanity Fair*, Martin Lawrence as Sha Ne Ne, and Sandra Bernhard and Morgan Fairchild as the loving lesbian couple on "Roseanne."

"If I was your girlfriend . . . Sometimes I trip on how happy we would be . . . We don't have to make love in order for you to

have an orgasm . . ." Back to Prince for a minute, because all that notwithstanding, he does represent the modern sexual persona. No matter what your sexual preference is, it's possible to feast on the pheromones swirling around in the man's entity. Most straight guys I know profess a love of Prince's music, but would feel a lot more comfortable if he wore sneakers. They're probably just getting turned on.

"Maybe I'm too demanding/Maybe I'm just like my father, too cold/Maybe I'm just like my mother, she's never satisfied . . ." In his lyrics, Prince offers us complex relationships charged with high-voltage sexuality and the psychological underpinnings that have complicated, nearly to ruination, the sex lives of the post-Freud, Jungian generation. If Prince were to stick his tongue in my ear, I'm sure it would tickle my brain. Prince was a harbinger of the franchising of pain in America; a lot of his lyrics have the raw confessional frankness of a daytime talk show. Think about Oprah and all the other talk shows on which people appear in their far-less-than-glamorous flesh to teletronically ease the pain.

"Twenty-two positions in a one-night stand . . ." Prince is in his highest form, perhaps, when discussing the lower drives. "Get Off" came (no pun intended) at just the right moment. The music world was swimming in the safe-sex message up to its ears. The future is, maybe, virtual sexuality, as the mating game becomes more and more dangerous. Who better to give your dirty mind some head than Prince?

Marvin Gaye went from the album *Let's Get It On* to *What's Going On?* Prince never got quite that far, he's not especially political, but he did make a brilliant double-haiku homage to the issues of the eighties with "Sign o' the Times." The isolation of AIDS at the Institute Pasteur in Paris was summed up in the line, *"In France a skinny man died of a big disease with a little name/By chance his girlfriend came across a needle and soon she did the same."* Homelessness and Reaganomics were scored like this: *"Sister killed her baby because she couldn't afford to feed it."* Kids killing kids encapsulated this way: *"At home, there are seventeen-year-old boys. And their idea of fun is being in a gang called the Disciples/High on crack and toting a machine gun."* You remember exactly where you were when the space shuttle Challenger blew up. The notorious o-ring disaster was partly blamed on President Reagan's wish that the launch coincide with his State of the Union address. The folly behind the disaster was subtly handled in "Sign o' the Times:" *"City know when a rocket ship blows, everybody wants to fly . . . Baby make a speech, star wars fly, neighbors just shy at home."* Prince mercifully boxed safe sex, that inexhaustible subject, in the phrase, *"Hurry baby before it's too late/Fall in love/Let's get married and have a baby."*

If I were going to set the eighties to music, Prince would definitely be the featured artist on the soundtrack for the coming-of-age tragicomedy written for my generation.

ODDS AND ENDS

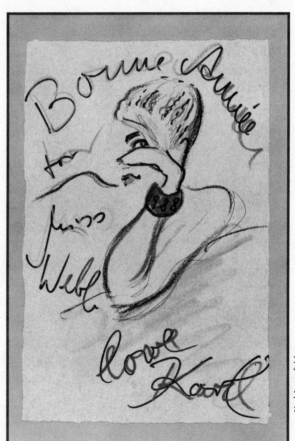

Karl Lagerfeld

DIGGING CHINA

What You See Is What You Get

D ig a hole. Take a slow boat. Those were the most popular routes to China when I was a kid. Now the other
side of the world is a manageable eighteen-hour air voyage
away. I knew nothing about modern Chinese culture before
making a trip to the mainland last month. Being a child weaned
on Cold War madness, my picture of the People's Republic was
formed by American anti-Communist propaganda. In Western
cultures, depictions of China beam in through television or
land on our doorsteps in the morning papers—sources not used
to portraying everyday people living in a country of complex
issues such as human rights, most-favored-nation status, or
swimming ashore through the rough surf off Long Island. The
evening news is still limited to snippets of high party officials
steadfastly toeing the party line, replays of riots four years ago
in Tiananmen Square, and misleading file footage of Chinese
marching in lockstep wearing blue Mao uniforms. What I

expected to see on the streets of Beijing were Chinese moving in this prescribed orderly fashion—like so many million blue worker ants, indistinguishable, serving goals of the state without freedom of choice.

Beijing's sleepy airport, a cinder-block construction with outdated dusty floors and computers, invites comparison with a desert island destination. Leaving the terminal, a jolly sculpture of two Candyland elves, one Asian and one Aryan, their hands joined by interlocking rings, symbol of the Olympic games, greets visitors with the slogan, A MORE OPEN CHINA AWAITS YOU 2000.

The first couple of days of my visit were shocking. China is not Japan. It is not a spit-shined world of sterile streets, wealth, and stifling gentility. Westerners stay in luxury hotels with $200-a-night price tags—a sum that amounts to more than one-third of the average Chinese yearly income. A walk across the lobby's red carpet to the curb brings third-world realities into view. A whiff of open sewage, or a sales pitch from an aggressive peddler, are the order of the day.

Beijing neighborhoods, which boast no green space, are a twisting series of alleys lined with one-story brick shanties topped by pagoda-style tin roofs—brick shacks simultaneously sheltering generations of the same family. Dust is everywhere from constant foot traffic and the ever-present threat of the encroaching Gobi desert not far from the city limits. The *houtong*, which means ally in Chinese, what we call the neighborhoood, usually has a low wall that serves as its parameter. Just outside the walls, a separate squat brick structure provides men's and women's toilets of the Turkish variety. A phone booth to service the residents can be found attached to the toilet house or at the corner store. The level of poverty this standard of living betrays is disturbing.

The best way to tour Beijing is on a bicycle. The fashions are as modern as those worn by the expatriate Chinese of New York or San Francisco's Chinatown. Mao suits are more likely to be seen on elderly people or peasant farmers visiting the capital. Pedestrian traffic is raucous. Oftentimes I found myself on the receiving end of an elbow, a gesture even the French would consider rude. "Chinese move like schools of fish," I was told.

One afternoon I ventured out beyond the city limits in a Jeep Cherokee assembled in Beijing. We reached an intersection where trucks from the thirties sat in a long line forming to our rear as the crossing gates descended over railroad tracks. The People's Steel Works Number One, a factory complex maintaining half a million workers, belched out smoke, a nuclear power plant was not 200 yards away.

What excited me about China was the realization that it is going from the nineteenth to the twenty-first century in one single bound. The "new market style economy," not to mention the death of Mao, has created a radically different society from the one we are allowed to see from our hemisphere. Kids are listening to Madonna, Michael Jackson, and LL Cool J records. Socialites take in jazz at Maxim's. Yuppies from the stock exchange talk on cellular phones and wear Pierre Cardin suits with the label left on the sleeve for effect. The sleeping giant wants to modernize.

Perhaps this economic reform can be linked to the fall of Communism the world over. Political reform without economic reform is chaos, as Russia's crass attempt at democracy has proven. A more tangible event on which to pin reform has to do with China's bid for the Olympics.

Beijing is all boom and bustle. The city recalls the legends of the Old West, as strange as that may sound, since China is the New East, a frontier full of promise and opportunities of riches, expansion, and invention. Colorful characters with get-rich-quick schemes abound in this "more open China." A used-car salesman named Mr. Shunkoo, a Mongol with the proportions of a warrior four feet wide and six feet tall, blew into town to import Oldsmobiles back to his home in inner Mongolia. If he was successful at crossing the Gobi with the cars, which would have to be hauled part way by a team of camels, he stood to make an enormous profit. When asked how much, he rolled his eyes with pleasure as if eating a morsel of creamy chocolate. It was obvious that for some, things in China were now living up to their wildest dreams.

FATAL EXTRACTION

Adventures with **le dentiste**

Jet-lagged and coming to consciousness without the aid of caffeine, only a lowly harmless bowl of granola to jump start me into a grueling fourteen-hour business day. Molars and incisors grinding and rotating, pulverizing and conquering the wheat and raisins. Umm, this bite is fabulously crunchy, umph, like a chicken bone—Ah! And fantastically painful — my blunt, weary senses clue me in with a minor delay. Voila! Half my right molar is fixed like a rough stone in the ugly setting of a massacred raisin. Bluch.

"This couldn't have happened at a worse time," saying the words out loud, scolding my shocked reflection—as if somehow my body was guilty, a turncoat, a traitor to the higher goals of the mind. "How dare you! We're in Italy. We're in the middle of Fashion Week. I treat you well. I brush you ungrateful teeth after every meal. I'll deal with you when we get to Paris."

The French, you see, are famous for their pharmaceutical

and medical care. The Institute Pasteur, after all, is where peni-
cillin was discovered and the first place to isolate one of the
AIDS viruses. I swear, there must be a pharmacy on every
other corner in Paris. There's a pill for everything here. The
RU486, or the "morning-after pill," relieves the need for a surgical abortion, if taken in time. Even little black boxes of powder noted for relief of "abdominal meteorites." (What you and I
call gas.) Telephoning for my appointment with the dentist, I
am certain the French must be leaps and bounds ahead of the
Americans in relieving discomfort.

Arriving at the address in the sixteenth arrondissement, one
of the most beautiful and bourgeois enclaves in the city of light,
I press the buzzer marked CABINET DENTAIRE. The sprawling
office, outfitted with leather couches, fireplaces, and picture
windows looking out onto a wooded courtyard gave me the
impression of convalescing. Five minutes dissolve and a blond
dental assistant leaves me reclining in a state-of-the-art
ergonomic dental chair that seems more like a clinical chaise
longue. My new dentist appears, cut like a young Omar Sharif,
with a pitted complexion not unlike that of James Woods.
Smiling in a way that reads slightly wicked, he tells me the tooth
must be extracted. "Can I have gas, please?" "No, we don't do
that in France." The shock. "I'll give you a shot." Producing a
needle about the size of the one on top of the Chrysler Building,
I know where it was headed. Too late. The needle has already
rocketed into my gums. In a flash he produces a gleaming pair of
silver pliers. Oh, God, no! The tool looks appropriate for, say,
working under the hood of a Mack truck, not between my
tongue and soft palate. Squirming uncontrollably, dodging the
attempts of the doctor, the warning comes. "If you don't stop
moving, I'll get people in here to hold you down." Hissing back
through now frozen and rubbery lips, "Go ahead. It might turn
into something better." Summoning four more blond assistants,
they pin me to the chair. The rest of the tooth comes out.

Glopping some blue Silly Putty on top of a flat steel instrument shaped like an apostrophe with a spoon handle, the doctor parts my lips very tenderly with his fingers, and orders me to "bite down hard." Watching him walk out the door, I play with the impression that he just might slap me if I disobeyed. He's so cute. I wiggle my teeth in defiance. Sensing rebellion, he strictly demands that I move no more. I whisper through my new impediment, "I hate you." The doctor responds instantly upon exit, "I hate you, too." A crippling enjoyment comes over me as I hear his laughter in the hallway. He tells me I would have to come back every other day for the five days I was staying in Paris.

Not thinking, the following day I dress in a major cleavage black leather jerkin with snaps down to the ground and find myself in the chair once again, *le dentiste* drilling gaily away. Eyebrows knit in concentration, he asks, "What do you measure, mademoiselle?" Countering the provocative question, I ask, "Why are you looking at my body, I'd like to know?" "Because it's stretched out here in front of me."

At my Lagerfeld fitting, after the dentist, with half my face frozen with Novocaine in the posture of a stroke victim, Karl remarks that I had put on a shirt for my treatment. "Yes, Karl," I say slyly. "But should I have unsnapped the skirt?" "Zis is zee classic fantasy, Miss Vepp," as he calls me, "to be mounted by the dentist, lying helpless here in ze chair. Zis happens quite often in France."

The final visit. "Doctor," I ask, trying to solicit pity with my gaze, "what's going to happen now?" The smiling face answers. "First, I'm going to put you in pain a little." Now cooing the punch line, "Then I'll give you a shot. The noise you make is very sexy," he says matter-of-factly, stretching my cheeks away from my jawbone in a grotesque Bozo the Clown smile and shoving the newly formed cap into the empty space. I gag. "I'm done, *ma petite mademoiselle*." "You're finished?" "*Oui!* Do you want a shot now for the road?" "Huh?" "I've saved you and your tooth!" Leaning over he gives me a French kiss. Not tongue to tongue, but on both cheeks, and went laughing out into the corridor. Lying there, I realize the French, after all, are famous for the guillotine and the Marquis de Sade.

—**Amsterdam, 1993**

PINS AND NEEDLES

Change Is in the Air

Change has a funny way of sneaking up on you. For instance, those coffee places like Starbucks: They didn't exist two years ago. These days I run up bills for cappuccino that rival my phone bill. The thing that gets me about fancy coffee places is the tip cup in front of the cash register. The reason I go to a counter in the first place is because I don't want to interact with my server. I don't want to use the time for exchanging pleasantries, and evaluating their service is a necessary act when calculating a tip. Following traditional etiquette, I'd pay for my cup of joe and go. But those clever folks at Starbucks have come up with their own brand of New Age guilt. Next time you go in for your favorite poison, take a closer look at that tip cup silently panhandling in front of the register; taped around its belly is a parable in bold print urging coffee drinkers to give. It says, KARMA IS A BOOMERANG. As I turn to leave, the phrase divides my attention between the business ahead and the debate as to whether or not to snap my wallet shut. What does this saying mean? If you don't tip the person who just made the milk on top of your coffee warm and fluffy, you may bring upon yourself the devastating misfortune of never being paid generously again. I put the money in the cup because, as we all know in the West, payback is a dog. I bet kids in Bombay say karma is a bitch.

Do you have voice mail? I do. Do you love it? I don't. I used to be really fond of the device. Years ago, it was the miraculous alternative to the answering machine. Voice mail rarely fails, and it affords one privacy, but what made me fall out of love with voice mail, despite its obvious and welcome attributes, was the voice-mail lady. At first, the sound of the artificially intelligent Indian guide who maneuvered me through kindergarten-level cyberspace was pleasant and mysterious. I wondered who she was as I was reassured by her smooth and unruffled manner. The voice-mail trail is easy to follow and quickly gives the illusion of making the user the master. "Please dial your mailbox number," voice-mail lady gives the firm but alluring order. "Please dial your password," is her next command to seduce you through the computerized layout. It's kind of cool to have those two little codes that only you can crack every day. Voice-mail lady is like the perfect domestic: Accurate and restrained, she gives me the number of messages, the time they came in and the option to replay, discard or save—all with the same unwavering emotion. I never really think of her as the robot she is—there's some part of me that lets her be human. As she leads me to the end of the messages, she invites me in her carefully modulated tone, "Press one for more options." Options? Okay. How about a male voice? Or language tapes so I can learn something while I get my messages? But all she says is "main menu" every damn time. I'm reduced to feeling like a rat trained to go through a maze. Who's the master now? She's trained me to run the maze, hit the wall and start all over again.

But if you try to bypass her system—press the star key one too many times looking for something new—and voice-mail lady will scold you ever so slightly with her pat phrase, "I don't understand what you dialed." She pauses, allowing you to regroup. "Please try again" is her patient sentence. Sometimes I like to insist on changing the order of things, and I continue to fiddle with the buttons. "Please try later" is the artificial-intelligence way of saying, "Tighten up your game, fool." Voice-mail lady has her rules. She swiftly lets me know I've been defeated. "Good-bye" is her tranquil victory cry. And then the dial tone leaves me floating, tethered to the handset.

Like I said, change does have a funny way of sneaking up on you. At this very moment I'm on a United Airlines flight between New York and Los Angeles. The folks at GTE who brought us the Airfone have taken things to the next level, bringing us phones that are capable of receiving incoming calls! So if you commute by air, your seat on the plane is just as good as being in your car on the way uptown. I think this is too good to be true. So good, in fact, it causes me to have rather morbid thoughts of how much I would have appreciated this marvelous invention had I been a passenger on the *Titanic*. I do say my best good-byes over the phone.

Back to reality. I call the GTE operator to sign up, and in moments I have a permanent pager number in the sky. I call a few friends who love exploring the frontiers of technology, and voila! My armrest is ringing off the hook. Fantastic! Except I have to enter a PIN number, which delivers me to the voice-mail lady! As usual, she's right there, blocking my hustle—her rules are even more complicated in the air. And, of course, she has the final "option." She hangs up on me. "Good-bye." *Plus ça change. . .*

—Los Angeles, 1994

THE ME NOBODY KNOWS

Smoke This

*Puff, puff. I'd love to quit, but what
habit would I replace it with?*

I have seen the face of evil. We first gussied up to each other in my teenage years and have been locked in a paralytic embrace for the last decade. I'm talking about my addiction to cigarettes. The reason I started smoking, like the reason I've done so many other things in my life, is because it looked so good in the movies. It seemed to be in some way the measure of cool, the mark of mystery; the heroes and the villains always did it with equal finesse. I'm not blaming the motion picture industry for this personality pitfall. Hollywood is truly not responsible, no more than Judas Priest is responsible for stoners in the boonies blowing their faces off after listening to "Stained Class." And anyway who feels mortal in high school?

I had high hopes when I first started smoking. I just knew I looked older and definitely more glamorous. I spent hours in the vacant lots of Detroit with my girlfriends, in what must have looked like a makeshift witches' coven sending our youth up in smoke, sampling different brands, and perfecting the hand gestures required to be a convincing smoker. I thought my pubescent little voice would be transformed into the sophisticated whiskey-soaked rumble of Bogie or Bacall. All I had to do was stick with it. No such luck. I've had a few sore throats in the pursuit, and more than my share of colds, and I still have the same high-pitched voice. There was a time that my cigarettes made a good companion, always at my side through bouts of nervousness when meeting new people, missing airplanes, heated arguments, and one of my more hated activities, talking on the telephone. Smoking was my quintessential, indispensable prop, like Hamlet with his skull. All through high school the excitement of smoking was that it was absolutely forbidden at home, in school, and under the law because of my age. I thought it was a most fearless and Bohemian gesture, the act of which firmly placed me in the netherworld of adulthood. I was sincerely laughing in the face of death. Now that I'm a little older and a lot wiser, and still hooked, evil has grafted its face onto mine and stuck its tongue down my throat. I wonder who's laughing at whom?

Cigarettes are evil. At times they rule my life like a narcotic. They are insidiously addictive, available everywhere at a nominal fee, and what makes it worse is that they are still basically socially acceptable. I've never been compelled by shame to hide out at work or a party when that old nicotine critter comes a-calling. *Au contraire mes amis.* The whole ceremony of lighting up is such a concentrated moment, a moment of such deep connection between human and object, it's a screwy instant of pride and belonging. I've never been one for groups, or cliques. I'm possessed of the impression that all the great loners smoked: Lorraine Hansberry, Brando, Bette Davis, it's a universal clique of one.

A few years ago, *Time* magazine published an exposé on the tobacco industry. When inundated with nicotine, smokers, they reported, think faster and are in a more relaxed state than non-smokers during the five-minute meteoric rush of the chemical to the brain. But, inhaling smoke also drastically reduces the quality of circulation of blood throughout the entire body, and smokers are more likely to suffer from cold hands and feet than nonsmokers. At the time I read that I didn't think it was a bad trade-off. I ignored the other statistics relating cigarette smoking to fatal cancers.

I never thought that smoking was bothersome or unfair until my oldest sister was pregnant with her first child. In the early stages of pregnancy most women's stomachs have an odor-activated vomit mechanism. I lit up one day during a visit with my expectant sister, and well, I don't need to spell it out. That was the first time my companion had embarrassed me. My cigarette failed to have the desired alluring effect. Ironically, my sister Jennifer is an oncologist, a doctor who treats patients with terminal cancers every day. It is to her deep dismay that I continue to smoke. Not as religiously as I used to, but still not a week goes by that I'm not seized by the urge to have at least one cigarette. Nowadays though, there are very few public places where a person can smoke in this U. S. of A., and those of us who smoke are relegated to smaller and smaller corners of offices and restaurants.

The shame associated with smoking is mounting. That's part of the thrill. My attitude toward the evil weed is changing too; suddenly, I hate the smell of smoke in my clothes and there are times when I manage to stay clean for a few weeks, when the presence of secondhand smokes incites me to outrage. Yet I cannot say that I am free of the desire to smoke. I tell myself, "But I'll quit smoking when I get pregnant. But I don't buy cigarettes anymore. But I don't smoke that much." Yeah, right. Puff, puff. Most people that I know who have quit smoking managed to do it in their early forties, after years of battling with this plant that no animal will eat, except a little green worm. Green worms are invertebrates, so worms don't need excuses. I have the hellfire and brimstone. I'm just missing the willpower. Happy New Year.

—Detroit, 1991

BURNED OUT

Smoking Under Fire

I've made up my mind to change and it scares me— because what I've decided to do is quit smoking cigarettes. Ugh! The idea! Ending my lifelong love affair with tobacco—it makes me want to sob. I made it easy on myself by allowing three weeks to savor absolutely every smoke I desired before severing my relationship. Committing to this deed is not pleasant. After all, cigarettes are my companions, my quintessential prop-sedative-digestive-laxative-stimulant—the all-purpose drug, a veritable medicine cabinet between my fingertips. It's a lot to give up. I tell my friends on the phone and at dinner parties of my new resolve. No matter how impressed, incredulous, or encouraging the listener may be, I can't disguise the crying in my voice.

In fact, I can't stop talking about it. I'm obsessed, okay? Like most addicts, I've tried to quit before and always went crawling back to the pack. I tried the patch, a fabulous invention for people who love nicotine. It's this Band-Aid–like thing permeated with the drug that you stick on your skin and let drench your veins for twenty-four hours a day. Real smokers, like me, take the patch off at the end of the day and have a cigarette. This is the true bliss of a nicotine rush. Such ecstasy. When I reported to my physician that I had failed with the patch and how I was abusing/enjoying it, he dropped his face into his hands and said, "Veronica, you can kill yourself like that." Smokers have a funny way of not being overly concerned with the odds of fate: Smoking is a way of showing the divine that you believe you are immune to death.

"If at first you don't succeed, try, try again." It's one of those nagging golden rules we're supposed to live by. I tried and tried every cigarette compromise I could think of: rationing, cigars . . . Each time, sooner rather than later, feeling guilty and tainted, I'd be back puffing on a fresh pack of butts. I just didn't care what it did to me. I loved it too much to let it go. But I could only think this way while consuming a cigarette. The rest of the time I was totally conflicted about smoking. The only smoking-related complication I used to vaguely worry about was lung cancer. When I was a kid, the big anti-smoking campaign was "Kick the habit: Join the young genera-tion." Well, I was the "young generation," so there was no enticement there, and I resented the government urging me to be a Goody Two-shoes. Over the past ten years, the surgeon general's antismoking campaign has mounted to the point where public consumption of a cigarette is not only socially disdained but damn near illegal. But the stronger the warnings and the legislation becomes, statistics say, the more teenagers seem to be smoking. Nobody wants to be told what to do by the government. For just $2.75, the price of a pack of cigarettes, anybody can be a rebel in our strange, politically correct times. And it's easy to be a rebel as long as you're too young to have a job, for just as the movement toward political correctness has modified speech and sexual behavior in the workplace for everyone's own good, it has also eliminated cigarettes from the workday to the same end. I have the good sense and a set of morals that would not allow me to sexually harass or racially insult anyone but, like a bigot who sometimes is embarrassed into silence, a smoker can be embarrassed into quitting.

If you smoke you know what I'm talking about. All of a sudden I'd find myself in the middle of a meeting and couldn't concentrate because there was no ashtray in the room, which meant no smoking, right? Then there's the mental debate over whether or not to ask if "anyone would mind . . ." Most of the time I would just sit there panting in anticipation of a moment to excuse myself because I couldn't cope with the awkwardness of people's reactions to the question. Then I'd find myself in a dank stairwell, not comfortable being away from the action, or definitely ill at ease out on the street in front of an office building. I didn't get that cool, rebellious feeling I used to get smoking a cigarette in the playground as a teenager. I felt like I was showing I was different in a negative way, and realizing that smoking cigarettes is too incongruous with conducting business in America. Peer pressure definitely works. That's how I got started. That's what made me decide to stop: It's too embarrassing to smoke cigarettes.

I thought about all this stuff a lot in order to motivate myself during my three weeks saying farewell to cigarettes. I didn't know if I could do it and I felt so emotional about letting it go. And then the day came. Everything was fine the first day and a half without smoking. But I soon found out that quitting smoking is one of those things like having a baby—if anyone ever told you the real deal, no way would anybody go through with it. It's like the time I was watching a documentary on childbirth with my sister, who's a mother of two. As the newborn's head emerged my sister said, "Right now she wants to shoot herself or the baby. I guarantee you." There was no way I could squeeze another detail out of Sister except: "It only hurts for a minute. Then you forget all about it."

It's over now and I'm relieved more than anything to know that every antismoking message isn't targeted toward me, and I don't have to flinch when the nightly news announces some new terrifying fact about cigarettes.

—New York, 1992

PLAYING TOUGH WITH JESUS

I hate Christmas. But, in true Christian spirit, I grin and bear it every year. The holiday season is overwhelmed by things annoying and things that have no relevance to the miracle. Christmas, they say, is about the spirit of giving. So, the office "gives" a cocktail party. You "give" fruitcakes or cufflinks to family and coworkers, or you "give" yourself a vacation. In between "The Charlie Brown Special," airplane rides, reunions with the loved ones and trying to contain the contempt the familiarity of the ritual can inspire after the fifth eggnog, I ask myself: What is it that I'm celebrating? I believe it's the birth of Christ. But, then why do I deserve a present? It's not my birthday. Why did God send Jesus here to Earth? "For God so loved the world," the Bible says, "that He gave us His only begotten son that the world might be saved." Talk about a gift.

What would happen if we all gave the thing most precious to us at Christmas? We'd all be pissed off. What do you want—

we're only human. Jesus was also human. Christ was the spirit living in him that was divine. The power of the story of Christ, I think, has very little to do with the appearance of the Three Wise Men who have degenerated over the centuries into icons of consumerism. When Mary Mother of Christ received the gold, frankincense and myrrh, I'm sure she didn't ask, "Is this stuff exchangeable?" The reason this myth endures lies in the universal lesson so abundantly racked up during the short life of Jesus Christ.

Jesus was highly individual, which is one of the most difficult states of being. For people to live the way they want to live, to make decisions informed by the third eye, to stand up and say what they believe to be the truth at all costs, is to be one's own person. Even when you have a crowd around, it's a lonely exercise.

Jesus couldn't tolerate bullshit. There was a part of Jesus that had no respect for any powers except for the voice inside of him that drove his actions. Before addressing a crowd in some dusty corner of the Roman Empire, Jesus warned his disciples, "Be on your guard against the yeast of the Pharisees, which is hypocrisy." Hypocrisy is an element of ruling authority that we, as subjects, have come to deplore and accept. Accepting this condition as a necessary evil gives everybody lots of leeway to stand around waiting to be corrupted. What fun! We all have to be corrupted before we can ask forgiveness.

From the beginning of organized society, love and rules have had a strong tendency to be in conflict. It is still not unusual for the faithful to be encumbered by all sorts of religious laws that serve no purpose other than to grant elders of the church control. Jesus was a rebel. On several occasions, Jesus was teaching in the temple on the Sabbath, and healing people suffering from dropsy, leprosy, demons, etc. The Pharisees, each time without fail, were horrified. News of the young iconoclast reached the attention of powerful King Herod. Herod, of course, had responded in kind.

The King sent news he wanted Jesus dead. Jesus answered the death threat by saying, "Go tell that fox" (which at the time was equivalent to calling someone a weasel) "that I will drive out demons and heal people . . . and on the third day, I will reach my goal. In any case, I must keep going today and tomorrow and the next day—for surely no prophet can die outside Jerusalem!" Like most leaders who are too outspoken, Jesus was usually on his way out of town.

Jesus' friends were not the most distinguished of men. Matthew was a grunt sleazebag tax collector before his transformation. Peter was plagued by cowardice. And Judas, well, he was plain greedy. Have you ever heard the saying, "Hell is other people"? After all the teaching and faith Jesus invested in Peter and Judas, in his final hour, they denied him. Betrayal is possibly the most corrosive agent to the soul. In Luke, Chapter 6, Jesus says two things: to lend expecting to be repaid in full is not generosity. And to love only those who love you is not to your credit. Anybody can do that.

Like most of us, Jesus did not always enjoy the life he was sent here to live. He was endowed with an empathy for the infirmity of the flesh and so he felt pain and fear. Being a prophet himself, and also having the aid of written prophecy in the Old Testament, he knew the crucifixion was coming. And because Jesus was human, he also knew that the thing most precious to the flesh, by all means, is life. Before his arrest, Jesus retreated to the Mount of Olives and prayed to be spared his fate until his sweat and tears turned to drops of blood. And God said no. And when Jesus was on the cross with less dignity than an insect stuck to flypaper, it seemed to him that God had forsaken him. But faith is not for the good times.

The story of Christ is the story of tough love. It's the gift that keeps on giving. Merry Christmas.

—Miami, 1993

● ●

ABOUT THE AUTHOR

Veronica Webb was the first African-American to sign a major cosmetics contract when she became a Revlon spokeswoman in 1992. She has been a board member of LIFEbeat, the music industry organization that raises money for people who are HIV positive and living with AIDS, since 1993. In addition to her work in fashion, she is an essayist and screenwriter. Her work has appeared in *Interview, Elle, Paper, Details, Esquire, The New York Times Syndicate*, and *The London Sunday Times*. She has also appeared in films, with roles in *Jungle Fever* and *Malcolm X*.